CONCEPTS
in CLOTHING

Other Webster/McGraw-Hill Titles in Home Economics

Barclay-Champion-Brinkley-Funderburk · *Teen Guide to Homemaking*
Carson · *How You Look and Dress*
Hurlock · *Child Growth and Development*
Landis · *Your Marriage and Family Living*
Morton-Geuther-Guthrie · *The Home: Its Furnishings and Equipment*
Paolucci-Faiola-Thompson · *Personal Perspectives*
Peck-Moragne-Sickler-Washington · *Focus on Food*
Shank-Fitch-Chapman-Sickler · *Guide to Modern Meals*
Sturm-Grieser-Lyle-Roberts · *Guide to Modern Clothing*

Webster Division, McGraw-Hill Book Company

New York · St. Louis · San Francisco
Dallas · Atlanta · London
Montreal · Sydney · Toronto

Judy Lynn Graef, M.A.

Coordinator, Home Economics
Bloomfield, New Jersey, Public Schools

Joan Buescher Strom, M.S.

Former Instructor, The Ohio State University
Columbus, Ohio

CONCEPTS in CLOTHING

Sponsoring Editor: Sally Pacheco
Assistant Editor: Patricia M. Channon
Editing and Styling: Faye Allen
Design: Lisa Delgado
Production: Renee Guilmette
Illustrations: Craven & Evans; Meredith Nemirov; Jack Weaver;
Graphic Arts International; Vantage Art; Cover Art: Bob Pardo

Credits for illustrations supplied by Butterick Fashion Marketing
Company, A Division of American Can Company, appear as
Butterick Fashion Marketing Co. Those illustrations supplied
by Simplicity Pattern Co., Inc., are credited to Simplicity Pattern
Co.

Library of Congress Cataloging in Publication Data

Graef, Judy Lynn, (date)
  Concepts in clothing.

  Includes index.
  1. Clothing and dress. 2. Sewing.
I. Strom, Joan Buescher, joint author. II. Title.
TX340.G73   646   75-31668
ISBN 0-07-023889-8

contents

preface

Today we are faced with a constantly changing world. Social changes, environmental concerns, and technological advances all require us to be able to evaluate and make decisions regarding new situations. Rules which once served as guidelines for what to wear and when to wear it no longer seem to exist. Today, personal values and preferences guide us in our clothing choices. As always, clothing is expected to do more than cover the body. But, now more than ever, our clothing helps to reveal a personality, to create an impression, and to answer a need for creativity.

CONCEPTS IN CLOTHING was written to help students become familiar with the many areas of clothing that affect them personally, financially, socially, and creatively. Designed for use in introductory clothing classes, the book is divided into two parts: a social look at the importance of clothing and a practical approach to clothing construction.

The traditional coverage of clothing has been written to appeal to all-boy, all-girl, or coed groups, emphasizing throughout the concepts of self-image, consumer intelligence, textile technology, clothing selection and management, and decision making.

To make CONCEPTS IN CLOTHING a relevant learning experience, behavioral objectives introduce each chapter, introductory career information is included, and the metric system (including conversion factors and dual dimensions) is used throughout. The Ideas for Action at the end of each chapter give the student the opportunity to express creatively the concepts learned in the chapter and provide, as well, the opportunity to explore the topics discussed.

The authors wish to thank Jeanne Hayden Brinkley, formerly with The Florida State University; Loree C. Likens, Seminole Junior College; and Dr. Maynette D. Williams, Texas Tech University for their helpful suggestions during manuscript preparation. The authors also wish to express their thanks to Linda Epstein for her overall contribution and especially for her invaluable help in the development of Chapter 3.

Judy Lynn Graef
Joan Buescher Strom

PART I

THE
IMPORTANCE
OF
CLOTHING

social-psychological aspects of clothing

After reading this chapter, you should be able to:

- *Discuss reasons for wearing clothes.*

- *Recognize the social forces which affect personal clothing choices.*

- *Identify the cultural influences on the clothing styles of a country.*

- *Choose clothing to communicate the first impressions, roles, and status that you want.*

- *Discuss how famous or important people can affect clothing styles.*

- *Describe five clothing fashions since the turn of the century.*

- *Explain how the historical events of a nation are reflected in its fashions.*

WHY WE WEAR CLOTHES

Look at the clothes you are wearing today and think about why you are wearing them. Just how did you come to have on these specific clothes and not others? Maybe the weather determined what you chose or maybe the fact that this is a school day. You might have some activity after school that helped you to make up your mind. Maybe what you are wearing today was the first thing that fell out of the closet, or possibly it was your last clean outfit!

We all wear clothing and we all wear different types of clothing. Yet, for the most part, we generally take it for granted. What we want to do is to begin to think about and to understand why we select the clothing we do. At the same time, we hope to gain some insight into other people's reasons for their clothing choices.

2

How does the clothing pictured here affect the people and their activities? *Cary Wolinsky, Stock Boston (left); Peter Menzel, Stock Boston (right)*

MODESTY

Probably the most obvious reason for wearing clothes is simply that in our society, people do not go around without them. We wear clothing for modesty. Those who have younger brothers or sisters or who babysit for small children know that young children do not feel embarrassed about going without any clothing. The need to have their bodies covered is something that they are taught.

Ideas about modesty are molded by the society in which we live. What is considered modest in one society might not be considered modest in another. Also, people of different time periods in the same society may have different ideas about modesty. For example, the bathing suits worn in the 1970s are quite immodest by the standards of swimmers of the early 1900s or even the 1950s. There are also occasions and places within the same culture and the same time period where the situation determines modesty. While it is acceptable to wear a swimsuit or bikini at the beach or at home, it is not appropriate to wear one at school or at work.

PROTECTION

What is another reason for wearing clothes? We wear clothing to protect ourselves from the environment—from weather, dirt, and pollution. When it is cold or hot, rainy or sunny, such things as boots, coats, and hats all serve to protect us.

Clothing can also protect us from physical harm. The astronauts have to wear space suits during their trips and during their walks on the moon. Fire fighters wear special clothing for protection from fire, smoke, and water, and steelworkers may wear protective aprons, glasses, gloves, and hats. Many sports activities, such as football, hockey, and rugby, require clothing that is specially designed to protect the players from injury.

Frequently clothing that is originally worn for protection becomes fashionable. Sunglasses

Standards of modesty have changed. All these bathing suits were considered both modest and immodest at different periods in our culture.

symbols. However, with the growing concern for wildlife conservation, the wearing of certain furs has lost its prestige. Groups within a society also have different ideas of status symbols. Blue jeans, a traditional work garment, were adopted as a nonstatus item for everyday wear in the sixties by those protesting a society too concerned with status and money. Jeans were low in cost and so durable that they seldom needed replacing. However, by the early seventies, the age, degree of fadedness and wear, and fit of one's pair of jeans became a symbol of its owner's status. Although jeans were popularized in an attempt to reduce the emphasis on money, you can now buy jean outfits costing several hundred dollars.

IDENTIFICATION

Wearing clothes for purposes of identification is not as common as it once was. We do, however, still identify some people by their clothing. This is especially true in the cases of people who wear uniforms, such as police officers, waiters, airline workers, and military personnel. Some jobs require the use of uniforms so that the personnel

were first worn to protect eyes from the sun and dirt. Now, however, they are oftentimes worn as a fashion accessory. Boots were used only in bad weather until they became stylish. Now we wear them in good weather, too.

In a somewhat similar manner, sneakers and sandals have now come to be worn for many different occasions rather than strictly for sports.

STATUS

A third reason for wearing clothing is to show status. It used to be true that you could identify people's social and economic standings, or their status, by their clothing. As stylish clothing became more and more available at reasonable prices, however, this fact became less true.

Of course, at different times in a society, different items are considered symbols of high status. In our society, furs have traditionally been status

Protective clothing also provides comfort for special activities. *Daniel Brody, Stock Boston*

4

Variations of denim and work boots, traditional nonstatus items, have taken on new social importance. *Simplicity Pattern Co.*

There is also an informal system of uniforms. Sometimes people of the same age or who have the same interests may dress alike to show a common bond. The "uniform" they choose may consist of a certain type of shirt, jacket, sweater, or pants that indicates the wearer is a member of the group.

ADORNMENT

What about wearing clothing just because you want to look attractive? This seems to be one of the basic reasons for wearing clothes.

One of the first forms of adornment was body decoration. This is still practiced today in some societies. It is done by etching or painting a series of designs on the body. The need to decorate and adorn the body seems to be one of the more universal drives of men and women and

Identifying these flight attendants would be easy at an airport, but perhaps not so easy away from their place of employment. *American Airlines Photo*

can be identified easily, present a unified appearance, and feel a sense of belonging to the group. In recent years, such businesses as banks have found that their employees like wearing uniforms.

Many of these uniforms look just like nonuniform clothes and can easily be worn by the employees when outside of their working situations. Often these uniforms are made so that the wearers can choose their own color combinations and styles and thus add their own personal touches to their outfits. When the uniform is purchased or cleaned at the employer's expense, the employee can save money or spend it on other types of clothing.

What evidence of traditional forms of adornment is there in clothing styles today?

can be found to some degree in all societies. Ear piercing, nail polishing, tattooing, and hair braiding and knotting are all forms of body decoration still used.

The desirability of such adornment is, like modesty, determined by society. Standards change from one society to another and within a society—from one period to the next or from one group to another.

WHY WE WEAR THE CLOTHES WE DO

As you can see, there is no *one* reason for wearing clothes. Instead, there are many reasons— conscious and unconscious. Some are the result of our ideas about what is modest, what is beautiful, and what is status. Some have to do with whether we live in warm or cold climates, what

kinds of jobs we have, or what kinds of activities and recreation we participate in.

What is the relationship between what we wear and the culture or society in which we live? Our society and, even more directly, our friends can have a great deal of influence over our clothing choices.

INDIVIDUALITY AND CONFORMITY

We cannot help noticing what other people are wearing. At the same time, they notice what we are wearing. Because we want to be part of a group, we sometimes use clothing as a means of being accepted. What we wear is often affected by what others are wearing. If this were carried to an extreme, we would all wear the same thing. Fortunately, though, while we want to belong, we also have a drive to be slightly different from the next person—to express our individuality.

FIRST IMPRESSIONS

Can you remember your first day at the school you are now attending? What was your first classroom like? What was your reaction to the people you met that day? Did you go home after that first day with a feeling that you were going to enjoy this school? Or did you have a feeling of dread about what the next day of school would bring? All the things you saw and experienced that first day helped to shape your first impression.

In much the same manner, when you meet someone for the first time, you form a feeling about the person, or a *first impression*. A first impression gives you an idea of the kind of person he or she is and may make you want to get better acquainted. However, a first impression and a true impression may not be the same. Sometimes you meet someone for the first time and come away thinking you really do not have much in common. Yet, when you get to know the person better, you find you actually have a lot in common. Maybe in time you even become good friends. Since we cannot really get to know most people we meet, it is important that our first impressions be accurate. In this way, we can take better advantage of our opportunities to meet, and learn about, new people. In the same way, they will know us better, too.

Clothing has a lot to do with a first impression. It is easily seen and is something everyone is familiar with. Clothing may express feelings and moods. It may indicate that you want to feel a part of the group or that you like to be different from others. Of course, the person seeing you for the first time will also have his or her own ideas about how you look. Most of the time, the idea will be the same as yours, but sometimes a person's previous experience affects how he or she sees you. Perhaps a favorite person always wore the style of garment you have on, and therefore, he or she will react to you in a positive manner. On the other hand, maybe a much disliked person always wore the color you are wearing, and so he or she will react negatively to you.

Whether for special or routine occasions, your clothing helps to shape first impressions. *Co-ed, Scholastic Magazines, Inc. (top); Wrangler Sportswear (bottom)*

ROLES

What other factors influence your clothing choices? Certainly your age, your sex, and your activities do. Sex roles are becoming more varied and less restrictive, however. Many cosmetics, hairstyles, fashions, jewelry, and accessories are now used by both sexes. In addition, many of the same clothing styles are being worn by children and adults. Can you think of some specific styles or items of clothing that are worn by both girls and boys? Young and old?

Your activities also affect your clothing. Although the pressure to dress up is less now than in years past, you may wear different clothing as a student than you would if you were working in an office. You might also wear different clothes for school, dates, and other occasions.

CULTURAL INFLUENCES ON OUR CLOTHING

The culture of a society has a great deal to do with the clothing of the people within it. Culture is shaped by such factors as tradition, important events, nationally prominent people, and the life-style of the average citizen. All these factors are further influenced by the nationality and ethnicity of the various subgroups within the culture.

TRADITION

Style of dress, culture, and environment are closely related. For example, the traditional Japanese culture has a great deal of respect for customs and formality. The traditional kimono has a long, narrow skirt and graceful, flowing sleeves. The narrowness of the skirt forces the wearer to take small steps and walk slowly. The flowing sleeves further add to a total effect of graciousness, refinement, and restraint.

The dress of the American Indian reflects a society that lived closely with nature. Traditional Indian garments are made from furs, animal hides, and fabrics woven from natural fibers. Jewelry, decoration, and trim are made of shells, wooden beads, feathers, and leather.

An agricultural society raises crops or livestock. This way of living was reflected in the everyday clothing of the European peasant. Garments were coarsely woven and the colors were primarily earth tones of brown, rust, black, and dark green. The clothing styles were functional, with little decoration. A sharp contrast can be seen in the bright colors, embroidery, and more delicate fabrics of European festive or ceremonial costumes.

Traditional dress is influenced by climate, too. Because of the hot climate, many African nations do not use elaborate clothing. Loose-fitting woven garments are worn by some tribes. Clothing and adornment of other tribes consists of body etching, painting, tattooing, beads, animal skins, and natural fibers.

The Eskimos use fur and skins to protect themselves from their cold, harsh climate. Because Eskimos have to be outdoors much of the time, leggings, boots, hooded parkas, and mittens are essential parts of their wardrobe. Decoration consists of fur itself plus some embroidery.

The many different climates of Mexico are reflected in its dress. Light, airy garments and wide-brimmed sombreros are comfortable in the dry, hot, sunny areas. Heavy blanketlike ponchos and serapes are used for warmth and protection in the cold or rainy regions. Influences of the Mexican Indians and early Spanish settlers are seen in the brightly colored, handwoven fabrics and the decorative festival clothing.

What about our mode of dress in the United States? Even though we are a culture made up of many others, our clothing reflects our life-style. We are, for the most part, easygoing and active—a nation constantly on the move. Likewise, our clothing tends to be comfortable and nonrestrictive. Whether we live in the city, on a farm, or on a ranch, we all want our clothes to have these same qualities.

Cultural differences in dress became less defined as the distance between cultures became less. Modern methods of communication and transportation have made this possible. However, traces of individual cultural groups do appear from time to time in current clothing styles.

Back-to-nature trends have resulted in the revival of designs of the American Indian and European peasant cultures. When Alaska and Hawaii became states, adaptations of their native garments, fur-trimmed parkas and muumuus, became fashionable.

ENTERTAINMENT

Can you think of what else affects what we wear? What about the movies? Singing groups? Many styles have come from the entertainment we enjoy.

The movie version of *Romeo and Juliet* (1968) greatly influenced the adaptation of twelfth-century styles to modern garments. Lush velvets, laced-up bodices, puffy sleeves, and crocheted caps were adopted by girls. Silky shirts with full sleeves and ruffles or embroidered designs were accepted by boys to be worn with their worn-out jeans. The movie *Dr. Zhivago* (1965) introduced long, fur-trimmed coats, knee-high leather boots, and embroidered peasant shirts for both sexes.

If you were a costume designer, you would create complete costumes for theater, movie, or television productions. Besides a background in art and design, you would need a knowledge of history. The costume designer is usually responsible for developing the total look of a character from clothing to hair and makeup. You might work for a theater company, a single production, a television station or network, or a movie studio.

When the Beatles became popular in the early 1960s, they not only revolutionized the music of the day, but they also set a new style for hair length and clothing trends.

What other areas of entertainment have influenced your ways of dressing now or in recent years?

Many items of clothing are worn for comfort and appeal by both girls and boys, and traditional play clothes are worn for all occasions. *McCall Pattern Co.*

FAMOUS PEOPLE

Frequently world leaders, royalty, and other prominent people help to bring about a new look or to establish a fashionable trend. They can do this through their travels, activities, or own style of dress.

Official visits by prominent United States citizens to such places as India, China, and Japan resulted in at least short-term American interest in the clothes of these countries. The people of these Far Eastern cultures responded with an increased awareness and use of Western-style clothing.

Fashions in the world of sports have also been influenced by famous people. Tennis whites were the traditional on-court uniform until popular professional players began to change them. The players helped to introduce individuality and color to the clothing as well as to the sport. In the early seventies, the "speed-suit" for Olympic swimmers caused quite a stir. Its sleek form-fitting look soon became popular even with sunbathers.

Some fashions take the name of the person responsible for its popularity. These include the Eisenhower jacket (later revived as the battle

Roles and activities, as well as the image to be presented, are all considered when clothing choices are made. Sometimes you are very aware of these considerations, and at other times you make decisions without really thinking about why.

11

jacket of the seventies), the Nehru jacket, the Chanel suit, and the "Garbo look," which included the wide-shoulder suit and the slouch hat.

HISTORY

History has a strong effect on what we wear. If you want to predict future styles, all you really need to do is carefully examine present clothing styles. However, just what will make these styles reappear is difficult, even impossible, to predict. Let's examine some fashions to see how they were influenced by history.

The early 1970s was an era of nostalgia. Old movies were shown on television and at film festivals, and admiration for the stars and styles returned. At the same time, music, movies, and shows were being produced to depict the years before and during World War II. There was a revival of the looks of the thirties and forties in clothing. If you compare the revival fashions with the originals, however, you will quickly notice that there is a considerable difference between them. When we talk about a revival of fashions from another era, we mean that clothing designers have adapted the look and the feeling of an earlier period in a current fashion.

If you were a clothing historian or researcher, you would deal with clothing of the past. You might work for a museum. Your responsibilities would include developing and caring for the historical section. You would also prepare showings of historical garments. You would identify pieces of clothing and textiles from past cultures and centuries and display them as accurately as possible.

FASHION: A HISTORICAL OVERVIEW

Thanks to the industrial revolution, people at the turn of the century had more clothes and a greater variety of them than ever before. Because they spent less time doing heavy physical work, they had more time and energy to devote to themselves and their surroundings. Massive and bulky everyday clothing, not practical for work, became a symbol of their new leisure.

The newfound leisure did something else, too. It provided opportunity for many activities— each requiring a different type of clothing. Less confining garments were worn for bicycle riding, tennis, golf, and drives in the newly invented "horseless carriage."

World War I presented a new fashion look. The soldier look was promoted as an ideal, and a lanky, natural-shoulder, youthful silhouette became fashionable. As women joined the work force in larger numbers, their clothing took on a more tailored appearance. Skirts were raised to ankle length and hair was worn shorter, requiring less care. The overall shift in style as the twenties approached was to clothing that was less confining—clothing that allowed easier, more comfortable movement.

By 1920, the struggle for equal rights began to reach some of its goals, and women achieved the right to vote. They felt a new equality with men, and their fashions showed it. The new look consisted of a straight, almost shapeless, boyish silhouette with a short skirt and a cloche hat pulled down over bobbed (short) hair. Men's fashions were as wild and youthful as the women's.

The effect of the Depression was to bring the styles of the 1930s back to a classical look. Thrift and economy became the guiding forces. Skirts and suits returned to more conservative styles. Skirts were longer but narrow, without flounces or decoration. Fashionable trousers for women were introduced for the first time.

The wartime influence on fashion in the early 1940s was seen in the broad, padded shoulders and military styling of men's and women's garments. World War II also brought rationing, with limited supplies of fabric for clothing. People wore uniforms and factory coveralls much of the time.

Postwar joy brought the "new look" for women in 1947. Fitted waists and fuller skirts

1900

teens

twenties

thirties

forties

fifties

sixties

seventies

were a drastic change in fashion from the Depression and war years. Men's fashion was just as dramatic after the war. A bold look of self-confidence and authority was achieved with broad shoulders, wide lapels, and striped ties. The desire to hold on to the postwar good feeling meant holding on to postwar fashions.

The full skirt got shorter as more layers of crinoline petticoats increased its width in the 1950s. The sleeveless, sheath silhouette became very popular as the decade continued and eventually ended in a style called the "sack." This one-piece dress was blousy on top and fitted from the hips down. Its acceptance was slow to come. The men's "bold look" evolved into the distinguished and confident "gray flannel suit"—the uniform of the decade.

Teen-agers in the later part of the decade seemed oblivious to these new fashions. Blue jeans, loafers, bobby socks, and "Dad's old shirt" seemed more than adequate.

The basic "sack" of the fifties became the shift of the sixties. Youth was again a strong force as the mini was introduced in London. The thigh-high skirts brought an interest in colored and textured stockings and chunky-heeled shoes and boots. With science fiction becoming a reality, designers showed space-age–looking clothes with boots, and a new fashion began. The silhouette was loose-fitting and long-legged and very much reflected the busy life of young women.

Men's fashion changed, too. The "peacock revolution" began in London. It gave men the opportunity to wear longer hair and bright colors and prints. It also gave them the go-ahead to be just as aware of fashion as were women. The chemical technology of the period introduced vinyls, fake furs, and knits, all of which were quickly adopted.

By 1970, the look of the sixties was far less popular. The silhouette was softer and more natural looking. Many styles were appealing to and suitable for both men and women. The unisex concept was greatly accepted because it answered the social need of the day. All types and styles of clothing were worn for all occasions. The casual look was seen in daytime and evening wear. Fashion offered a wide range of choices, but the look was natural with a classic styling.

Each period influences the one following. Sometimes the style change is radical; at other times there is a gradual merging of one period with the next. As the century has progressed, the clothing industry has had less influence on fashion. Instead, the new styles frequently come from and are reinforced by the people.

As a clothing historian or researcher, you could work for a theater or for a movie production studio. You would study the clothing styles for the time period presented in the production. You would share this information with costume designers so they could accurately create the clothing for the characters.

As you can see, there are many things which influence the clothing you are wearing today. Some come from far back, in history and tradition; others are as current as today's movies. Your own personality, mood, age, and sex also play a large role in determining what you wear.

● IDEAS FOR ACTION

1. Using magazines, find examples of clothing worn for modesty, protection, adornment, status, and identification. Use photos to make a mobile for your classroom. Discuss each picture with your classmates.

2. What are some of the status clothes at your school right now? Bring an example to class and discuss why it has become so important.

3. What would be some of the problems and pleasures of living in a society where everyone wears exactly the same clothing? Get together in small groups and pool your ideas. Then try to make up an ideal "uniform" for everyone.

4. Take a trip to your favorite clothing store. Make a list of the most popular styles. Are they useful and comfortable? What sort of first impression would you make wearing them? Are any of them status items? Report to the class.

5. Study the traditional costume of a country. Write a short paper on the conditions and customs in that culture which influenced the style of dress.

6. Plan a bulletin board to show how entertainment has changed clothing styles. Include the people or productions that prompted a fashion trend. (Hint: Your parents can think of some great ones!)

7. What is this year's new fashion look? Do some research to find out if this is a revival of a style from the past. If it is, what has influenced the comeback? If it is not, what brought about its acceptance?

8. Take a look at the clothing styles for the past ten years. What political, economic, or social factors have affected them? What things might influence styles in the next ten years?

● DO YOU KNOW

adornment
body decoration
conformity
ethnic clothing
fashion revival
first impression

kimono
modesty
protective clothing
roles
status
tradition

consumer know-how

After reading this chapter, you should be able to:

- *Explain what is meant by consumer personality.*

- *Name five types of stores that sell clothing and describe a major feature of each.*

- *Apply the steps of better decision making to your clothing selections.*

- *Discuss the use of credit to purchase clothing.*

- *Recognize and evaluate construction features important in buying and caring for clothing.*

- *Identify and use permanent care labels in the upkeep of your own clothing.*

- *Explain the importance and usefulness of clothing labels and hangtags.*

SPENDING MONEY WISELY

We are all confronted with the same shopping problems—what, when, where, and how much to buy.

Being a wise consumer means using all your resources to make the right decisions and to get the greatest satisfaction from what you buy. What can you do to make intelligent choices? You can begin by learning to know your own consumer personality.

Different people have different buying habits. Do you buy too quickly? Do you take a lot of time thinking over the choices and then later feel that you did not really make the best selection after all? Do you like to shop to raise your spirits? Do you and friends shop together just for fun? Do you spend more money than you can afford when there is a charge card available? Do you shop during sales to save on items you

Our consumer personalities affect when, where, and how we shop. *J. C. Penney, Co.*

would ordinarily buy anyway? Do you compare items before you purchase?

Your answers to these questions and your clothing choices are based on your *values* and *goals*. Your values are what you care about, such as comfort and physical health and appearance. A goal is something you want in the future that you are willing to work for or toward. For example, would you prefer having many different items of clothing or a few outfits that mix and match? Would you rather buy one coat or purchase a less expensive coat and two pairs of slacks for the same amount of money? Your feelings and attitudes are reflected in your values and goals, and all these things influence your clothing choices.

You also make decisions based upon your current *wishes* and *needs*. You might want a new record or tape or you might want a new pair of dungarees, but you could get by without them. However, you may have a real need for a new

jacket or pair of shoes. You will probably shop differently for items that you need than for items you can really do without. As a member of a family, you must also remember the needs of others. For most families, money is limited and must be divided to meet many needs. The family budget must pay for food, shelter, health care, transportation, and recreation, as well as for clothing. When a lot of money is used in one area, less can be spent in another. Understanding this and learning to share are the responsibilities of all family members.

Each of us has a distinct buying, or consumer, personality. This personality can change as our values, needs, and available money change. Whatever your consumer personality, you can be a satisfied shopper. When you are aware of the many factors that influence your purchases and you base your choices on that knowledge, you will probably make satisfactory decisions and spend your money wisely.

17

Hangtags and labels provide information to help you compare items and make wise decisions.

MAKING WISE DECISIONS

You can became a good consumer if you know yourself, what you want, and the technique of wise decision making. Identifying your goal or the problem to be solved is the first step in decision making. Next, you must think through possible answers to that problem. For example, if you want to buy a pair of slacks, you must decide on several things: the style, color, and fabric you want; the amount of care you wish to give the slacks; the price you can pay; and the place to find them in your shopping area.

Some questions you might ask yourself before deciding to buy the slacks are:

- Do I need them?
- Is the style suitable for many occasions?
- Where will I wear them? Where can they be worn?
- Will they soon be outdated?
- Is the fit correct, or will I outgrow them quickly?
- Do I have a shirt, sweater, or blouse that can be worn with them?
- Can I afford to make the purchase?
- What will it cost me to take care of them?

When you have actually selected and purchased the slacks, you will have put your decision-making plan into action. Many people believe this is where the decision-making process ends, but there is still one more important step—evaluation. You must decide if your selection was a wise one.

The best way to learn and understand how to make wise decisions is to practice making them. Making satisfactory decisions is easier when you consider all the facts, possible choices, and possible results of each choice. Careful evaluation of your decisions will help you to live with your choices.

The steps to better decision making are:

- Identify what you need.
- Compare the available products which meet your needs. Consider all the facts.
- Make the best choice you can.
- Evaluate the results of your decision.

BUILDING A USABLE WARDROBE

Many people have a closet filled with clothes and still complain, "I have nothing to wear!" This statement might actually be true. Building a

Consider how the colors and styles of new items will go with the clothes you already own.

workable wardrobe requires careful thought. As you examine your wardrobe, you will begin to see some of your own buying mistakes.

Before you go shopping, consider what you already own. To make this chore easier, make a list of what you have and what you need but do not have. Keep the inventory up to date by adding the new clothes you buy and removing those that are no longer suitable or that you have not worn for several years.

Take a good look at your present wardrobe. What basic line or style is dominant? What colors do you like best? Have you selected clothing that can be mixed in different ways to make many attractive outfits? Have you thrown out garments that no longer fit? Do your clothes reflect the type of life you lead? Do you have clothing to use for different occasions?

Climate and the local styles of dress affect people's needs. A person living in Maine needs warm winter clothing. A Florida resident does not. Clothing suitable for city life may be very different from the clothing required for the country. After you have considered your own needs and your budget and you have developed a spending plan, you are ready for action.

If you were a fashion buyer, you would select and purchase garments from the market that meet the wishes and needs of customers. You would work closely with the department or store manager and be responsible for decisions involving the spending of budgeted money. You might work for one store; for a large central store, buying for other stores in the chain; or for several small stores.

WHERE TO SHOP

Where you shop is influenced by where you live and how much money you have to spend. Stores cater to the interests and budgets of their different customers. They offer a variety of goods and services. You must judge the merits of each store before you buy. To choose where to shop,

it helps to compare the type of merchandise stores display and the services they provide.

Charge accounts, delivery service, the acceptance of returned merchandise, free gift wraps, and alterations are customer benefits that cost the store money. The price on a tag includes a markup to cover these services. Each item you buy helps to pay for these services even if you do not use them.

Stores may be grouped according to the type of ownership, the quality and quantity of merchandise available, and the services given.

Ownership varies from the individual to large corporation.

- The individual shopkeeper is a person who owns and operates one or more stores. All expenses and any profits belong to him or her.
- In a partnership, two or more people share the operation, expenses, and profits of a store or stores.
- A corporation is managed by a board of directors. They represent the people who own stock in the company. The profits of the company are shared by the stockholders.
- The cooperative is owned by a group of people who combine their money to purchase goods. When merchandise is sold and the expenses paid, the profits are divided among the owners according to the amount of money they have invested.

These basic types of ownerships can be combined in different ways to produce a great variety of store ownerships.

Specialty shops and boutiques cater to a certain market, figure type, or size range. Some sell only leather goods, or jewelry, or sleepwear, or shoes. The small specialty store owner often has an understanding of local needs. The income and success of the store are directly related to neighborhood satisfaction.

Chain stores operate in centrally located areas. Because goods and services are bought and sold in volume, it is possible for you to buy goods at a lower price. A chain store in a large

There are many kinds of stores where you can buy clothing and accessories. *Sears, Roebuck, and Co. (bottom right); Bob Capece (others).*

city often has many branch stores. Savings can result when advertising is handled centrally, with one advertisement listing the names and addresses of all the local stores in the chain.

A chain that operates in many areas of the country is often popular with families who move often. The chain store provides them with a familiar name, as well as goods and services to which they are accustomed.

Manufacturers' outlets provide products at lower prices than chain, branch, or individually owned stores. They can do this for several reasons. Outlets usually deal with extra merchandise from normal production. Some of the merchandise is damaged or inferior and should be labeled as a "second" or as "imperfect." When buying from an outlet, you should inspect every detail carefully for damage or flaws in the workmanship or fabric. Usually outlets do not allow returns. All sales are final. Prices are lower because the costs of operating are less. There are few services available and you must pay cash.

Discount stores are found in all regions of the country but are especially prominent in manufacturing areas. The discount store sells both labeled and unlabeled goods at lower prices than other types of stores. Sometimes merchandise is not returnable. Cash is usually required, although personal checks and credit cards are sometimes accepted.

Always inspect all garments before you buy and know whether the store deals in first quality merchandise or in seconds. Garments with a defect, or flaw, that happened during manufacture are called *seconds.* They can be good buys if the imperfection does not show and does not affect the wearability or life of the garment.

Mail-order business became an important part of our marketing system years before the development of rapid transportation and large shopping centers. Ordering by mail is convenient for families who live in rural communities or for customers who cannot or do not want to travel to do their shopping. Catalogs are published several times a year and are sent to prospective customers, who can then make selections at home. Some mail-order houses have stores where customers can order from samples or from a catalog. Prices are often slightly lower than in other stores because overhead is less.

It is also possible to order items advertised in newspapers or magazines. The purchases can be made by telephone or in writing and can be paid for by check, charge card, or COD (cash on delivery). A service charge is usually added to the bill of a COD order.

There are some disadvantages in shopping by mail. It is important to consider color and proper fit, quality of construction, and fabric when buying clothing. It is very difficult, if not impossible, to determine these points from a picture or a written description. Returning unwanted merchandise costs money and can be a bother.

Thrift or secondhand shops can be good sources of bargains. They are also excellent places for your family to recycle outgrown or discarded clothing. You may receive a small payment when your items are sold, or your family may use the total value of the items as a tax deduction. Often, worthwhile community projects are supported by the sale of donated clothes.

If you were a store or department manager, you would supervise activities of other employees. You would plan sales and work with advertisers. If you managed a small department or store, you might also be responsible for buying and inventory control.

WHEN TO SHOP
You can be well dressed and spend less money if you are careful when you shop. Before you go shopping, know what you want and how much money you can spend. Inspect all garments. Do not ignore seconds.

Clothing sales occur frequently. Watch for advertisings that tell when sales are held. Sales occur at the end of a season to make room for new stock; to celebrate special events such as Election Day, Columbus Day, or the Fourth of

Sales can save you money. They can also tempt you to make unplanned purchases. Buying needed items at sales is a wise consumer practice. *Bob Capece*

July; and to serve as postholiday clearances, such as after Christmas. Certain types of apparel, like underwear, shoes, or stockings, are reduced for brief periods of time by individual stores at least once a year. It pays you to know when sales are held in your area.

Shopping takes time, energy, and money. Conserve these resources. Your answers to the following questions may help you determine when and how to shop.

- How much money do you have to spend?
- Do you need the item now, or can you wait for a sale?
- Should you buy only first quality merchandise even if seconds are available?
- Can you save by purchasing end-of-season merchandise? Will the styles and fit be usable the following year?
- Can you rely on your own shopping skills or do you need the help of others?

If you were a comparison shopper, you would visit stores to compare merchandise quality, prices, advertising, and displays with those in your own store. You would collect facts necessary to answer customers' questions on products, prices, and services available at your store and other stores. You might work for one or several departments, or for an entire store.

CREDIT

Many Americans depend on credit to buy goods and services. "Buy now—pay later" describes what credit is. When you purchase an item with credit, you are actually pledging future income to pay the bill. The receipt that you sign during the sales transaction is a promise to pay when the bill is due.

Use of credit has advantages and disadvantages. Charging often enables you to purchase items when you do not have cash. When you have to save for a sale item, it might not be there when you are ready to buy. Using credit, therefore, can help you get more value for your money. Also, you do not have to carry cash, which cannot be regained if lost or stolen.

Some stores give better service to charge customers than to cash customers. Credit customers tend to buy more than cash customers and help keep sales steady by shopping in the stores which allow them credit. When merchandise has to be returned, it is often easier to have the credit listed on your account than to wait for a cash refund. Another advantage is that charge customers are notified of special purchases or sales before they are advertised to the public. Also, you can phone in an order and use your charge account number. The person who uses credit wisely has the satisfaction of enjoying his or her purchase before the bill is due.

Credit cards are convenient and easy to use. For some people, though, credit is an obvious disadvantage. Many people do not budget their spending to stay within their ability to repay. The same rules should govern the use of credit as cash. Using credit can make it easier to overspend.

People who use credit establish a credit rating. A credit rating is a record of one's buying and bill-paying habits. Paying bills promptly helps you maintain a good credit rating and makes you a good credit risk. A good rating permits you to borrow money or open new charge accounts with ease. Information related to your paying habits is kept on file by a credit bureau. Those who do not pay their bills on time earn poor credit ratings and have difficulty in opening new accounts. The person who uses cash to purchase goods and services does not have a credit rating and may also have difficulty opening charge accounts.

There are a variety of charge accounts available. It is just as important to know about them as it is to know how to shop.

The regular, thirty-day charge account is available in many clothing and department stores. With this arrangement you must pay within one month or before the next billing date. There is no extra charge for this type of credit.

The revolving charge account is similar except that the customer has the choice of paying the entire bill or just part of it. When partial payment is made, a finance charge on the unpaid balance is added to the next monthly statement. This finance charge is the cost of credit. The rate is usually $1\frac{1}{2}$ percent per month on the previous month's unpaid balance. This charge is equal to an 18-percent, simple annual interest rate ($1\frac{1}{2}$ percent per month times twelve months per year equals the simple annual interest rate). This type of credit does cost money.

DEVELOPING YOUR SHOPPING SENSE

Style, color, and fabric of clothing attract you in a store. How well a garment fits, its price, and its appearance will narrow your selection for final purchase. Many people do not judge the quality of the clothing they select mainly because they do not know how. To get more satisfaction from the money you spend, you should be able to evaluate the cut, construction, and finish of a garment.

LOOKING FOR QUALITY

Grainline is a major consideration when buying clothes or fabric. Grain is the direction in which threads run in a piece of fabric. If you inspect a piece of woven cloth carefully, you will see that there are lengthwise threads and crosswise threads. In a plaid fabric, for example, each of the colored threads in the pattern reveals the grainline. The lengthwise and crosswise threads of a fabric should be at right angles to each other. If they are not, they may cause a garment to sag at the hemline or lose its shape.

When a plaid is cut and sewn, its lines of color should meet at the seams. This is called a

Checking grainline, seams, and other construction details will help you to select quality merchandise.

"matched" plaid. It takes more time, skill, and often fabric to complete a garment with matched plaids. Clothes with matched plaids usually cost more than clothes with plaids that do not match. The care the manufacturer takes in construction is included in the price you pay.

Bias is any angle to the grainline. Fabric cut on the bias has more stretch, and this affects the finished appearance of the garment.

Seams give us the basic line and shape of our clothes. Check to see that seam allowances are at least ½ inch [1.27 centimeters] wide. Narrow ones do not lie flat and often fray, leaving no room for repairs. Wide seam allowances give a more pleasing appearance to the outside of a garment. They also provide more opportunity to adjust a garment for fit when necessary. Always check to see that the back and side seams hang straight without ripples or puckers. Al-

ways check the back view in the mirror when you try on a garment.

Stitching should be small, even, and straight. There should be no loose threads showing inside the garment. Points of stress in high quality merchandise are double-stitched for strength. These areas include the crotch of pants or shorts and the underarms of a blouse, shirt, coat, or jacket.

If a garment is made from a stretchy knit fabric, give the seams a gentle tug to see if they will give, too. If they do not, the stitching will probably break when the garment is worn.

Closures, including buttons, hooks and eyes, and snaps should be secure. Machine-worked buttonholes are covered with thread stitched along the edges. If there are no loose threads, buttonholes will remain intact through long wear. Fasten the garment to be certain the closures are flat, smooth, and spaced correctly.

Zippers should lie flat and, unless decorative, should have a flap of fabric covering them. Always be sure the zipper works smoothly and does not have broken or missing teeth.

Hems should be neat and should not show on the outside of the garment. They should be of even width. The width often varies from one type of garment or fabric to another. If you think you may have to increase the length of a garment, check to see if there is enough fabric to do so.

If the garment is lined, the lining should not be too stiff for comfort and ease of movement. A lining bears the stress of wear. If it is too small for the garment, it will pull apart at the seams. Unlined jackets or coats should look as neat on the inside as on the outside. Look for finished seam allowances and trimmed threads.

When you try on a garment, take a good look in the mirror. Do you like what you see at first glance? How does it fit? Is the size correct? Can you move comfortably? Crush a small portion of the fabric in your hand and release it. The fabric should bounce back into shape. If it does not, the garment will wrinkle easily when worn.

Does the collar fit comfortably—not too tight or too loose?

Are the left and right sides of the collar the same length and width, and are they wrinkle–free?

Are the sleeves smooth around the armholes?

Is the fit trim but not too tight across the front and back?

Do the buttons look sturdy? Are they sewn on firmly? Do the buttonholes look like they will not unravel?

Are the seams smooth and even?

Is topstitching even and unbroken?

Are the cuffs even and neatly finished?

Are the shirttails even in length and shape? Are they long enough to tuck into pants or skirt?

Do the hangtags and labels show a guarantee that the garment will not fade or shrink?

Is the waistband snug, but not tight, and even in width? Are band fasteners secure?

Is the zipper completely covered, with closure flat and neatly stitched?

Does the crotch depth allow for movement, that is, is it not too long or too short?

Is the length right for you? Is the hem even, with stitching that does not show or pull?

Is the fit smooth across the hips? Do pockets lie flat?

Are the side and leg seams smooth, straight and even, and neatly finished?

Is the fabric cut on the grain and matched, if necessary?

Are the cuffs even in depth and securely tacked?

If you were a garment-test laboratory technician, you would experiment and report on different articles of clothing to see if they meet the claims made by the manufacturers. Flammability, soil and wrinkle resistance, and shrinkage are just a few of the properties you would conduct tests for. You might work for an independent test laboratory, for a textile or clothing manufacturer, or for a government test bureau.

WHAT'S IN A LABEL?

Quality of construction and how the garment looks and feels on you are only two of the many points you must consider before you make the decision to buy. Your final satisfaction is strongly related to the care you must give to the clothes you select. Care labels and hangtags are your best guides for the correct methods of clothing care.

In 1970, the Permanent Care Labeling law went into effect. According to this law, all clothing and yard goods must be labeled with care instructions. On ready-made clothing, these care labels are sewn into a seam. The end of a bolt of fabric contains a label with complete care instructions. When the cloth is cut from the bolt, the salesperson should give you a care label for the fabric so that you can sew it into your garment. You may have to ask for such a label.

Before permanent care labeling became law, the hangtag on the garment was the only way to know how to take care of it. Unless you saved these tags to follow the instructions, you might have washed what should have been dry-cleaned or dripped dry what should have been tumbled dry. You also had to remember what needed special care.

Permanent care labeling became necessary when the textile industry grew from producing cloth of pure natural fibers such as cotton, linen,

Hangtags often combine advertising with important information about the product.

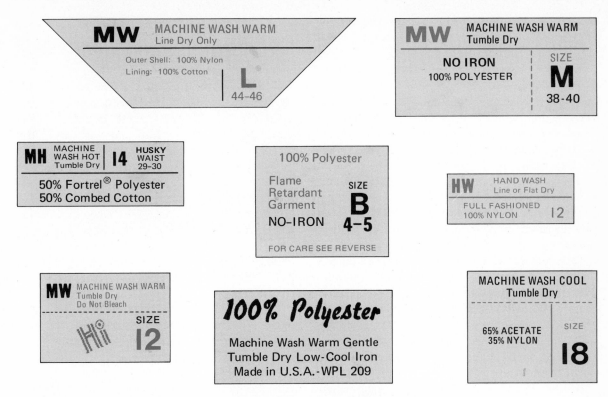

Care labels are sewn into garments, or attached to them, for easy reference.

silk, and wool into an industry which produces many synthetic fabrics.

Many people refuse to buy a garment that says "dry-clean only" because of the additional cost or time involved in caring for it. The real cost of any clothing is its purchase price plus the cost of keeping it wearable. The pair of white slacks with a low price tag but with a "dry-clean only" label is less of a bargain than a more highly priced pair which can be laundered at home. Know the care you are willing and able to give and follow the instructions carefully.

Low labeling is a technique used by some manufacturers to avoid giving instructions for all types of care which could be given. A "dryclean" label on a garment that could also be washed is an example of low labeling. Manufacturers are only responsible for the cleaning method they recommend on the label.

If you follow care instructions and the garment does not perform as you expected, return it to the store immediately. You should bring your sales ticket or other proof of purchase with you. Stores want satisfied customers, so they will usually respond to a legitimate complaint.

BEING A SATISFIED SHOPPER

Part of the thought process that will help make you an effective shopper is being able to recognize both the best and the worst qualities of any purchase. After a garment has been purchased, you evaluate it in terms of performance, care, and durability. There are certain standards that you expect the clothes you buy to meet. When these expectations are met, you are happy with the purchase. When they are not, you should complain. No one wants color to fade or fabric to shrink or hang limp with the first washing. Who would want slacks to wear out or bag at the seat or knee, or a sweater to pill after being worn only a few times?

The emphasis on consumer awareness and wise buying habits in the United States has become strong in recent years. It is interesting that it has not been only the consumer who has taken an active part in this movement. The government has been responsible for introducing many of the laws that protect consumers. The purpose of these laws is to guard the rights of those who buy products and services within the United States.

Government action alone, however, cannot eliminate the buying problems of the public. The government cannot protect people against their own mistakes, but it can encourage the growth of protective agencies in local communities who listen to complaints and handle consumer problems. The consumer must likewise become involved.

In 1960, President John F. Kennedy established the first Consumer Advisory Council, and by 1964, the first Special Assistant to the President on Consumer Affairs was appointed. In a public message President Kennedy outlined the rights of the consumer:

- The right to be protected against the sale of products that are dangerous to health or life
- The right to be informed about or to be protected against misleading information and to be given the facts to make informed choices
- The right to choose from a variety of products
- The right to be heard when something goes wrong

For each of these rights, you, as consumers, must be willing to accept responsibilities to make the system work.

You have the right to expect textile products to be safe. In 1967, an amendment to the Flammable Fabrics Act was passed to prevent the sale and use of textiles that could easily burn in clothing and in home furnishings.

Returning items that do not live up to expectations is one of our consumer responsibilities.

You also have the responsibility to guard against potential fire hazards and to keep matches and other fire-producing agents out of the reach of young children.

You have the right to be informed. The Textile Fiber Products Identification Act and the Permanent Care Labeling law require certain specific information to be on labels. It is the consumer's responsibility to look for and use this information. You must also care for the product as instructed. If you do not, the manufacturer cannot be held responsible for possible damage.

You have the right to select from a wide variety of merchandise in a broad range of prices. You have the responsibility to consider the pros and cons of each purchase and to make the best selection possible according to your needs.

You have the right to be heard when your complaint is legitimate. You have the responsibility to be fair and honest when you do complain. A letter to the store president or to the manufacturer might be necessary when you have a complaint. Write clearly and supply as many facts as you can. Only those who make their problems known will solve them.

Sometimes it becomes necessary to contact a local Better Business Bureau, Chamber of Commerce, or other agency for additional help.

Machine Washable

When label reads:	It means:
Washable Machine washable	Wash, bleach, dry, and press by any customary method including commercial laundering.
Home launder only	Same as above but do not use commercial laundering.
No bleach	Do not use bleach.
No starch	Do not use starch.
Cold wash Cold setting Cold rinse	Use cold water from tap or cold washing machine setting.
Lukewarm wash Warm wash Warm setting Warm rinse	Use warm water (hand comfortable) 90° to 110°F (32° to 40°C).
Medium wash Medium setting	Use warm water (medium washing machine setting) 110° to 130°F (43° to 55°C).
Hot wash Hot setting	Use hot water (hot washing machine setting) 130°F (55°C) or hotter.
No spin	Remove wash load before final machine spin cycle.
Delicate cycle Gentle cycle	Use appropriate machine setting; otherwise, wash by hand.
Durable press cycle Permanent press cycle	Use appropriate machine setting; otherwise use medium wash, cold rinse, and short spin cycle.
Wash separately	Wash alone or with like colors.

Non-Machine Washing

When label reads:	It means:
Hand washable Wash by hand	Launder only by hand in warm water. May be bleached. May be drycleaned.
Hand wash only	Same as above, but do not dryclean.
Hand wash separately	Hand wash alone or with like colors.
No bleach	Do not use bleach.

Home Drying

When label reads:	It means:
Tumble dry Machine dry	Dry in tumble dryer at specified setting—high, medium, low, or no heat.
Tumble dry Remove promptly	Same as above, but in absence of cool-down cycle remove at once when tumbling stops.
Drip dry Hang dry Line dry	Hang wet and allow to dry with hand shaping only.
No squeeze No wring No twist	Hang dry, drip dry, or dry flat only.
Dry flat	Lay garment on flat surface.
Block to dry	Maintain original size and shape while drying.

Ironing or Pressing

When label reads:	It means:
Cool iron	Set iron at lowest setting.
Warm iron	Set iron at medium setting.
Hot iron	Set iron at hot setting.
No iron No press	Do not iron or press with heat.
Steam iron Steam press	Iron or press with steam.
Iron damp	Dampen garmet before ironing.

Miscellaneous

When label reads:	It means:
Dry-clean Dry-clean only	Garment should be dry-cleaned only.
Professionally clean only Commercially clean only	Do not use self-service dry-cleaning.
No dry-clean	Use recommended care instructions. No dry-cleaning materials to be used.

Adapted from *Consumer Care Guide for Apparel*, © Copyright 1971, The American Apparel Manufacturers Association, Inc.

Know your local agencies and what aid they are equipped to give. Use them only when you really need to.

There is help available at the local, state, and federal levels. Agencies such as the Federal Trade Commission and the Consumer Protection Council take action on large-scale problems and help regulate the selling practices of big companies. They attempt to control practices such as regulation of interest charges on installment accounts, improper labeling of fabrics, and false advertising.

If you were a consumer specialist, you would keep records and investigate and solve problems for people who have already done everything possible to solve their own problems. You would also take action to protect consumers from illegal business practices.

People are becoming more aware of the roles they play as consumers. It is important to be a knowledgeable buyer since your selection determines your degree of satisfaction. Laws may help regulate business practices, but they cannot make your consumer decisions. To be a more effective, satisfied consumer, you should:

· Plan for your shopping needs.
· Look for styles that are suitable for your figure type, age, and activities.
· Select clothes that fit into and add to the versatility of your wardrobe.
· Plan ahead and compare merchandise for quality of fabric and construction, cost, and care.
· Read hangtags and care labels for desired performance characteristics.
· Be aware of the names of the manufacturers that produce the clothing you like.
· When necessary, complain effectively.

● IDEAS FOR ACTION

1. Conduct a survey of consumer personalities. Ask your friends and family about their buying habits and preferences. Are there any characteristics that are common to many of the people interviewed? Why do you think these similarities exist? Are there differences, too? Why?

2. Bring to class advertisements related to dress and appearance. Discuss radio and television commercials for clothing. How do the companies present their products to make them appealing? How does this advertising affect you? Your clothing selection? Your budget?

3. Make a list of the clothes you have but do not wear. Next to each item, explain why you do not wear it. What do you plan to do with these clothes? How might you put them to use?

4. Name the garments you plan to buy this season. Develop a list of the points you will consider when shopping for these garments.

5. Make a list of the types of stores available for clothes shopping in your area. List each store's advantages and disadvantages. Which store is your favorite? Explain why.

6. Use the information gained from activity 5 to construct a bulletin board about stores in your area. For each store, show the type of clothing and methods of payment available, the sales and services offered, and the advertising used.

7. Bring an article of clothing to class. Point out the construction features. Discuss how careful evaluation of these features can be important in the selection and care of the garment. Collect clothing hangtags and labels. Compare the information found on each. Look for the manufacturer's name, fiber content, and care instructions.

8. Present a series of brief skits about a consumer trying to return an item of clothing. Show a legitimate complaint and an unfounded complaint each receiving appropriate attention. You might want other class members to suggest ways of solving consumer problems.

9. Sometimes what seems like a bargain turns out to be a poor buy. Give examples of when this can happen. How can you avoid making these mistakes?

10. If you had $30 to go shopping for clothing, what would you buy? How would your values, goals, wishes, and needs influence your purchase? Are there any sales or special buys available? What other consumer information can you find? Consider your time, travel expenses, and any taxes as part of the cost of your purchase.

● DO YOU KNOW

bias	decision making
blend	fiber content
charge account	goods and services
consumer	grain
consumer responsibilities	hangtag
consumer rights	interest
credit	permanent care labeling
credit rating	second

fibers and fabrics

After reading this chapter you should be able to:

- *List fibers from animal and plant sources.*

- *Compare the characteristics of several natural fibers.*

- *Explain the difference between natural and synthetic fibers.*

- *Describe how synthetic fibers are made.*

- *Explain how fibers are made into yarns.*

- *Identify the main types of fabric construction.*

- *Give examples of fabric weaves.*

- *Discuss the reasons for and effects of fabric finishes.*

TEXTILES

You have just returned home from school, and you enter the living room. You take off your jacket and put it on the sofa. You open the curtains to see who is walking down the street. You use your handkerchief. You take off your shoes and socks and wiggle your toes on the carpet. You may not know it, but nearly everything you have just touched is a textile. Clothes, curtains, carpets, upholstery, and handkerchiefs are all made of fibers. Fibers make fabric, and both are textiles.

Before the twentieth century, fibers for fabrics came from nature. Wool, silk, cotton, linen, and a few others were the only known fibers then. Wool came from sheep and alpacas and llamas. Silk came from silkworms, which make fiber for cocoons. Cotton and linen came from plants.

There were fur and leather fabrics then, too. Both came from animals such as birds, snakes, goats, cows, pigs, deer, minks, raccoons, musk-rats, and many others.

Today we need not depend only on animals and plants for our textiles. Synthetic fibers, which are made from liquid chemicals, have revolutionized the worlds of clothing and home furnishing.

Fibers are made into yarns, and yarns are made into fabrics. For thousands of years, the fiber content of a fabric determined its qualities and how you cared for it. Recently, though, a number of fabric finishes have enabled us to have cotton that need not be ironed, linen that repels dirt, and wool that resists damage by moths.

NATURAL FIBERS

Linen, cotton, silk, and wool are the most important natural fibers. Hemp and jute are natural,

too, but they are not used for clothing. Fur and leather must also be mentioned. Although they are not true textiles, they are used as fabrics.

LINEN

Nearly everyone has heard of flax. But who can remember what it is? Ancient Egyptians knew: flax is the plant that linen is made from. Linen is not as common as many other fibers, but it makes the most beautiful tablecloths and lint-free towels and suits, slacks, and dresses, too.

The best linen comes from the tallest flax. To get the fibers from inside the woody stem of the plant, the outside must be soaked in water. The water rots the outside and frees the fibers within. Magnified, flax fibers look like bamboo sticks. Their thick-thin structure makes the texture of linen somewhat bumpy. Linen is very strong, durable, and absorbent.

Linen is easy to clean. Though bleach may damage it, linen can be washed and ironed at high temperatures. Ironing gives linen a luster,

Flax is soaked, stacked, and left in the fields to dry again. It will then be crushed, separated, and combed. The combed flax looks like human hair. *The Belgian Linen Association*

From cotton flower to cotton boll—the harvest is only the first step in the production of cotton fibers for fabrics and clothing. *Cotton Incorporated*

or rich sheen. If you own something made of linen, you already know that it wrinkles easily, and you have to iron it often.

COTTON

Cotton is known to us all. It is a part of our culture, a part of our history as Americans. The economy of the pre-Civil War United States depended on it. Eli Whitney invented a machine, the cotton gin, to remove seeds from cotton, and the fiber became even more popular. Today the United States is still the largest producer of cotton in the world. In the nineteenth century we sold our cotton to England, and now we sell it to many different countries.

Cotton is still the most commonly used natural fiber. All of us wear cotton. It is what blue jeans are made of, and T-shirts, and handkerchiefs, and terry cloth, and diapers.

There are several varieties of cotton plants producing fibers, or *staples*, of various lengths from $\frac{1}{2}$ inch to 2 inches [1.27 to 5.08 centimeters]. The different length fibers make fabrics with different looks. The longer varieties produce fine, somewhat shiny fabrics, used for expensive dresses and shirts. The medium staple, the most common, is coarser and costs less than the finer varieties. The cotton used in peasant blouses and shirts is coarse and dull and is an example of the short staple type.

It is hard to believe that sheer, delicate organdy and voile come from the same fiber as canvas, sailcloth, and muslin. One of the most valuable properties of cotton is this variety of possible

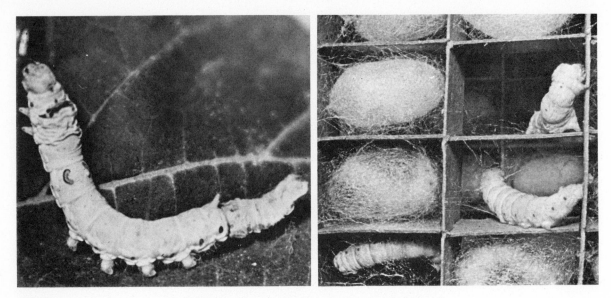

The silkworm eats every two to three hours, night and day, for five weeks before it attaches itself to a twig and spins its cocoon. *International Silk Association*

weaves and fabrics. Another advantage of cotton is that it is very absorbent. Nothing can match it as a diaper or a towel. The main drawback of cotton is that it wrinkles easily.

You can bleach cotton, wash it in hot water, iron it, starch it, dye it, and wear it in the sun without ruining it. Cotton really is nature's miracle fiber.

SILK
Silk is another of nature's miracles.

One of the world's most expensive fibers, it comes from the mouth of a worm. Cultivated silkworms, which eat only mulberry leaves, spin long strands for cocoons. These strands, called *filaments*, average in length from 300 to 1800 yards [274 to 1644 meters]. The silk fabric woven from these filaments is fine, smooth, and delicate.

Silkworms can also grow wild and live on a diet of oak leaves. These worms produce an uneven, rough-textured, tan-colored filament. Sometimes two silkworms encircle each other while spinning their cocoons. The resulting silk filament is knotted and thick or thin in different spots.

Silk must be dry-cleaned or hand-washed in warm water with mild soap or detergent. It can easily be scorched. The sun can discolor and weaken it. Today, many new fibers look and feel much like silk and are less expensive and easier to care for. As a result, silk is a rarity in our wardrobes.

WOOL
Like silk, wool is an animal fiber. It comes most often from the fleece of sheep. Like cotton, wool is part of our culture. Sheep are raised all over the world. In addition to raising sheep, the United States is also a leading maker of wool products. Most of us, even if we live in a warm climate, own something made of wool.

The wool fiber, or staple, is rough and scaly. As a result, it sheds water and other liquids. It has a built-in crimp (a natural curl), which makes it elastic, strong, and slow to wrinkle.

The appearance and texture of raw wool is due to its natural crimp and oils (lanolin). *American Wool Council*

WOOL BLEND

PURE WOOL

COTTON INCORPORATED

These registered trademarks can help you to identify products made of cotton or wool. They appear on labels, hangtags, and in advertising.

Llamas, alpacas, vicunas, cashmere goats, as well as several kinds of sheep, all give us wool. The length of the staple can vary from 1 inch to 12 inches [2.5 centimeters to 30.5 centimeters]. The length and appearance of the staple depend on which animal it comes from. Long staples are woven into smooth fabrics called *worsteds.* Shorter staples are woven into *woolens.*

Wool clothes and fabrics can be made from virgin wool, reprocessed wool, or reused wool. Wool, or *virgin wool*, is made of fibers that have never been used or made into finished fabric. *Reprocessed wool* is made from shredded scraps of unused wool fabric and *reused wool,* from cleaned, shredded scraps of used wool fabric. Both are much cheaper than virgin wool. Reused and reprocessed wool go into carpets and coat linings and, sometimes, blankets. Virgin wool is the strongest of the three types. For this reason, it is the wool we choose most often to wear.

If you care for your wool clothes, they will repay you with years of wearability. Most of them must be dry-cleaned. If they can be washed, it must be done in cool water. Hot water will shrink them. Press wool clothes with a warm, not hot, iron on the wrong side so they do not scorch or become shiny, or use a press cloth. Do not use bleach on wool and try to keep it out of direct sunlight. Both bleach and sun quickly yellow the fiber.

Wool clothes need a rest after wearing. Let them hang on padded hangers for at least a day between wearings to allow the fibers to pull themselves together. Fold wool knits instead of hanging them to keep them from stretching. The clothes moth and carpet beetle are especially fond of wool fibers and can cause damage to wool clothes and home furnishings. You can protect your woolens from moths and beetles by dry cleaning or mothproofing them.

JUTE AND HEMP
Other natural fibers from plants include jute and hemp. Neither is used in clothing. Burlap and sacking are made from jute. Hemp is used mainly for twine and rope.

Animal	Fiber name	Where found	Characteristics	Uses
Angora goat	Mohair	Turkey South Africa United States	fine, silky, shiny fiber that is strong and easily dyed	suits sportswear knitted garments
Cashmere goat	Cashmere	Kashmir China Tibet Mongolia	very soft, fine fibers	outerwear suits
Camel	Camel's hair	Mongolia Tibet China	underhairs are fine, soft fibers that can protect the wearer from extreme hot and cold temperatures	outerwear suits sportswear
Alpaca	Alpaca	South America	fine, soft, shiny fiber	suits dresses plush linings
Llama	Llama	South America	fine, soft fiber	same as Alpaca
Vicuna	Vicuna	Andes Mountains, South America	very soft, lightweight, fine, and shiny fiber	coats suits outerwear
Angora rabbit	Angora	France Italy Japan United States	long, fine, soft, and fluffy fibers	knitting yarns knitted garments

38

Straw, like hemp and jute, is used to make hats, bags, belts, and other accessories.

FUR AND LEATHER

Fur and leather are natural clothing materials, too, but they are not true textiles because they are not made of fibers. Both fur and leather are more expensive than most textiles. This is because the animals they come from are limited in number.

Since the ecology movement of the late 1960s, some people have come to feel that killing animals for clothing is not necessary. Killing of certain animals has nearly wiped out entire species, and the balance of nature has been upset.

Many leathers are made from the skins of animals raised for food. But even this source is limited. Leather is made by treating the skins chemically, after the hair has been removed. The process is called *tanning*.

Both fur and leather are exceptionally durable but expensive to buy and care for. For this reason, synthetic fur look-alikes, leatherlike vinyls, and synthetic "suede," have become popular substitutes.

Today, many synthetic fabrics are popular substitutes for real leather and fur. *Russel Taylor's Ben Kahn Collection with Verel Modacrylic (bottom)*

SYNTHETIC FIBERS

There was once a movie (*The Man in the White Suit*—1951) about an inventor who had developed the ideal fiber. This fiber was wrinkle-free, easy to clean, elastic, lightweight, and exceptionally strong. It dyed beautifully, could be woven or knitted into any texture, helped the wearer to stay cool in the summer and warm in the winter, and did not accumulate static electricity. It was also easy and inexpensive to produce.

Nice as they are, natural fibers are not like the ideal described above. Production of natural fibers is subject to natural disasters—cotton and flax plants can get diseases, and insects can damage them. Cotton and flax must be planted and harvested. Both plants and animals can be affected by weather conditions. Sheep must be shorn. Silkworms have to be fed and their cocoons unwound. These things take time and add to the cost of fibers. The need for greater amounts of textiles for clothing and home furnishings also raises the cost and uses up the natural supply of fibers. Natural fibers wrinkle. They can be hard to clean. Some are inelastic, or heavy, or limited in what types of fabrics they can be made into.

If you are interested in a career in the textile industry, there are many different areas to investigate. There are jobs in all the stages of the processing of natural and synthetic fibers and the making of yarns and fabrics. Marketing, manufacturing, research and development, advertising, engineering, and design are general fields in textiles that offer a number of job opportunities.

Synthetic fibers are not always ideal either, but they do offer variety. Fibers made by people have greatly increased our choice of textiles for clothing and home furnishings.

The silkworm provided the idea for the technology of synthetic fibers. The silkworm makes silk filaments by forcing a liquid through its tiny mouth; the air makes the filaments solid. Observing this, scientists thought that if they forced a liquid through a tiny hole, perhaps they could make filaments, too. The problem was to find

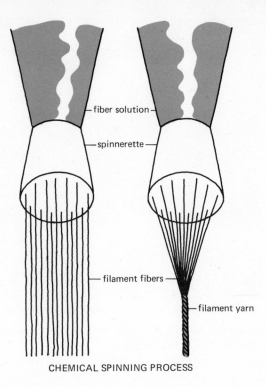

CHEMICAL SPINNING PROCESS

the right liquid. This took from 1850 until 1889, when "artificial silk" was made successfully in France. By 1905 it was being produced commercially, and it was called *rayon.*

The liquid that rayon is made from is itself made from cellulose. This liquid is found in tree bark and cotton seeds, so rayon is not considered a true synthetic. *Acetate* is also made from liquified cellulose, with some chemicals added. Like rayon, it is not considered a true synthetic.

True synthetics are made in the same way as rayon and acetate. A liquid is forced through the tiny holes of a round device called a *spinnerette.* The filaments are then treated to make them solid. The liquid used to make true synthetics, however, is totally chemical. There are many formulas, of course, and different ways of making the filaments solid. For the most part, though, the chemicals are made from oil products, and the fibers are made solid in air, water, or a chemical bath.

RAYON AND ACETATE—
SEMISYNTHETICS

Rayon and acetate seemed miraculous in the early years of their use. They are nearly as soft as silk and are easier to care for. They are less expensive than silk, too. They dye well. These qualities make rayon and acetate good substitutes for silk. Rayon is used for shirts, blouses, and scarves; acetate, for linings, lingerie, satins, shirts, dresses, and ties. However, because they have a natural base, rayon and acetate absorb moisture. They dry slowly and do not repel liquid stains. They wrinkle easily and must be ironed. If you use a hot iron, they will melt.

TRUE SYNTHETICS

There are presently about fifteen types of true synthetics. The ones most widely used are *nylon, polyester, acrylic,* and *modacrylic.* They have a lot in common. They are wrinkle-resistant, quick to dry, lightweight, and durable. Like rayon and acetate, they all melt easily, so you must use a cool iron.

Unlike rayon and acetate, the true synthetics repel moisture, and as a result, they attract static electricity. This causes them to cling to other fabrics and to the wearer, as well as to sometimes give the wearer electric shocks. When synthetics are rubbed in the course of normal use, the fiber ends, which would break off in less durable fabrics, accumulate in little lumps on the surface. This is called *pilling.*

The four important true synthetics have different uses. *Nylon,* which was the first to be developed, has replaced silk in stockings, lingerie, and nightclothes. Lightweight and water-repellent, nylon has made the modern ski jacket and camping gear possible. It is also used for parachutes and umbrellas, mesh bags, and lightweight clothing.

Polyester fiber can look and feel a lot like cotton. Yet it is wrinkle-resistant and quick to dry. Since it can be fluffy and warm, it is used to fill quilts, comforters, and winter jackets. Pillows and upholstered furniture can also be stuffed

with it. Polyester is used to make a wide variety of woven and knitted clothing. Often, polyester is combined with natural fibers to add its drip-dry quality and extra strength.

Acrylics are fluffy and lightweight, too. Most often, acrylic is used where wool might have been used before. It is used to make machine-washable sweaters, resilient double-knit fabrics for men's and women's suits, and other medium-weight clothing. Blankets made of acrylics are much easier to find now than those made of wool. This fiber is usually less expensive than wool—both to buy and to maintain.

Modacrylics are similar to acrylics, as the name implies. They are heavier, though, and are often used in carpeting, home furnishings, and wigs. Fake furs and pile linings are also made of modacrylic fibers.

Of course, there is some overlap in the uses these synthetics are put to. For example, nylon is used to make carpets. Polyester is used to make underwear and nightclothes. When blended with natural fibers, the synthetics expand their range even further. The advantage, of course, is variety. If you cannot have a fiber ideal for every purpose, you can have one fiber that is ideal or almost ideal for any purpose.

FAMILY GROUPS

Each of the true and semisynthetic fibers we have discussed (rayon, acetate, nylon, polyester, acrylic, modacrylic, and others less well known) includes fibers with different names. Every company that produces a synthetic fiber has a registered name for it. To simplify things, the Federal Trade Commission has grouped fibers with the same chemical composition under the family names given above. For example, Antron and Qiana are both nylon, and Dacron and Kodel are both polyester.

BLENDS

Blends are made of two or more fibers. Most often, a synthetic and a natural fiber are combined to gain some of the advantages of each.

Alone or combined, both natural and synthetic fibers provide us with an almost limitless variety of fabrics for all occasions.

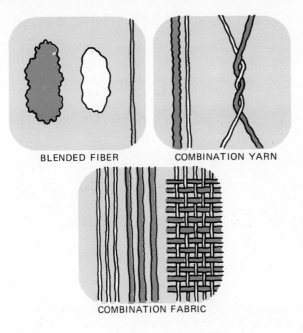

BLENDED FIBER   COMBINATION YARN

COMBINATION FABRIC

ning. During spinning, each fiber is twisted around itself and other fibers. Spinning adds strength and length. Shorter fibers are twisted more than longer ones to help them to stick to one another. Try it yourself by twirling some wisps of wool or cotton or lengths of thread between your fingers.

Natural fibers require preparation before spinning. Sheep get stained and have twigs and leaves in their wool. Cotton and flax grow in the dirt—they can be soiled in the picking, too. These natural fibers must be washed. They are sorted according to length, and the longer fibers are combed. Synthetics are spun as they come out of the spinnerette. Fibers of different origins can be spun together to make blends.

Spinning can add special features. Boucle yarn, for example, is made by looping fibers during the spinning. Loops and other variations produce what are called novelty yarns.

An example is the blend of cotton and polyester that is used for no-iron shirts. The blend makes the shirts wrinkle-resistant and quick to dry, like polyester, and soft and absorbent, like cotton. Shirts made entirely of polyester can make wearers uncomfortable by repelling their perspiration. Shirts made entirely of cotton need to be ironed.

As a rule, the care for a fabric that is a blend of fibers is the same as the care for whatever fiber is used most in the blend. For example, a fabric that is 55 percent acrylic and 45 percent wool should be cared for as you would care for an acrylic fabric.

In 1969, the Textile Fiber Products Identification Act was changed to require manufacturers to label the fibers in their fabric by percentage of the total weight. You can tell how much of each fiber is in a blend by looking at the label.

HOW YARNS ARE MADE

To make fabric, you need yarn. To get yarn, you must process fiber. The process is called *spin-*

HOW FABRICS ARE MADE

Once the yarn is spun, it is ready to be made into a fabric. There are several different ways this can be done. Weaving, knitting, felting, and bonding are the methods used most often. Each produces a different type of fabric.

WEAVING

Yarns can become fabric if they are woven. This means one yarn is passed over and under other yarns. The yarns that run up and down, called *warp yarns,* are held at right angles to the yarn passing across them, called the *filling yarn.*

Weaving would be hard to do if there were no *looms.* Perhaps, as a child, you made hand-woven pot holders out of nylon loops. If you did, you had to pull the filler loops over and under the warp loops with your fingers. Looms do this for you. They divide the warp yarns so that the filler yarn can go straight across. Then they divide the warp yarns the other way, so the filler yarn can come straight back.

Steps in the production of fibers and fabrics range from spinning, weaving or knitting, and finishing to final inspection. *American Textile Mfrs. Inst.; Cotton Incorporated* (*top left and bottom middle*)

Looms come in all sizes. The big ones used by fabric manufacturers are power-operated and turn out yards and yards of fabric in just minutes.

There are three common weaves: the *plain weave*, the *satin*, and the *twill*. These weaves can be tight or loose depending on how close together the yarns are placed. Tighter weaves are stronger. Sheets are often labeled with the number of threads (yarns) per square inch: the higher the number, the more durable the sheets.

Sheets made of muslin or percale are an example of the *plain weave*. Gingham fabric is another. Each filler yarn is passed over one warp yarn and under the next, over the next, under the next, and so on. Most fabric is woven this way.

If you were a textile designer, you would be responsible for developing new patterns and designs to be used in the making of fabrics. You might sketch a design and transfer it to a silk screen or a printing roller. You might design a new pattern for a weave or knit to be done directly on a loom. The selection and mixing of colors would be another of your responsibilities. You might work for a textile mill or for a design studio.

Satin fabric is, of course, an example of the *satin weave*. Each filler yarn in satin is passed over four or more warp yarns before being passed under one. Satin is shiny because the filler yarns on the surface reflect light. Satin is strong because the yarns must be close together. Otherwise, the shiny effect would be lost. Satin is usually made of acetate or silk fiber. When it is made of cotton, it is called *sateen*.

Twill is most likely known to you in the form of denim. In *twill weaving*, the filler yarns are passed over two warp yarns and under one, over two and under one, and so on. That is why blue jeans, when looked at closely, have diagonal lines running along the fabric. As you know, blue

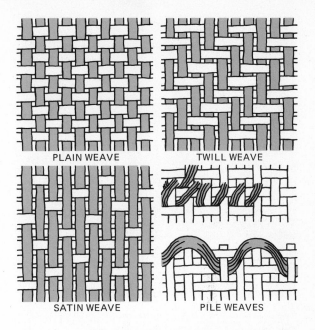

PLAIN WEAVE TWILL WEAVE

SATIN WEAVE PILE WEAVES

jeans are tough and long-lasting. This is because twill, like satin, is closely woven. Other examples of twill are gabardine and wool flannel. Herringbone is a twill variation in which the direction of the diagonal is reversed at regular intervals, resulting in a striped effect.

The three common weaves are not the only possible ones. Combinations and variations account for the pile weaves of corduroy, velvet, and terry cloth, for example. Detailed designs can also be woven into fabric with specialized looms. Pictures woven into fabric are called *tapestries*.

KNITTING

Yarn can also become fabric if it is knitted. In recent years, with the invention of double knit, this method of making fabric has become very popular. Knitted fabric has built-in stretch and a casual look. It seems especially appropriate for easy-care synthetic fibers.

There are two ways to knit yarn into fabric. The first way, similar to what handknitters do to make a sweater, is called *filling knit*. In this kind of knit, one yarn is brought horizontally across the fabric in a row of interlocking loops.

The Jacquard loom is known for the detailed patterns it can produce. *American Textile Mfrs. Inst.*

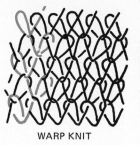 

WARP KNIT   FILLING KNIT

As in weaving, the *filling yarn* runs across the width of the fabric. Filling knit is used for both single-knit and double-knit fabrics. For both, only one yarn is used, but double knit has two layers of interlocking loops. These layers cannot be separated. As a result, double knits stretch less and hold their shape better than single knits.

Sometimes filling knits are made on circular knitting machines. These machines produce fabric formed like a tube, with no seam. Usually the tube is cut before the fabric is used. Stockings, socks, and some underwear and hats are knitted in and remain in small-size, specially shaped tubes.

Stockings are a clue to the big disadvantage of filling knits: they run. If one stitch is broken, all the loops in the line can pull loose and the fabric can be ruined.

Warp knit does not run because it is made of a series of parallel yarns, each controlled by a separate needle. The interlocking loops go the long way, up and down the length of the fabric, just like the *warp yarns* in weaving. Warp knit

is less stretchable than filling knit. Tricot used for underwear, lingerie, and blouses is a common example of a warp knit.

FELTING AND BONDING

There are two other ways to make yarn into fabric: *felting* and *bonding*. Neither of these is as common as weaving or knitting.

Felting is used primarily for wool but sometimes for cotton or fur. It combines the fibers by wetting them, heating them, and pressing them together. The result is an inelastic fabric that does not fray. Felt is used for decorative garments, for decoration on other fabric, for toys, for accessories, and for hats.

If you were a textile tester, you would be responsible for checking different fibers, fabrics, or finishes before they were introduced to the public. How they look, feel, and act after wear and care are only a few of the characteristics that are tested. Your knowledge of textiles and chemistry would be important for this job. You would work for a textile mill or an independent testing laboratory.

Bonding combines fibers in a way similar to felting but with the addition of an adhesive. *Interfacing*, the layer of fabric that fits between the finished outside and inside of collars, lapels, and waistbands is often bonded. Paper products such as those used to make disposable diapers are also examples of bonded fabrics.

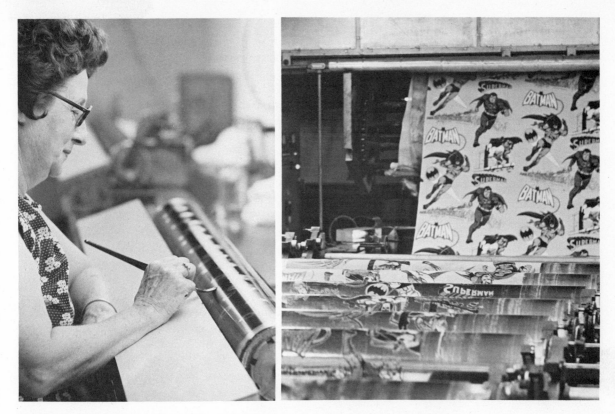

Rotary screen printing produces clear, colorful prints at great speed. Dye is forced through holes in the cylinders, and the cylinders are rolled over the cloth, leaving the print. *American Textile Mfrs. Inst.*

Bonding is also used to combine two fabrics. This kind of bonding strengthens loosely woven fabrics and very stretchy ones.

FINISHES

It was only recently that stain-repellent and anti-static finishes were invented for fabrics. Yet chemicals and mechanical procedures have been used to treat fabrics almost since the beginning of fabric making.

A finish is anything that is done to alter the appearance, feel, or performance of a fiber, yarn, or fabric. Ironing is a finish, for example. When ironing is done by the manufacturer, by running a damp fabric through heated rollers, it is called *calandering*. Ironing, or calandering, makes fabric look smooth and slightly shiny. Sometimes designs or textures are pressed into the surface of the fabric by calandering. This is how embossed, pleated, and moiréd fabrics are made.

Calandering and another mechanical finish called *tentering* are used to restore the straight grain of fabric, which has been pushed or pulled out of shape in weaving or knitting. To tenter a fabric, the manufacturer pins it to two parallel belts, stretches it, and runs it through a drying box. This places the filling and warp yarns permanently at right angles to each other.

When a pile fabric, like terry cloth, is *sheared,* it is treated by a machine that resembles a lawn mower. This machine trims the fibers to make them all the same height. On flat fabrics, shearing removes loose threads, fibers, and knots.

Another finish that is a combination of the mechanical and chemical finishes is called *sizing.* When you do it at home, you call it *starching.* Chemicals are added to the surface of the fabric to make it stiff and smooth. Sometimes cheap, lightweight fabrics are sized to make them look

Many fabrics can be treated to make them water resistant. *Simplicity Pattern Co.*

heavier. Sizing usually disappears when you wash or dry-clean the fabric.

We may think of chemical finishes as very new. They are, but they are also the oldest kind of finish. The most common chemical fabric finish and the earliest known is *dyeing.* Natural fabric colors are attractive but limited. So, extracts of berries, tree bark, and vegetable roots, in addition to a variety of chemicals, are used to dye, or color, fabrics. Prints are made by applying dyes to the fabric surface in patterns.

Other chemical finishes are *bleaching, acid treatment,* and *mercerization.* At home, you bleach fabric to whiten it. This is the industrial purpose, too. Just as often, however, fabrics that will be dyed are bleached first; this is done so that the fabrics will take on true, even color. Acids of various kinds are used to make fabric translucent or to create an interesting surface. Designs can be etched into fabric with acid, or fabric can be puckered. Mercerization means treating the fabric, usually cotton, with caustic soda to increase its strength, luster, and ability to absorb dye. Nearly all cotton thread is mercerized.

Other chemical finishes can make fabric water-repellent, flame-retardant, and quick to release soil. Mildew, moths, and molds are repelled by still other finishes.

TEXTILES AND YOU

As more and more new fibers, fabrics, and finishes are used in clothing, it becomes increasingly difficult to know what you are buying. How to take care of what you have bought can also be a problem. The manufacturers' care labels and hangtags are your best guides. However, knowing some general information about textiles should be helpful when you purchase or care for your garments. It will also be helpful when you are selecting fabric to make your own clothing. More information on the selection and buying of fabrics is included in Chapter 9.

FABRIC FINISHES

The finish	And what it does
antistatic	prevents the buildup of static electricity and helps to keep the fabric from clinging to the wearer or other garments (often used in underwear and sleepwear)
colorfast	helps the fabric keep its dyed color during normal wear and care
flame-resistant	prevents the fabric from supporting a flame
mercerization	applied to cotton fibers and fabrics for added strength, luster, and the greater ability to accept and hold dyes
moth-resistant	makes wool fabrics resistant to attacks by moths and carpet beetles
sanforized	controls shrinkage to less than 1 percent; usually applied to cotton and linen fabrics
soil-release	helps fabrics to give up soil and spots when washed; durable press fabrics need this finish
stain- and spot-resistant	protects fabrics from spills by not allowing them to penetrate the fibers
water-repellent	helps fabrics to resist water, but does not make them waterproof
waterproof	closes the pores of the fabric, preventing any water from penetrating
wrinkle-resistant, wash-and-wear, durable- or permanent-press	helps to improve the wrinkle-recovery and shape-retention qualities of the fabrics and garments

1. From a piece of 100-percent-wool fabric, cut three 3-inch [7.6-centimeter] square pieces. Machine wash one square in hot water and dry it in a clothes dryer. Wash the second piece by hand in cool water and allow it to air dry. Compare the two washed pieces of wool with each other and then with the unwashed sample. Discuss your findings.

2. Cut three small pieces of fabric made of different fibers—animal, plant, and synthetic. Mount the fabric samples on cardboard and label their fiber content. Cover one half of each sample with another cardboard. Place the samples in a window with good sun exposure. Keep a record of approximately how many hours of sun they receive each day. After a two-week period, remove the cardboard covers. Note any differences between the covered and exposed halves. What does this tell you about the effect of sun on each of these fibers?

3. Give a presentation on how yarns are made from both natural and synthetic fibers. Use a variety of yarns from sewing and knitting scraps to demonstrate. Show differences in crimp. Ask each student in the class to bring one yarn sample to untwist and compare with all the others.

4. Make a display of different types of weaves —plain, twill, satin, and others you may find. Use actual fabric samples and simple drawings of each weave. Include a description of the characteristics and clothing uses of each weave.

5. Find out the fiber content of a garment you own. Trace each fiber back from garment to original source. Include a brief description of every stage of production. You might even illustrate your story.

6. Prepare a bulletin board entitled "What's Hiding in Your Closet?" Name weaves, knits, finishes, and fibers found in your clothes and accessories.

7. Investigate flammability standards for clothing. Check your library for recent newspaper and magazine articles. Write to the Federal Trade Commission, Washington, D.C. 20580, or to your representative in the United States Congress or state assembly to find out what is being done in this area of clothing safety. Report on your findings. How does the legislation being enacted now affect you and members of your family? What do you think about flammability and clothing?

● DO YOU KNOW

bonding	plain weave
fabric	satin weave
felting	spinnerette
fiber	spinning
filament	staple
finish	static electricity
knitting	synthetic
natural fiber	textile
permanent press	twill weave
pilling	weaving

4

selecting clothing

After reading this chapter, you should be able to:

- *Identify four types of clothing lines and their visual effects on the human body.*

- *Recognize the basic clothing shapes.*

- *Discuss how pattern and texture add interest and variety to a wardrobe.*

- *Understand the relationship of primary, secondary, and intermediate colors.*

- *Use a basic knowledge of color in personal clothing selections.*

- *Explain the term* optical illusion *in relation to the elements of clothing design.*

- *Discuss how planning and coordinating a wardrobe can result in efficient use of your clothing dollar.*

HOW YOUR CLOTHES LOOK ON YOU

What goes into the makeup of a garment? What makes a garment look and feel the way it does even before you put it on? What gives it style? What makes it fit? Every garment has basic elements. They are line, shape, color, and texture. When combined in different ways, they make different styles of dresses, jeans, shirts, and jackets.

Clothing that is right for you expresses your individuality and looks good on you. To a certain extent, this depends upon your body build. As you study your figure or physique, you will find some guides to selection, but there are no written rules as to what you *must* wear.

YOUR BODY BUILD

Take a good look at yourself in a full-length mirror. Check for overall proportions, that is,

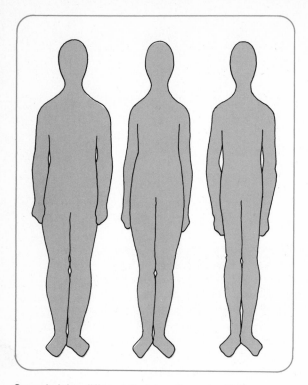

Same height, different limb lengths and widths.

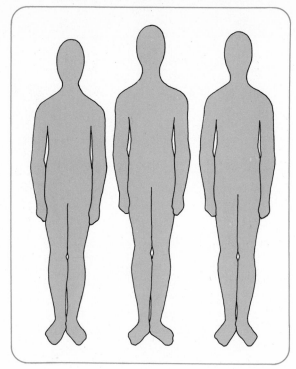

Different heights, same limb lengths and widths.

how one measurement compares to others or how height, weight, and bone structure are related to one another. You probably already know how tall you are and how much you weigh. *Bone structure* is the size and shape of the bones of your skeleton. Bone structure and muscles give your body its basic proportions and shape. People who are the same size have different proportions, shapes, and weights because of their bone structure and muscles. For example, you and a friend may be the same height, but you might look bigger and weigh more because you have a large bone structure and your friend has a smaller one. You both might wear the same size, but you may have to shorten your slacks while your friend must make them longer. This is because your proportions differ. Your bone structure is hereditary and cannot be changed. However, you do have some

control over your weight, shape, and overall appearance. The clothes you choose to wear can have a positive or negative effect on your appearance. As you study the basic elements of clothes, you will see how and why this is.

OPTICAL ILLUSION

The human eye is constantly making observations and comparisons. For this reason, you can make something appear different from the way it actually is. You can also trick the eye into seeing something which is not actually there. This is called *optical illusion*. Food and exercise are the best ways to improve your physical appearance, but illusion can help those areas that cannot be changed.

Here are some of the techniques of optical illusion:

Weight Chart (in pounds)

Female Height	Age 13	14	15	16	17
5'	85–90	85–90	85–90	86–91	87–92
5'1"	85–93	85–94	85–95	86–96	87–97
5'2"	88–98	89–99	90–100	91–101	92–102
5'3"	91–103	92–104	93–105	94–106	95–107
5'4"	96–108	97–109	98–110	99–111	100–112
5'5"	100–113	101–114	102–115	103–116	104–117
5'6"	105–118	106–119	107–120	108–121	109–122
5'7"	109–123	110–124	111–125	112–126	113–127
5'8"	112–128	113–129	114–130	115–131	116–132
5'9"	118–133	119–134	120–135	121–136	122–137
5'10"	123–138	124–139	125–140	126–141	127–142
5'11"	128–143	129–144	130–145	131–146	132–147
6'	132–148	133–149	134–150	135–151	136–152
6'1"	136–153	137–154	138–155	139–156	140–157
6'2"	141–158	142–159	143–160	144–161	145–162

Male Height	Age 13	14	15	16	17
5'	93–98	94–99	95–100	96–101	97–102
5'1"	93–101	94–102	95–103	96–104	97–105
5'2"	98–109	99–110	100–111	101–112	102–113
5'3"	101–114	102–115	103–116	104–117	105–118
5'4"	108–120	109–121	110–122	111–123	112–124
5'5"	111–125	112–126	113–127	114–128	115–129
5'6"	118–131	119–132	120–133	121–134	122–135
5'7"	121–136	122–137	123–138	124–139	125–140
5'8"	128–142	129–143	130–144	131–145	132–146
5'9"	131–147	132–148	133–149	134–150	135–151
5'10"	138–153	139–154	140–155	141–156	142–157
5'11"	141–157	142–158	143–159	144–160	145–161
6'	148–164	149–165	150–166	151–167	152–168
6'1"	151–169	152–170	153–171	154–172	155–173
6'2"	158–175	159–176	160–177	161–178	162–179

How tall are you in centimeters? How many kilograms do you weigh? Multiply your height, in inches, by 2.5 to get centimeters and your weight, in pounds, by 0.45 to get kilograms. *Metropolitan Life Insurance Company*

- Vertical lines help to make you appear taller. Horizontal lines widen the body and make you look shorter.
- Shape can emphasize or camouflage physical characteristics. Tubular shapes add height and hide a thick middle.

Dull, rough textures decrease body size, while smooth, shiny textures increase it.

- Large and bold patterns emphasize the areas they are used on.
- Warm colors increase apparent size while cool colors decrease it.

LINE

What you saw in the mirror will help you choose lines, shapes, colors, and textures that are flattering to you. *Lines* are the details of a garment or an outfit that divide it into smaller areas. The different possible line choices are:

- Vertical—lines that go up and down
- Horizontal—lines that go across
- Curved—lines that are rounded or that have no straight parts
- Diagonal—lines that slant (not vertical or horizontal)

Garments with different lines have different effects on your appearance when you wear them. They can also convey special kinds of feelings to onlookers.

To see vertical lines, your eyes must move up and down. This creates an effect of height and slimness. Vertical lines can convey feelings of strength, poise, dignity, and formality.

This plaid fabric adds width, as well as texture and pattern, to this poncho. *Simplicity Pattern Co.*

How does the design of the fabrics give these blouses two different looks? *Butterick Fashion Marketing Co.*

What optical illusions are created here? *Butterick Fashion Marketing Co.* (left); *Simplicity Pattern Co.* (right)

All clothing designs are made from variations and combinations of straight and curved lines. What lines are used above? *Butterick Fashion Marketing Co.; McCall Pattern Co. (top left)*

Horizontal lines cause eye movement from side to side. They add width to a thin figure and divide the length of a tall person. Horizontal lines can make us feel relaxed and calm.

Diagonal lines add height to a short figure or width to a thin figure. Because of their very direction, diagonal lines are strong and draw your attention to the area where they are used.

The curved line is a variation of the straight line. Curved lines tend to draw attention and therefore increase the apparent size and shape of

tubular   bell   back fullness

the figure. There is a definite movement with curved lines, but it is more relaxed than with straight lines. The feeling expressed by curves is soft, gentle, and youthful.

SHAPE

Shape of a garment generally refers to the silhouette or the outline. There are three basic shapes found in clothing: tubular, bell, and back fullness. Each of these basic silhouettes appears and reappears in one way or another throughout fashion cycles. Shape is reflected in the cut of a jacket, the fit of a bodice, and the fullness of slacks and skirts.

A shape that is most flattering to you is one that will emphasize your good features. At the same time, it will camouflage, or hide, other features. For example, if you are very tall, a tubular shape would make you look even taller. A better choice would be a bell shape or back fullness to emphasize width and cut height. On the other hand, if your waistline is especially small, the bell

shape would help to emphasize its smallness. A tubular shape helps to hide a large waistline.

TEXTURE

Another part of the overall design of the garment is the *texture*, or surface quality. You can both see and feel this surface quality. A dull or rough-textured fabric absorbs light and makes the wearer appear smaller. A smooth or shiny texture reflects light, making the wearer appear larger than he or she actually is. There are times when this rule does not hold. For example, long-haired fur, though rough-textured, increases figure size because of its bulk, which is more dominant than its texture.

It is possible that you will want to use a combination of a smooth, shiny texture on one area of the body and a rough, dull texture on another area. The combining of textures can be an exciting aspect of clothing selection. Textures which are used together should not be so different that they cause confusion in the design. Instead, they

Texture, pattern, color, trims, and accessories work to produce three very different looks. *McCall Pattern Co.*

Making your own combinations of different patterns and colors can be fun. *Wrangler Sportswear*

should be different enough to be interesting and similar enough to belong together.

PATTERN

Pattern is texture that you see rather than feel. Pattern can be woven or knitted into a fabric. It can also be dyed or printed. The terms *pattern*, *design*, and *print* are often used to mean the same thing. *Realistic* patterns are made by reproducing actual photographs, drawings, or paintings. A T-shirt printed with a photographic design is an example. *Stylized* patterns are simplified copies of nature. For example, a fabric designer might see a flower as it grows in the field and then draw it, without every petal, leaf, and vein. Stylized patterns are often used for clothing. Another type of patterning is *geometric*. It includes such shapes as squares, circles, triangles, and straight lines, as well as combinations of these shapes. Stripes, plaids, and polka dots are examples of geometric patterns.

Similar colors or designs in patterns make

them look well together. Patterns in fabric can be small, medium, or large, and subtle or bold. Large and bold patterns attract attention and emphasize the areas where they are used.

Printed fabrics with realistic, stylized, and geometric patterns. *American Thread*

Your choice of colors for clothing can make you look and feel good. *Butterick Fashion Marketing Co.*

highlights in your hair, or warm your complexion.

Select colors that you like and that look good on you. Experiment with different colors to see which ones are best for you.

A color wheel can be used as a guide for choosing and combining colors. A color wheel shows the relationship of all the colors in a spectrum. A color spectrum is like a rainbow: a band of colors ranging from red to violet. When this band is closed, a circle, or *color wheel,* is formed.

There are three basic colors. All other colors are combinations of them. These colors are red, yellow, and blue. They are the *primary* colors. When equal amounts of two primary colors are combined, a *secondary* color is made. Orange, green, and violet are secondary colors. These colors are placed on the wheel between the two primary colors they are made from. When a secondary color is mixed with one of the two primary colors next to it on the color wheel, an *intermediate* color is produced. For example, yellow and orange make yellow-orange; blue and green make blue-green.

If you were a fashion designer, you would create new designs for all types of clothing and accessories for men, women, and children. A background in art, fashion, and clothing construction as well as a keen awareness of fashion would be your best assets. You might work for a large or small manufacturer, a private store, a commercial pattern company, or a high-fashion design house.

COLOR

Color is an important part of our lives. Think for a moment how many times a day you use color. If you were asked to describe something, you would probably include color in your answer. Color influences your feelings, too. For example, you might like a friend's new bicycle because it is your favorite color. You might feel happy and talkative in a bright-colored room or calm and quiet in a soft-colored one. Consider your reaction to the color of a traffic light or the color of your food. Color is just as important in your selection of clothing. Colors you wear can help to brighten your eyes, bring out the

Complementary colors are opposite each other on the color wheel. Colors next to each other on the wheel are called *analogous* colors. Analogous colors combine well because they have some of the primary colors in common. For example, blue and green make pleasing color combinations. The *triad* color scheme consists of three colors equally distant from each other on the

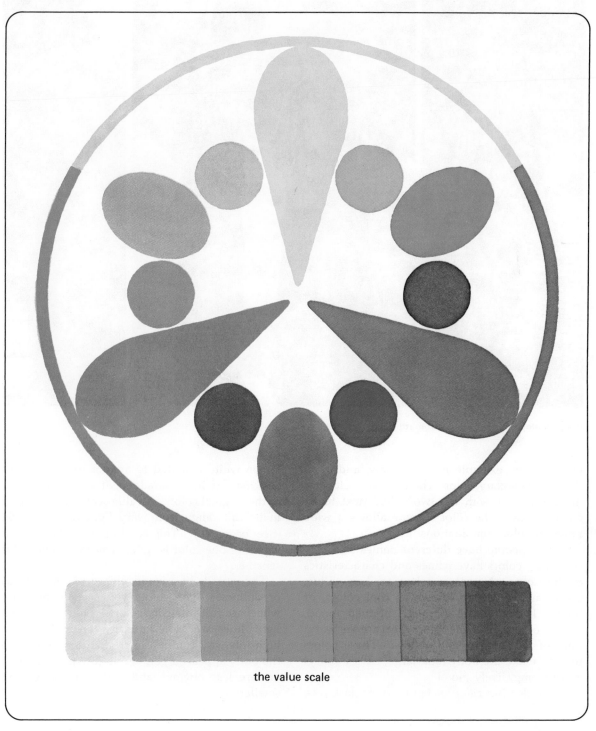

the value scale

Triad, analogous, and monochromatic color schemes . . .

wheel. One example is red, yellow, and blue. *Split complementary* color schemes are made by mixing a color with the two colors next to its complement. The color scheme allows a wide range of color combinations.

Just as people have different names and personalities, colors have names and characteristics of their own. Names of colors are *hues*. Blue, green, and violet are known as cool colors, or hues. They indicate a quiet, subdued mood. On the other half of the color wheel are the warm hues of red, orange, and yellow. These colors tend to make the body look large. They reflect an outgoing, lively mood.

Color also has *value*, or lightness or darkness.

When white is added to a color, the new color is a *tint*. If black is added, it is called a *shade* of the original color. A value scale shows a color in its full range from very light to very dark. (See page 59.) The combination of different values of one color is called a *monochromatic* color scheme.

The *intensity* of a color refers to its brightness or dullness. The colors you see on the color wheel are full-intensity colors. Dull, faded, and light hues are low-intensity colors. Bright, high-intensity colors attract attention and make the body appear larger. Dull, low-intensity colors are less obvious and make the body look smaller.

complementary and neutral color schemes. *Simplicity Pattern Co.*

WHAT IS BEST FOR ME?

How do you decide what looks best on you? Consider your good points and how you can emphasize them. Are there any features you would like to camouflage? Study the clothes you already have. Notice what lines, colors, and textures are most complimentary to you. Your present wardrobe can be the basis of your future one.

WARDROBE PLANNING

Have you ever had a long-range plan for your wardrobe, that is, all the things you wear, for the coming season, year, or even longer? Perhaps you have planned your clothing needs for a special occasion or a vacation. Knowing what you presently own and what you will need in the future will help you to plan your wardrobe. The plan will help you to avoid costly buying mistakes. It will also help you to choose colors and garments that can be combined or coordinated to make the most of the clothes you now have.

YOUR CLOTHING DOLLAR

You probably already use part of your money to buy clothing. Do you plan this spending, or does it depend on how much money you have on hand? To help you decide what part of your income to spend on clothing, ask yourself the

Three coordinated tops and bottoms can be mixed to make nine different outfits.

If you were a professional wardrobe coordinator, you would show consumers how fashion items can be combined and help them to plan and make clothing choices. You would need a knowledge of color, design, and body proportion. You would have to keep up with the latest styles and fashion developments. You might also plan fashion shows. You could work for a retail store, private designer, or modeling agency, or you could free-lance your services.

following questions: What is the total amount of money available? What are my costs for food, school, entertainment, and other expenses? How much money is left for clothes? How can I best use my clothing dollar?

CLOTHES FOR ALL OCCASIONS

With all the considerations and demands on your clothing dollar, it is important to get as much for your money as possible. When planning a wardrobe, keep in mind your life-style and activities. It will do you no good to have many dressy clothes when you have no place or reason to wear them. What kind of activities do you participate in? Do you have a hobby or sport that requires special clothing? Do you need special clothes for school, church, or social activities? Careful planning and coordination make different outfits suitable for many occasions.

FADS AND FASHIONS

Among the decisions that must be made in planning a wardrobe, there is the selection of a particular style of clothing. The choice is limitless,

Variations of traditional "safari" clothing can be fads or fashion at different times. *Simplicity Pattern Co.*

The faddish hats, bow tie, and shoes are a fun way to update these slack outfits. *Wrangler Sportswear*

and knowing what you like and what looks good on you is a big help. Be aware of the difference between a fad and a fashion. A fad can be an article of clothing, a way of wearing your hair, or even a dance style. A fad is usually very noticeable and is popular only with a particular group. Fads usually last a short time—a few weeks or months. While it is sometimes enjoyable to purchase faddish clothes, you should realize that once they are out of style, you may not enjoy wearing them. An inexpensive fad item can be fun. An expensive one might be a costly mistake for you and your budget.

If you were a fashion promoter, you would be responsible for setting and promoting the styles of retail stores. It would be up to you to seek out new trends and determine which would be best for your retail market. You would work with buyers, direct style shows to introduce new fashion looks and items, and supervise display and promotion plans. Experience in copywriting and advertising would be most useful. You might work for a clothing manufacturer or an advertising agency.

Do you remember any of these fad items? Are there any you still wear? What new fads are popular?

Unlike fads, fashion items have good, basic designs and lasting qualities. They usually remain in style for many months and sometimes even for years. Fashionable clothing looks current but is not so new or extreme that you quickly tire of it. Many classic styles, such as the blazer, the skirt, slacks, and sweater combinations, were originally fashion items. Their lines and general appeal have kept them in style. While it is not necessary that your wardrobe be made up of all classic-style clothes, it is a good idea to have some. You can help keep them up-to-date by wearing some fad items with them. In this way, you can have fun and be practical at the same time.

PUTTING IT ALL TOGETHER

Now that you are aware of what goes into wardrobe planning, you are ready to begin your own plan. Start by analyzing your present wardrobe. Allow yourself the time to look over your clothes completely. It can be done once or twice a year or seasonally.

Do you have a few favorites you wear very often? What do you like about them? Do you notice anything similar about them? The styles? The colors? Are the clothes you wear only some of the time for special occasions? Could you wear them more often? Would you want to? Does care (cleaning and pressing) have anything to do with why they are rarely worn?

Did you find any garments that you forgot you owned? You will have to spend more time with these clothes and make some decisions about them. Try on each item that you do not wear often. Ask yourself: Does it fit? Is it fashionable? Why do I wear it so rarely? What can I do to improve it or make it more useful?

Your clothing choices are influenced by special occasions and activities. *Tampax Inc.*

Should I discard it? Save it for a younger member of the family? Trade it with a friend for something else? Donate it to a charity or a thrift shop?

To get the most out of your future clothing purchases, remember the following points:

· Choose basic styles that can be used for different occasions. A suit can be casual or dressy, depending on the accessories used.
· Plan around one or two basic colors so that clothes and accessories can be mixed and matched.

· Choose accessories to go with different outfits. One belt, pair of shoes, or hat can go with a number of garments.
· Use separates to extend your wardrobe. Three coordinated tops and three bottoms can be mixed to make nine different combinations.
· Look for garments that you can wear most of the year or year-round.
· Avoid fads or extreme designs in garments to be worn often or over a long period of time. They usually do not stay in style for long.

● IDEAS FOR ACTION

1. Identify examples of each of the different types of lines in clothing. Prepare your examples for display in the classroom.

2. Collect pictures of current fashions. Determine the basic shape of each—tubular, bell, or back fullness. Explain how these shapes can enhance or camouflage the body build.

3. Experiment with water colors to make secondary and intermediate colors from the primary colors. Make a value scale for one color.

4. Prepare a bulletin-board display of clothing color schemes.

5. Plan to have you and your classmates bring into class—or wear—some current fad items. Discuss why these items are so popular. What other clothing and accessories are popular?

6. Plan a weekend wardrobe for yourself or someone else for a special event or vacation. Describe the activities of the weekend and how they will influence your choices. Use your knowledge of clothing selection and color to coordinate the outfits.

7. Plan and stage a small fashion show with all your classmates wearing their favorite garments. Let each model describe his or her outfit in terms of line, shape, texture, and color and explain why it is his or her favorite.

8. Answer the clothing question: What is best for me? Study your body build. List your best features and those you would like to improve. Determine what lines, shapes, textures, and colors are most flattering to you. Explain how the clothes you now wear do or do not meet these requirements.

● DO YOU KNOW

body build	pattern
color	shade
color wheel	shape
fad	silhouette
fashion	texture
hue	tint
intensity	value
line	wardrobe
optical illusion	wardrobe planning

the look of quality

After reading this chapter, you should be able to:

- Discuss the importance of food to good health and appearance.

- Explain the relationship of food energy and physical exercise.

- Give reasons why correct posture is important when sitting, standing, and walking.

- Describe the care necessary for healthy, attractive skin and hair.

- Explain how eye, hair, and skin color can be used as a guide for choosing clothing.

- List things to consider when choosing accessories.

FEELING GOOD

What makes people attractive? Is it clothes, skin, hair, personality, the way they walk or talk? Is it a combination of some or all of these? Clothes are important for creating an individual look or style, but they have their limits in making someone attractive. Even the nicest clothes cannot make a tired, rundown person look attractive. Good health is essential to looking and feeling good—to being attractive.

FOOD AND ENERGY
There are few things in your everyday life that affect your health as much as food does. Food gives you the energy you need to go to school, to play or watch sports, to grow an inch taller,

What makes people look attractive and well-groomed? *Simplicity Pattern Co.* (*bottom*)

Activity	Approximate calories used per minute
badminton	3½
bicycling	8
bowling	7
dancing	4
jogging	15
rowing	7
skiing	10
skating	4
sitting	1
standing still	1½
standing, light activity	2½
swimming	10
tennis	6
walking	4½

to get a good night's sleep, and to cope with situations around you. How much energy you have depends on the foods you eat.

In the same way a foot is used to measure distance, a calorie is used to measure food energy. Different foods provide different amounts of energy, or calories. For example, a 10-ounce can of soft drink contains about 120 calories, a slice of pizza, 180, and a cheeseburger, 400. The total amount of energy or calories you need is related to how old you are, how tall you are, how hard you work and play. Even such things as the weather and where you live affect how many calories you need each day.

You use up calories with everything you do. You use more energy riding a bicycle, swimming, or dancing than you do watching a movie, standing talking to friends, or sleeping. When

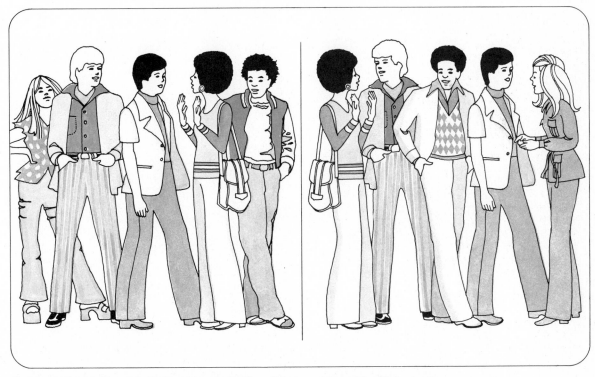

Clothes are important to your appearance and self-confidence, and good health is a major ingredient in helping you look and feel your best.

your body uses all the calories your food provides, your weight remains the same.

Calories that are not used are stored in your body. Stored calories become extra weight or body fat. To lose weight, you have to use up more calories than you take in. To gain weight, you have to take in more calories than you use up. It takes 3500 extra calories to lose or gain one pound.

NUTRIENTS

While your body needs energy, it also needs nutrients. Nutrients are necessary for growth and for keeping all the parts of your body in good working condition. Proteins, carbohydrates, fats, vitamins, and minerals are the basic groups of nutrients.

Protein provides energy and is needed for growth and repair of your body cells. Your skin, hair, nails, muscles, blood, and bones are all made of protein. Since very little extra protein is stored in the body, it is important to get some every day.

Fats supply the greatest amount of energy for your body—more than twice as much as the same amount of protein or carbohydrate. Fats regulate body temperature and support and protect your bones and vital organs. Even your brain and muscle tissues are made partly of fat. Fat helps to give your body shape.

Carbohydrates, sugars and starches, are a good source of energy. These forms of energy can be used quickly by the body. When your body uses carbohydrates for active energy, fats and

When you use the same amount of food energy (calories) as you take in, your weight stays the same. If you take in more or less food energy than you use up, you will gain or lose weight.

Nutrients	Needed for
proteins	growth building and repairing body tissues fighting infection energy
carbohydrates (sugars and starches)	energy
fats	energy essential fatty acids carrying fat-soluble vitamins A, D, E, K
vitamin A	clear, smooth skin resisting infection controlling bone growth protecting against night blindness healthy eyes
vitamin B_1 (thiamine)	normal appetite and digestion healthy nervous system preventing irritability releasing energy from food utilizing other nutrients
vitamin B_2 (riboflavin)	helping cells to use oxygen releasing energy from food clear vision healthy eyes, skin, tongue, and lips
niacin	healthy nervous system healthy skin, mouth, tongue, and digestive tract helping cells to use other nutrients

Nutrients	Needed for
vitamin C (ascorbic acid)	holding body cells together firm, healthy blood vessels resisting infection healing wounds and broken bones
vitamin D ("the sunshine vitamin")	helping the body to use calcium and phosphorus
vitamin E	preventing stored body fat from breaking down and combining with other substances that may become poisonous in the body all functions are not fully known
calcium and phosphorus	building bones and teeth clotting blood helping muscles and nerves to work regulating the use of other minerals in the body
iron	making hemoglobin, the red substance in the blood that carries oxygen to the cells
iodine	forming thyroxin, a hormone that controls metabolism (sum of all the activities of the cells)

proteins are then more efficiently used for their specific purposes. However, carbohydrates that are not used are eventually stored in the body as fat.

Vitamins and minerals help the body to grow and function normally. Vitamins, themselves, are not used for energy or to build cells. However, they make it possible for these things to happen. Minerals are needed for strong, healthy bones, teeth, and other body cells. They also help your body to digest the foods you eat. You are most likely familiar with the names of common vitamins and minerals—vitamin A; vitamin B complex (niacin, riboflavin, thiamine); vitamin C (ascorbic acid); vitamin D; vitamin E; calcium; iron; phosphorus; and sodium.

If you were interested in a career in foods and nutrition, you would have many different areas to explore. You could explore the business world for jobs which might include research, product and recipe development, test-kitchen operations, and consumer services. You could look for jobs in education, from elementary to postcollege level. Jobs in health care might interest you. They include consulting and out-patient services for many government and social agencies and hospital patient care. Many of these jobs require a professional degree; however, entry-level jobs do exist.

THE BASIC FOUR

To help you select a combination of foods to stay healthy, nutritionists have divided all foods into four groups. These groups are called the Basic Four—milk and dairy products; breads and cereals; fruits and vegetables; and meat, fish, and poultry. A nutritious daily diet for teenagers would include four servings from the milk and dairy group; four servings from the bread and cereal group; four servings from the fruit and vegetable group; and two servings from the meat, poultry, and fish group.

The Basic Four food groups and your calorie requirements can guide you in your choice of foods and how much you eat. Eating a variety of cooked and raw foods of different colors, textures, and from different plant and animal sources will help you to get the nutrients you need to stay healthy.

Not only is what you eat important but also when and how much you eat. Skipping meals is hard on your body. Often, when you skip a meal, you overeat at the next one. When your body has to process a large amount of food at one time, it does a less efficient job, and some nutrients are lost. During the period of not eating, you may be lacking the energy you need to function.

Snacks give you energy between meals. Snacks can also provide nutrients and should be considered as part of your total daily food intake. Snacks that are heavy in sugar and artificial flavoring give you energy but provide little, if any, other nutrition. Foods that only provide energy and lack nutrients are called "empty calories." There are many snacks that are rich in nutrients *and* taste good, too. Fruits, vegetables, milk, ice cream, cheese, pizza, hamburger, and peanut butter are some.

EXERCISE

Good nutrition will help build strong bones and muscles but there is more to keeping your bones and muscles strong and healthy than just eating. You have to work, too. This work involves exercise. Exercise uses up energy, tones and strengthens muscles, and increases the blood's circulation.

You may think of exercise as hard work or the kind of activity that only athletes and overweight people have to be concerned with, but exercise can take on many forms. Just the simple act of getting out of bed and stretching each morning is exercise. There are many other things you

BASIC FOUR

fruits and vegetables

breads and cereals

milk and dairy products

meat, fish, and poultry

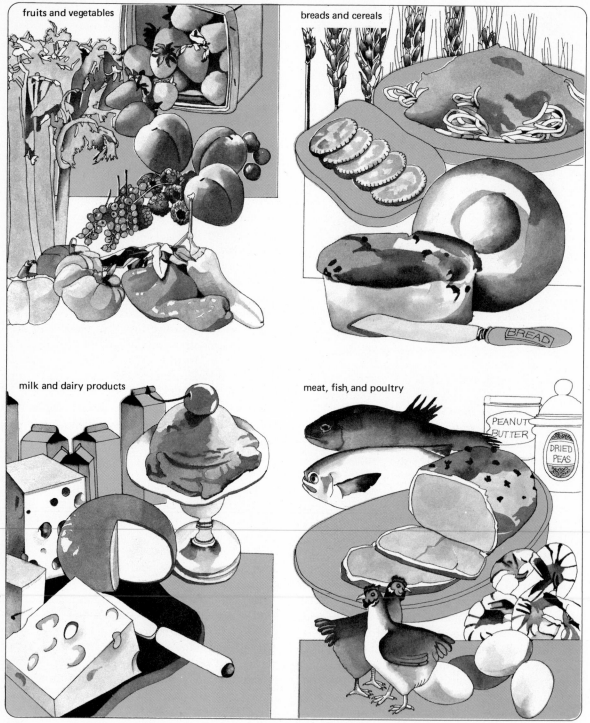

PEANUT BUTTER

DRIED PEAS

BREAD

normally do that you probably do not think of as exercise. Stretching to reach a high shelf, bending to pick up something, straightening your room, cleaning your bicycle, walking the dog—all help to tone and strengthen the muscles. These simple movements and activities help you to feel healthy and alert.

If you were a consulting dietitian, you would work with individuals to plan meals for their specific health needs. You might advise people recovering from a serious illness or operation or people trying to lose or gain weight. You could work for a hospital, clinic, or social agency. You would need a professional degree in dietetics.

We can all take a hint from the athlete or coach who "limbers up" before beginning a strenuous activity. Your muscles and bones are limber when you can bend or flex them easily without pain or later soreness. Simple activities and exercises will keep you limber and prevent strain or serious damage to your muscles.

Naturally, such activities as swimming, bicycling, running, golf, tennis, as well as other sports, athletic exercises, and gymnastics are very effective for toning and strengthening muscles. It is important to remember, though, the everyday movements and activities that put your muscles to work.

Certain activities, like gymnastics, are very effective for toning and strengthening muscles. *Tampax Inc.*

POSTURE
Have you ever unexpectedly seen yourself in a full-length mirror? Did you wonder who that slumped-over person could be? Were you surprised to find it was you?

Sport	Important muscles used
bicycling	leg
golf	leg, arm, wrist, midsection
skating	leg, arm
skiing	leg (especially thigh), arm
surfing	arm, shoulder, leg
swimming	arm, shoulder, leg
tennis	leg, arm, wrist

sit-ups

push-ups

hopping

bicycling

running in place

squat thrust

Simple exercises can help keep you limber and alert.

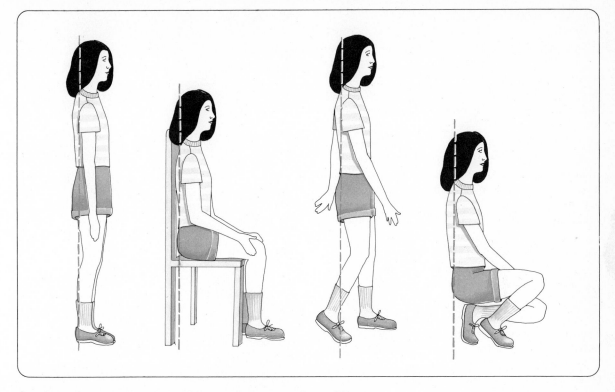

Standing, sitting, walking, or bending—good posture makes a difference.

You have control over the way you stand, walk, and sit. One of the easiest and quickest ways to look more attractive is to stand up straight. When you stand straight with your shoulders back, head up, and stomach and buttock muscles pulled in, you suddenly feel and look more trim. Your clothes hang and fit better, too, when your posture is correct and relaxed. Try this in front of a mirror and see the difference it makes in your appearance.

To stand correctly, put your shoulders back, pull in your stomach and buttock muscles, and keep breathing regularly. Hold your head high and stretch "tall," as if you were being lifted by your ears. At first this may feel strange, but with practice, it will become second nature to you. You will even find it comfortable.

Keep this same posture when walking and sitting. Resist the urge to let your whole body collapse, especially while sitting. Relax against the chair with the base of your spinal column touching the chair back. Keep your head and rib cage up straight. When you walk, let your legs lead the rest of your body. Your knees should be relaxed and your arms should hang easily at your sides.

Sitting, standing, and walking correctly not only work to make you more attractive but also to make you feel better. How often have you sat slumped over or stood shifting your weight from foot to foot for a long time? Do you remember how you felt when you got up or began to walk? You may be able to almost "feel" the soreness, yet! Good posture can help to prevent this type of strain and tiredness and to keep your muscles and bones in condition.

PROFESSIONAL HEALTH CARE

A healthful diet and exercise are ways to promote good health. A routine physical examination will further ensure good health. The doctor keeps records and is familiar with your overall health picture. Regular medical checkups can help to avoid any problems that may occur. Weight control and skin problems are often a concern to many teenagers. Your doctor or local health-care clinic can answer your questions about these and other health and body concerns.

Routine health care should also include a dental examination twice a year. However, there are some ways that you can help make these visits more trouble free. Good eating habits is one of the simplest and best ways to prevent tooth decay. Frequent and thorough brushing and use of dental floss can further reduce cavities. Plaque, a film of bacteria, forms on your teeth when you eat. When plaque combines with sugar from food, it forms an acid that can cut through your tooth enamel. The tooth is then unprotected and can decay easily. Brushing and flossing soon after eating will help you to avoid many decay problems.

LOOKING GOOD

Once you have made every effort to see that you are as healthy as possible, your hair and your skin should reflect the positive results. Further care of hair and skin is necessary to keep them in their best condition.

Ready-made products for hair and skin care are abundant and popular. Before these products were so easily available, people made their own. Many foods, flowers, spices, and herbs have been used for centuries as ingredients for lotions, creams, conditioners, soaps, shampoos, perfumes, and other "mystical mixtures." Many commercial products are also made with natural ingredients. You have most likely heard of such things as egg shampoos, herbal lotions, milk baths, strawberry cleansers, lemon rinses, cucumber skin fresheners, lime colognes, and spice creams.

Electric combs, dryers, and stylers are among the many special kinds of grooming equipment available today.

HAIR

Hair, like clothing, says something about you. Hair should always be as clean and neat as possible. You should wash it as often as is necessary. This may be anywhere from once a day to once every couple of days or weeks. Your hair type, your activities, the weather, and where you live can all affect how often you have to wash your hair.

Use a shampoo that will not dry or damage your hair or scalp. When shampooing, be sure to work up a foamy lather. Massage the scalp with your fingertips by moving them in a circular motion back and forth over your head. Massaging stimulates circulation, hair growth, and natural oils. Rinse your hair with clean water. You will know your hair is completely rinsed when you can pull your fingers along the hair and it squeaks. Many times what you think is oily or dirty hair is hair that has not been rinsed properly. Even the slightest amount of soap left in the hair leaves a dull film that also attracts dirt and dust.

Healthy, clean, shiny hair is the beginning and basis of a good hairstyle. The style you choose to wear should make you feel and look good. It should also be suitable to your everyday living. A hairstyle that takes a lot of time and effort to look presentable would soon limit your activities. Many casual, natural-looking styles are easy to care for. These require little more than a good cut, clean hair, and brushing and combing.

Finding the right hairstyle or styles for you can be fun. The shape of your face is often a factor to consider when choosing a hairstyle. To determine your face shape, stand before a mirror, with your hair held back away from your face. Look very carefully at the outline of your face. Sometimes tracing the outline on the mirror with a wet bar of soap will make the shape easy to recognize. Faces generally follow the basic geometric

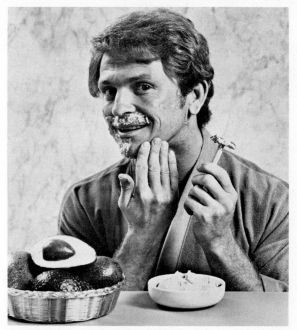

An avocado shave? Whip half an avocado with a teaspoon of oil to make a natural shave cream. *California Avocado Advisory Board*

Natural Hair-Care Products

Preshampoo conditioners part hair and rub ingredients onto scalp with cotton	dry hair olive or vegetable oil oily hair equal parts water and vinegar oily hair whipped egg white
Shampoos add to your regular shampoo for each washing	one beaten egg ¼ cup milk
Conditioners apply after shampooing, let stand a few minutes, and rinse	whole egg, beaten milk olive oil and herbs warm beer
Final rinses dissolves filmy soap residue, highlights, and makes hair manageable	lemon juice grapefruit juice lime juice vinegar mixed with herbs

shapes—square, round, rectangular, oval, diamond, and triangular. A hairstyle can emphasize the shape or camouflage it. You should also look at your features—your eyes, nose, mouth, ears, jaw, chin, and forehead. Again, a hairstyle can emphasize certain features and de-emphasize others. Once you have determined your facial shape, you are ready to think in terms of specific hairstyles.

Any hairstyle, long or short, gets its shape by the way it is cut. Hair cutting is best done by a skilled person. Even when you are letting your hair grow, you will need to have the ends trimmed periodically. Hair ends dry and split from tangling, combing, washing, drying, and exposure to the weather. Natural oils from the scalp do not always reach the hair ends. Cutting or trimming will get rid of dry, split ends and keep your hair looking healthy.

If you were a hairstylist, you would need a complete knowledge of hair and scalp. You would have to learn, practice, and perfect the skills of cutting and styling hair. Keeping up-to-date on new hair care products, hairstyles, and styling techniques would be important. You might be licensed to specialize in men's or women's hair, or both. You could be self-employed or work for an owner-operated business, a chain of beauty and hair salons, or a theatrical company.

SKIN

There are two different types of human skin—facial skin and body skin. The care of the skin on the body is relatively easy. Regular washing with plain soap and water reduces the growth of

VARIATIONS OF BASIC HAIRCUTS

80

BASIC FACE SHAPES

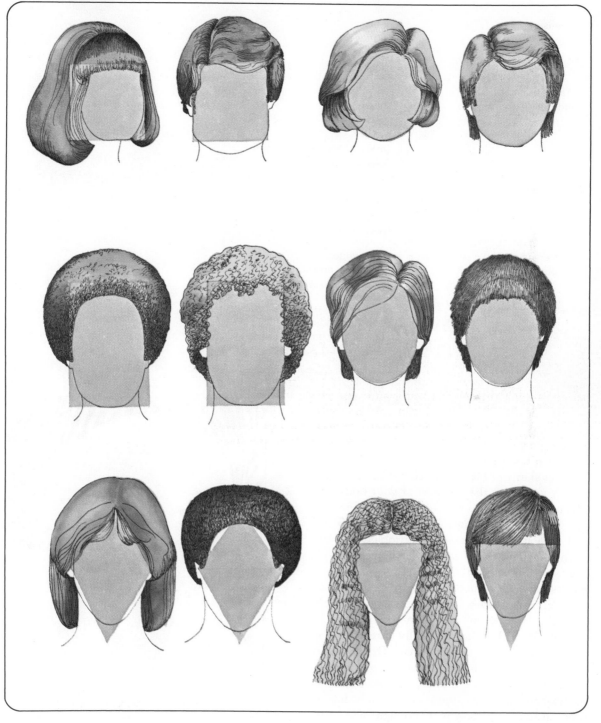

81

Natural Skin-Care Products

Cleansers	milk buttermilk yogurt sour cream
Moisturizers and conditioners	vegetable oil olive oil peanut oil honey mashed honeydew melon avocado paste
Astringents	vinegar oranges lemons grapefruits
Tighteners for pores	egg whites cornmeal-and-water paste oatmeal-and-water paste
Fresheners	mashed cucumbers and water peaches-and-cream paste bananas-and-cream paste strawberries-and-cream paste

bacteria—the source of body odor and skin irritations. Many people use deodorants and antiperspirants to prevent body odor and wetness. Talcum powder and cornstarch can also be used to absorb body perspiration.

Facial skin is a little more complicated to care for. Your face is the one part of your body that is constantly exposed to the elements. Dirt and oils can cause breakouts and blemishes. Stress and tension can also cause skin problems. Staying healthy and rested can help to keep your skin clear. While adolescent acne is caused by hormones rather than foods, a healthy diet and good skin care can help to control an acne problem.

You need to know your skin type to care for it properly. There are basically three types of facial skin—dry, oily, and normal. Dry skin may feel somewhat rough and have a chapped appearance. Oily skin has a shiny or wet look. In contrast to these two types, normal skin has an even and smooth look with no sign of oiliness

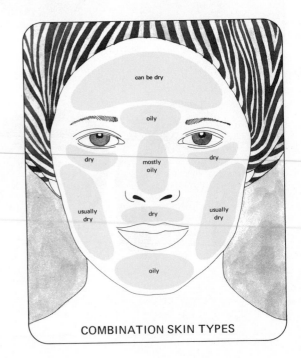

COMBINATION SKIN TYPES

There are two ways of cleansing facial skin—with soap and water or with a cleansing cream or lotion. Both methods are satisfactory. You are the best judge of which is most successful for you. Soap is generally more drying to the skin and, therefore, is helpful for oily skin. Facial soaps are more gentle than body soaps for your face. Your drugstore and supermarket have many to choose from. Cleansing creams and lotions are milder and less drying than most facial soaps. They can be used on dry and normal skins.

As you cleanse your face, use a gentle, upward motion with your fingers or facecloth. Do not stretch or pull your skin. Follow product directions carefully and rinse thoroughly. If you have oily skin, an astringent can help to dry up excess oils. An astringent is a lotion made with alcohol. The alcohol closes the pores of the skin making it harder for bacteria and dirt to get into

Wearing your favorite colors can make you feel good about the way you look. They may even highlight your personal coloring. *Butterick Fashion Marketing Co.*

or dryness. While it is called "normal," few people actually have this third type of facial skin. More people have a combination skin type with some oily, some dry, and some normal areas. The areas around the nose, chin, and forehead are often oily, with the remaining skin being either dry or normal. Each facial area needs to be cared for according to its skin type. Skin types may change with the seasons, causing you to have dry skin when it is cold and oily skin during warm weather.

If you were a product representative of a cosmetic company, you would be responsible for introducing new grooming products to salespeople and buyers. You would have to demonstrate the new products and answer questions about them. You might work in one or many areas of grooming. You could work from a central office or travel to different cities, states, or countries.

There are many color choices available to complement or contrast both warm and cool hair and skin colors. *Butterick Fashion Marketing Co.*

the skin. Alcohol, used full-strength or diluted with water, or witch hazel can also be used.

Moisturizing lotions and creams can help to keep skin on your face, hands, arms, legs, and feet smooth and comfortable. Such products are especially helpful in extremely hot or cold weather. Sunscreens and tanning lotions provide protection from the burning and drying effects of the sun.

PERSONAL COLORING

Personal coloring includes the color of hair, skin, and eyes, and their total color tone together. Skin tones are classified as either warm or cool. Warm skins have red or orange tones while cool skins contain blue or green tones. Most yellow, brown, red, olive, and suntanned skins can be classified as warm tones. Ivory and black skins, with bluish casts, are cool tones. Hair and eye color can be warm or cool, too. Warm hair colors are those with red highlights such as auburn, chestnut brown, dark brown, red, and even blond with a reddish cast. Yellow, gold, blue,

Color helps to add individuality and style to your appearance. *Butterick Fashion Marketing Co.*

A flattering color near your face can attract attention and bring out the best in your skin, hair, and eyes.

and silver highlights are the clues to cool hair colors. White, blond, gray, black, and some light-brown shades are usually cool. The warm eye colors include most shades of brown, and cool eye colors include most shades of blue and green.

You can use your personal coloring as a guide in selecting clothing colors. Remember the color wheel and how warm and cool colors relate to one another? How analogous color schemes soften colors and how complementary color schemes make colors more striking? If your skin, hair, and eyes are all cool, then the cool clothing hues will blend with your cool coloring, while warm clothing hues will contrast with it. Both effects can be very pleasing and becoming to you, or you may not like one or the other.

It is not at all uncommon for a person to have warm hair and skin, but cool eyes. There are any number of possible combinations of warm

and cool tones. If your skin, hair, and eye coloring are different, it is usually best to plan your color scheme according to your skin. For example, if your skin is warm, but your hair and eyes cool, warm colors will blend with your skin while emphasizing the cool contrast of your hair and eyes.

To help you decide what colors are best for you, hold a piece of fabric close to your face. Stand in the same type of lighting as when you will be wearing that color garment. How does it look? What does the color do for your skin, hair, and eyes? Sometimes a certain color will bring out hidden tones in your skin. A yellow shirt may bring out the yellow in your complexion, just as a red shirt would bring out redness in another's skin tone. You may or may not like the effect. If a color you like does not look particularly good on you, it does not mean you cannot or should not wear that color. Just keep

Accessories can add variety to your wardrobe and that something extra to your appearance. *Simplicity Pattern Co. (bottom left); Butterick Fashion Marketing Co. (others)*

The same basic garment can be worn by different people and still reflect an individual personality, mood, or look.

it away from your face. You can use it for an accessory color or for slacks or a skirt. If you do wear an unflattering color near your face, add a collar, scarf, or tie of another more becoming color. This second color can attract attention away from the first and bring out the best in your skin, hair, and eyes.

What else do you remember about color? How do the different values, intensities, and personalities of colors produce different looks? A shade or tint of a favorite color can add variety to your wardrobe and may even be more flattering to you than the original color. Bright colors and warm colors are outgoing and attract attention. Dull colors and cool colors are quiet and are less obvious. You can call attention to or underplay different areas of the body by the intensity and other characteristics of the colors you wear.

SOMETHING EXTRA

Accessories include such things as belts, bags, scarves, ties, shoes, stockings, jewelry, and sunglasses—things you wear in addition to basic garments. Shoes, watches, and belts are accessories and can be decorative, but they are usually basic to your wardrobe. Some accessories may be for looks only, such as jewelry, scarves, and ties.

Accessories add interest and individuality to your wardrobe. Did you ever look at an outfit or garment and say, "that's me" or pass up another with "no, that just isn't me"? Well, accessories can help to make your clothing more of an expression of you. For example, two people might have the same suit. One person adds a brightly colored vest and scarf and jewelry. The other will choose a matching shirt or sweater to

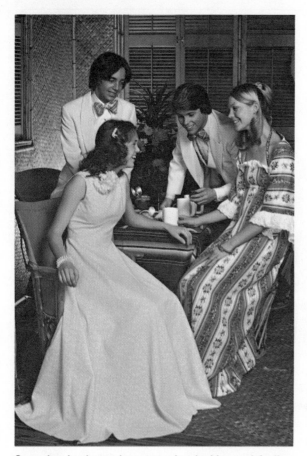

Grooming is always important, but looking and feeling good makes special occasions even nicer. *Co-ed, Scholastic Magazines, Inc.*

A sincere smile adds the finishing touch to a well-coordinated outfit. *Butterick Fashion Marketing Co.*

wear with the suit. The different outfits reflect the personalities or moods of the individuals wearing them.

Accessories are often a small part of an outfit, but they can be very important. Well-chosen accessories may make the difference between a dull outfit and a really great one. Accessories can also provide an inexpensive way to make an old garment look new.

Accessories attract attention. Be careful not to clutter an outfit with too many points of interest—one or two are usually enough. If you wear

a scarf around your neck and one on your head, too, each scarf can detract from the other. In the same way, you may not want to divide the body at too many points. If you wear very noticeable accessories at your neck, waist, legs, and wrists, you may present a confusing image—a lot of little pieces that do not pull together. When you want to use many accessories, a common color, texture, or theme can help to give your outfit a total look.

As a general rule, accessories should be in scale with the garment and the wearer. This means that the size and impact of accessories should not overpower the garment or the person wearing them. For example, you would not usually want people to look at you and see only a hat or belt or bag or pair of boots. There are times, however, when the wearing of an oversized item by a smaller person or the wearing of a small, delicate item by a larger person makes an attractive contrast. Think of the occasion and the total look you wish to create when choosing accessories.

When you purchase clothes, give some thought to the kinds of accessories that will look best with them. Notice the types of accessories being used in magazine and store displays. When selecting accessories, think of their lines, colors, and textures. Consider how many garments they will go with and how often you will be able to use them. Accessories can be relatively inexpensive or very costly. Remember the rules of wise decision making when buying any clothing or accessory items.

The look of quality is also a feeling of confidence that you are your best. *Wrangler Sportswear*

Good health and grooming and comfortable clothing contribute to your having fun. *Maverick Sportswear*

● IDEAS FOR ACTION

1. Make a bulletin board that shows a nutritious diet for one day. Include all meals and snacks. Use posters, advertisements, magazine clippings, or drawings to show how the menu has satisfied the Basic Four requirements.

2. Make a list of snacks that you and your friends eat most often. Which of these snacks could be included as part of your daily Basic Four? Are any of them "empty calorie" snacks? Can you suggest some ways to make "empty calorie" snacks nutritious? Suggest nutritious substitutes for "empty calorie" snacks?

3. Take a survey to find out what your classmates eat for breakfast. How many skip breakfast? Make a bulletin board or chart showing the results of your survey. Give some suggestions for new ideas for breakfast. Try to include some that are different, yet easy and quick to prepare.

4. Work with some of your classmates to prepare a demonstration of "good" and "bad" posture. Show examples of posture in typical situations—sitting at a desk, carrying books, going up and down stairs, and standing. Ask members of the class to point out which postures look best and why.

5. Make a mobile or a collage showing current hairstyles for boys and girls. Indicate the care required for each. You could also show, on several different face shapes, the most popular hairstyle. Is the style equally becoming to all the shapes?

6. Have each member of the class choose accessories for a basic garment. Use actual accessories, drawings, or pictures cut from newspapers and magazines. Display the completed outfits. Discuss how the chosen accessories make each outfit different. Do any of the outfits reflect the individuality of the people who selected them?

7. Name your two or three most favorite colors. How does each color affect the looks of your hair, eyes, and skin? Do you wear the colors a lot?

● DO YOU KNOW

accessory	energy
astringent	exercise
Basic Four	health
calorie	limber
color	nutrients
dental care	posture

creative stitchery

After reading this chapter, you should be able to:

- *Discuss how craft-making can be personally satisfying and culturally enriching.*

- *Select tools and materials for each of the crafts discussed, and demonstrate how to use them correctly.*

- *Identify the basic needlecrafts of embroidery, needlepoint, and knitting.*

- *Describe how weaving, hooking, and knotting are related.*

- *Explain how, when, and why quilting, patchwork, and appliqué can be used together or separately.*

We read that adornment is a major reason for wearing clothes. This basic desire to make ourselves attractive plays an important role in other areas of our lives, too. We adorn ourselves with clothing and our environments with colors and textures in many forms. Walls, floors, and furniture may be adorned with any number of crafts. For example, a picture or a design printed, painted, or embroidered on fabric may hang on a wall or cover a chair or pillow.

The reasons for doing any form of craft are as many and as varied as the crafts themselves. Primarily, though, crafts are creative. They can help us to express an idea or a feeling, to fulfill an emotional need, or to share some part of our lives with others. The fact that we can look at craft items from many centuries ago and from many different cultures and know something of the life-style of the designers is evidence of this.

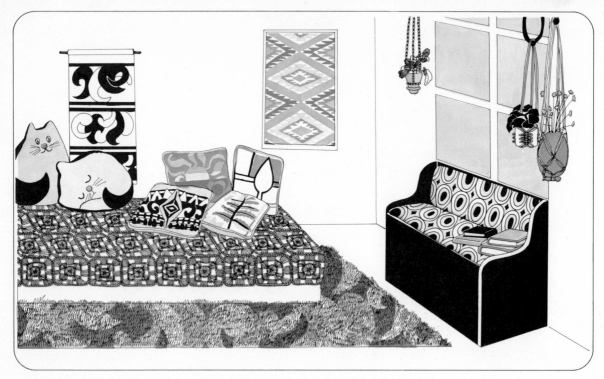

Handcrafted items add a creative, personal touch to our environment.

Today many of the traditional crafts used for personal and environmental decorating are made by someone else. When you buy a fabric, the design is already printed on it. The picture hanging on the wall was painted by someone else. The furniture in your house was designed and made by someone you have never met.

In an attempt to bring back individual creativity, many people are turning to crafts during their leisure time. These arts and skills allow them to be creative and put something of themselves into their surroundings. Many people get personal satisfaction, relaxation, and pure enjoyment from creating crafts while developing the necessary skills.

As you read about and try each of the following crafts, remember that they are just a beginning. Only basic information is given here, but you can interpret the techniques and develop them into something that is uniquely your own.

NEEDLECRAFTS

The use of a needlelike tool to make or to decorate fabric was one of the first crafts developed. It was primarily used to shape fabric into a garment by joining two pieces together. Today, needlecrafts include everything from simple hand sewing to elaborate crewel embroidery and knitting and crocheting.

EMBROIDERY

Embroidery refers to a decorative design applied to fabric with a needle and thread. It is usually a colorful decoration adding a raised texture to the fabric. Any type of background material can be used for your embroidered design, but a tightly woven fabric is the easiest to work on.

Embroidery can be done on just about everything from clothes and accessories to wall hang-

Embroidery done in traditional or modern designs is a fun way to decorate clothing.
Simplicity Pattern Co.

ings and pillows. You might want to start with a ready-made kit that includes the design already stamped on the material and instructions for doing it. You may also copy a favorite design or draw one of your own onto a background fabric. Browsing through craft and needlework books will give you many ideas for a project. If you do transfer a design to fabric, use a light-color tracing paper. Trace the outline of the design with a sharp edge to insure a clear and accurate guide for stitching.

Your choice of threads will depend upon the design, the background fabric, and what you want the finished effect to be. Cotton, linen, or sometimes silk thread, *floss,* is used for embroidery. The sheen and fineness of these threads are best suited to a fine fabric and a delicate design with many details.

It is also possible to use wool yarns for embroidery, and the effect is very interesting on a heavy background fabric. This type of embroidery is referred to as *crewel* embroidery. Crewel yarns are heavier than cotton, linen, or silk, but are still not as heavy as a sweater yarn.

For your embroidery project, you will find a crewel needle easiest to work with. It has a short body and a long eye. Be sure that the eye is big enough to accommodate the embroidery floss you are using. A thimble will be helpful, especially if you are using a heavy background fabric. Use one that fits snugly on your middle finger. While most embroidery can be worked in your hand, a hoop or frame holds the fabric taut and helps you make even stitches. The hoop also reduces the amount of puckering caused by the stitches in the fabric.

A peasant look is achieved with the colorful flowers embroidered on this blouse. *Butterick Fashion Marketing Co.*

There are many stitches used to do hand embroidery. The more stitches you know, the greater variety you can have in your finished work. In the beginning though, try to learn just a few of the basic stitches. The charts on pages 96 and 97 will show you some of the most frequently used embroidery stitches. You might want to check Chapter 13 for some additional hand stitches that can also be used for decorative embroidery.

When you are ready to begin, thread the needle and make a small knot in one end of the thread. Hold the hoop or frame with one hand and stitch with the other. Bring the needle and thread up from the underside of the fabric at the point where you want to begin.

Try to develop a rhythm to your stitching, as this will help to insure an even tension on the thread. Be careful not to pull the stitches too tight. Wool yarns in particular stretch more easily and can cause your finished design to pucker.

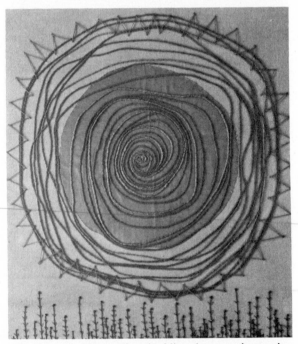

Crewel embroidery and embroidery done on the sewing machine make interesting pictures for wall hangings. *McCall's Needlework & Crafts Magazine*

94

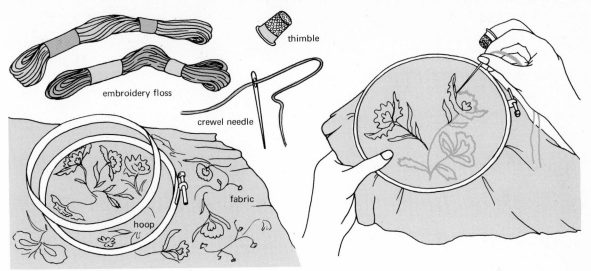

TOOLS FOR EMBROIDERY

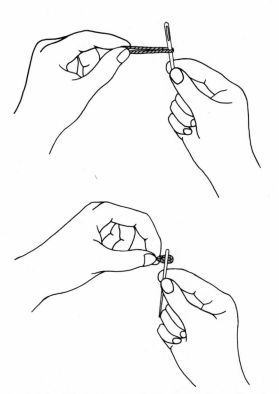

To keep the floss or yarn from separating when you thread the needle, wrap it around the needle and pull it taut. Slip the floss off the needle and thread the loop through the eye of the needle.

When you are ready to end a stitch, bring the thread to the wrong side and make a small back stitch. Weave your needle in and out of the last few stitches until you feel the thread is secure. Then cut the thread close to the work.

Embroidery can also be done on some sewing machines. The stitches usually consist of combinations of straight and zigzag stitches. Machine embroidery is faster than hand embroidery, and the results are similar.

There are only a few simple rules to remember with machine embroidery. A tightly woven background fabric usually works best. If you want to use a loosely woven fabric, back it with another piece of fabric or with an iron-on interfacing before beginning to embroider. Sometimes it is suggested that a hoop be used for machine embroidery. Check your machine instruction booklet for additional directions.

NEEDLEPOINT

Another type of stitchery is *needlepoint*. Wool, acrylic, or cotton yarns are used to make stitches in a mesh canvas background. The needle used is called a *tapestry needle*. It has a blunt point, since it does not have to make holes, and a large eye. The durability and beauty of needlepoint have allowed many pieces to remain in use for

EMBROIDERY STITCHES

Straight stitch	used for any short, straight lines
Running stitch	used for lines and outlines can be used as a filling stitch with open spaces
Back stitch	used to make clear, sharp outlines also used as a solid filling stitch when worked in close rows
Stem stitch	used for lines and outlines should be worked with two threads
Blanket stitch even uneven slanted	used for making edges, for filling, and for attaching appliqués
Feather stitch basic variation	made and used much like the blanket stitch
Chain stitch	a decorative outline or filling stitch
Lazy daisy stitch	closed, it makes a simple petal or leaf open, it makes a V-shaped design
Cross stitch	used for borders and filling

EMBROIDERY STITCHES (Continued)

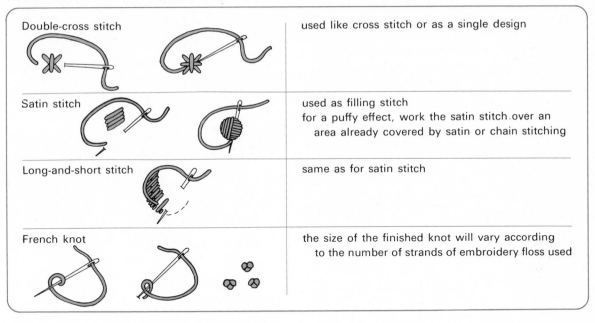

Double-cross stitch	used like cross stitch or as a single design
Satin stitch	used as filling stitch for a puffy effect, work the satin stitch over an area already covered by satin or chain stitching
Long-and-short stitch	same as for satin stitch
French knot	the size of the finished knot will vary according to the number of strands of embroidery floss used

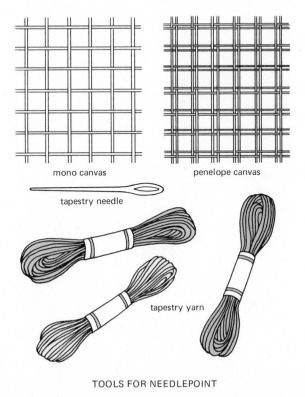

mono canvas

penelope canvas

tapestry needle

tapestry yarn

TOOLS FOR NEEDLEPOINT

centuries. Originally an expensive art pursued only by wealthy women, needlepoint is done today by people of all ages and economic backgrounds. Pillows, rugs, wall hangings, belts, bags, and even tennis racket covers are just a few of the things made more attractive with needlepoint.

Needlepoint projects are sold many different ways. The most commonly found types already have the design printed on the canvas. Some also have the major part of the design worked in needlepoint, so that all you have to finish is the background. Many kits are available with the colors and amount of yarn required to complete the picture. Needlepoint canvas and yarns can be purchased separately also, for you to do your own designing and color coordinating.

The canvas used for needlepoint is specially made for this craft. The size of your stitch depends on the number of meshes, or holes, per inch in the canvas. Very fine needlepoint, known as *petit point*, often has as many as forty meshes per inch. Some designs are worked on canvases that have five meshes per inch.

Needlepoint is another means of making pictures with stitches. *McCall's Needlework & Crafts Magazine*

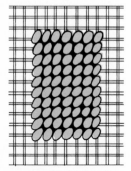

front: continental and half-cross stitches

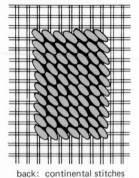

back: continental stitches

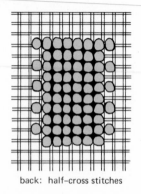

back: half-cross stitches

Any type of smooth, firmly twisted yarn may be used for needlepoint. These are usually called *tapestry yarns.* The yarn must be thick enough to fill the holes in the canvas evenly, but not so thick as to stretch the mesh or to fray while being pulled through.

When you are ready to begin, bind the raw edges of the canvas with masking tape to prevent them from raveling. Cut each piece of yarn about 18 inches [46 centimeters] long. A longer strand can easily knot and may fray or break because of the excess pulling through the canvas. Thread the needle but do not put a knot in the yarn. Stitches are made with a single strand. The design is always worked first and the background, last.

The stitches used for needlepoint are slightly slanted. The easiest and most commonly used stitches are the *continental* and *half-cross* stitches. Both of these look identical on the front surface. It is only when the design is turned over that you will see a difference. On the back of the canvas, a diagonal design is formed by the conti-

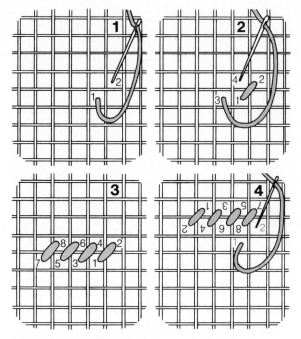

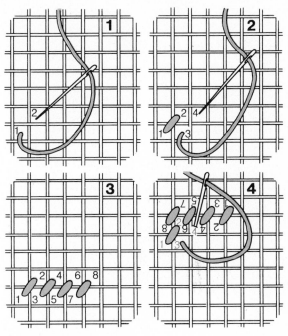

THE CONTINENTAL STITCH

1 Begin in the right-hand corner of the design. Bring the needle up through the lower left hole of the first stitch.

2 Cross over diagonally to the next opening above it and to the right. Insert needle.

3 Cross behind the stitch to the lower left opening next to 1.

4 Continue across the design until you complete the row. Turn the canvas around and stitch the next row in the same way.

THE HALF-CROSS STITCH

1 Begin in the lower left-hand corner of the design. Bring the needle up through the lower left hole.

2 Cross over diagonally to the next opening above and to the right of 1. Insert needle.

3 Bring needle up through opening just below 2 and to the right of 1.

4 Continue across the canvas until you complete the row. Turn the canvas so you can stitch the next row in the same left-to-right direction.

nental stitches and a vertical design is formed by the half-cross stitches.

To begin stitching, put your needle through one hole from back to front. Leave a tail of yarn hanging in the back. As you work the first five or six stitches, hold this tail so that it will be caught by the stitches, thus anchoring it in place.

The continental stitch is worked across the canvas from right to left. After you have completed one row, turn the canvas upside down so that you will still work from right to left on the next row.

The continental stitch is very durable. It is especially recommended for needlepoint projects that will be used as pillow or seat covers. The major disadvantage of the continental stitch is that it pulls the canvas out of shape. Blocking the canvas with steam and pressure after the design is completed restores the canvas to its original shape.

The half-cross stitch is worked across the canvas from left to right. When one row is completed, the canvas is turned so the left to right stitching continues. The half-cross stitch re-

star stitch

leaf stitch

cubed cross–stitch

SOME DECORATIVE NEEDLEPOINT STITCHES

This pillow combines the two crafts of needlepoint and Bargello. The detailed flower design is needlepoint; the rippled border, Bargello. *McCall's Needlework & Crafts Magazine*

quires less yarn than the continental stitch. It is also less durable. Half-cross stitches are best used for needlepoint projects to be framed or used as wall hangings.

Whichever stitch you use, try to keep the tension even on your yarn. Pull it tight enough to eliminate any slack but not so tight that the background can be seen. If your yarn becomes twisted, let the needle and the yarn dangle so that they can unwind. When there are only a couple of inches left to the strand of yarn, weave it through a few of the stitches on the wrong side of the canvas, then clip.

There are several other more decorative needlepoint stitches for you to learn. The continental and the half-cross stitches give a smooth, bead-like finish to the needlepoint picture. Some of the other more elaborate stitches add shapes and texture to designs. The leaf, star, and cubed-cross stitches are only a few examples. A more detailed craft book or magazine can give you instructions for doing these and other varieties of needlepoint stitches.

A craft very similar to needlepoint is *Bargello*. Instead of the small, diagonal stitches used for needlepoint, Bargello stitches are vertical and usually cover four rows of canvas. These straight-up-and-down stitches are worked in a variety of ways to create different designs. Geometric designs are the most popular.

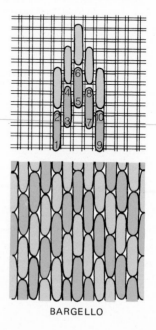

BARGELLO

The skills of many crafts are used to make and decorate articles of clothing.

KNITTING

In Chapter 3, you learned that knitting is a way of forming fabric through a series of interlocking loops. Hand knitting has been a craft for centuries. Pieces of knitted fabrics have even been found in some Egyptian tombs. Sweaters, socks, hats, baby clothes, afghans, and mittens are just a few items that have traditionally been knitted.

To accomplish a knit project of your own, you will need knitting needles, yarn, a knowledge of basic stitches, and a little practice. Knitting needles range in size from hairpin thin to as large as 1 inch [2.5 centimeters] in diameter. The thin needles are used with fine yarn and the thick needles, with heavy yarn. They come in different lengths and types, too. They can be single- or double-ended or circular.

While wool yarn might first come to mind for knitting, most any type of yarn can be used. Cotton, linen, blends, and many synthetics such as nylon and acrylic are frequently used. The type of yarn and the needle best suited for the

KNITTING

Terms and Abbreviations

k	knit	mc	main color
st(s)	stitch(es)	cc	contrasting
yo	yarn over		color
sl	slip	p	purl
inc	increase	rnd	round
tog	together	sk	skip
dp	double-pointed	pat	pattern
psso	pass slip	dec	decrease
	stitch over	lp	loop
beg	beginning		

project are usually suggested in the directions.

The following charts should help to acquaint you with the basic stitches. As with other types of needlework, you control the tension on the yarn while you make the stitches. By keeping the tension the same for each stitch, you can be assured that they will all be the same size.

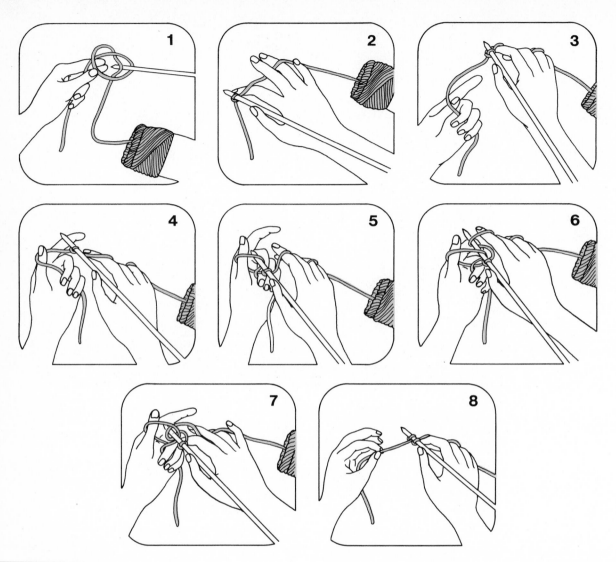

CASTING ON

Putting the first row of stitches on the knitting needle is called casting on.

1 Make a slipknot 12 inches [30.5 centimeters] from the end of yarn. The loop of this knot counts as the first stitch.

2 Hold the needle and the yarn from the skein in your right hand.

3 Hold the loose end of the yarn in your left hand.

4 Loop the loose end of the left-hand yarn around your left thumb.

5 Insert the needle through the loop on your left thumb.

6 With your index finger, loop the right-hand yarn around the point of the needle.

7 Draw the yarn and the needle through the loop on your thumb.

8 Ease the loop off your thumb, and pull the yarn in your left hand to tighten stitch. The second stitch is now cast on the needle. Repeat steps 4 through 8 to continue casting on until you have the desired number of stitches on the needle.

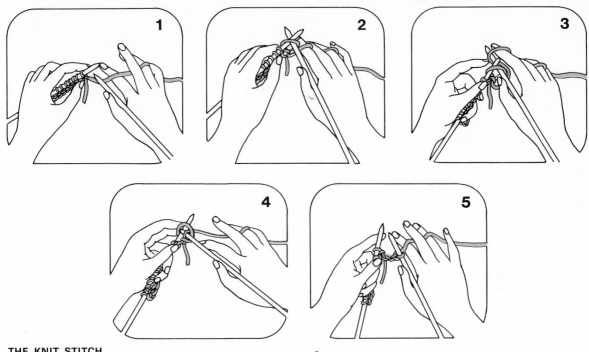

THE KNIT STITCH

The movements in knitting are the same as in casting on. Push the stitches on the left needle up toward the point of the needle as you work. At the end of a row, the needles change hands—the full needle is held in the left hand; the empty needle, in the right.

1 Hold the needle with cast-on stitches in the left hand and the empty needle and yarn in the right hand.

2 Slip the point of the needle into the first stitch.

3 Loop the yarn around the point of the needle with your index finger.

4 Draw the loop and needle through the stitch.

5 The right needle holds the new stitch and the old stitch is slipped off the left needle. Work all knit stitches the same way.

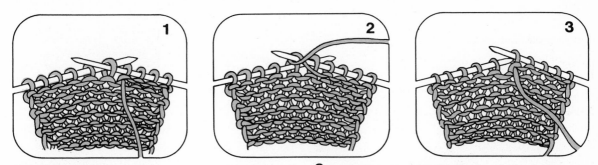

THE PURL STITCH

1 Hold the needles the same as for the knit stitch, but with the yarn in front of the right needle. Slip the point of the needle in each stitch from the back.

2 Loop the yarn around the point of the needle.

3 Draw the yarn and needle through the stitch and slip the old stitch off the left needle. Work all purl stitches the same way.

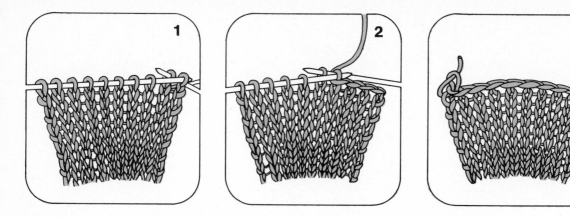

BINDING OFF

Finishing a row of stitches so they will not ravel is called binding off.

1 Knit two stitches *loosely*. Pass the first stitch over the second stitch and off the right needle.

2 One stitch remains on the right needle. Knit the next stitch *loosely* and repeat step 1.

3 Bind off all stitches except the last one. Cut the yarn and draw the end through the last stitch, pulling gently to make a knot.

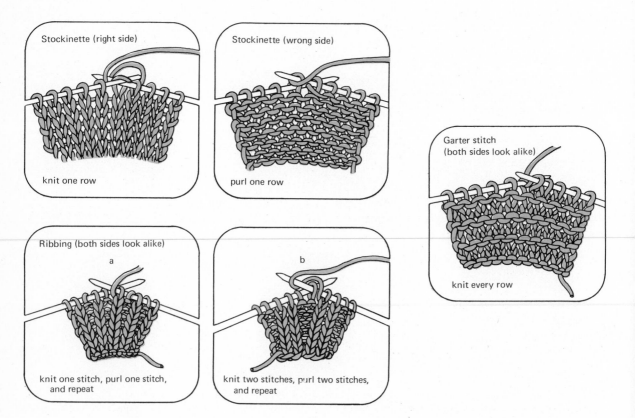

Stockinette (right side)

knit one row

Stockinette (wrong side)

purl one row

Garter stitch
(both sides look alike)

knit every row

Ribbing (both sides look alike)

a

knit one stitch, purl one stitch, and repeat

b

knit two stitches, purl two stitches, and repeat

BASIC STITCHES

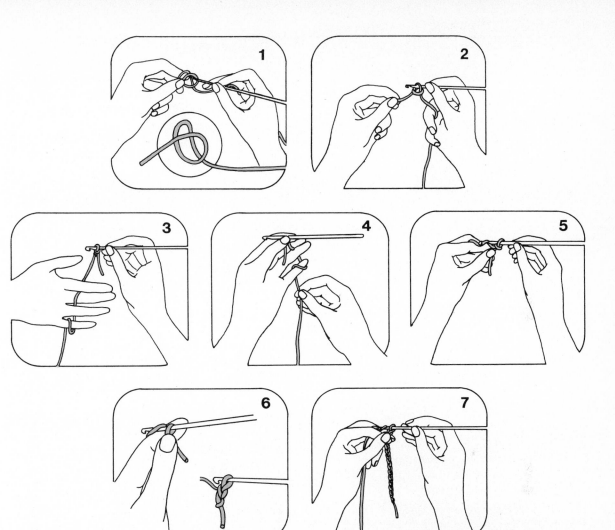

TO MAKE CHAIN STITCHES

1 Hold the hook with your thumb on the flat part of it. Make the first loop as shown and put the hook through it. Catch the yarn with the hook and pull it through the loop.

2 Pull both ends of the yarn to adjust the loop. It should be close to the hook, but not too tight.

3 As you hold the hook with one hand, arrange the yarn around the other hand. Wrap the yarn once around the little finger, then under and over the other fingers.

4 Hold the hook and the loop with your wrapped hand. Pull the yarn gently around your hand.

5 As you work, hold the hook in one hand and the stitches with the other. Do not hold the hook or the stitches too tightly.

6 Catch the yarn on your forefinger with the hook and pull it through the loop on the hook. You just made one chain stitch. The loop should be loose enough so that the hook and yarn can go through it easily.

7 Continue catching the yarn with the hook and pulling it through the loop. Hold the top stitch with the thumb and forefinger of the yarn-wrapped hand. Keep the tension on the yarn even so all your stitches come out the same size. One stitch always remains on the hook and is not counted as a stitch.

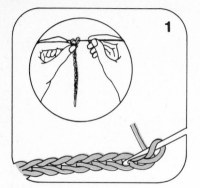 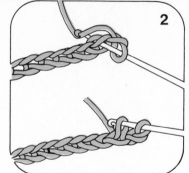 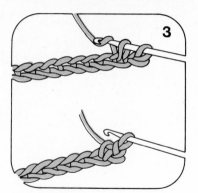

 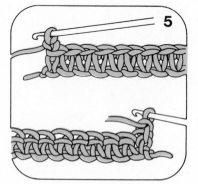

TO MAKE SINGLE CROCHET STITCHES

1 Insert the hook in the second chain stitch. Remember, the stitch on the hook is not counted, so count back two chain stitches from the hook.

2 Catch the yarn and pull it through the stitch. Watch how the hook goes into the stitch through the space and under the yarn in back.

3 Catch the yarn with the hook and draw it through the two loops. You have made one single crochet stitch.

4 Make one single crochet in each chain across. Do not let the chain twist. The hook goes through the front of each chain stitch—into each space and under the back yarn.

5 When you finish the row, count the single crochet stitches. (The directions for your project will tell you how many stitches are required for each row.) To get to the next row chain one, then turn. Continue to make single crochet stitches in each stitch across the row.

CROCHETING

Like knitting, crocheting is a series of interlocking loops. However, only one needle is used to pull the yarn through the loops. From the very simplest of crocheted chains to elaborate lace designs, the technique is basically the same. You can crochet vests, sweaters, hats, tablecloths, pillows, and wall hangings.

Like knitting needles, crochet hooks come in different sizes for different thicknesses of yarn. Traditionally, cotton cord was used for crocheting, but now wool and synthetics are used just as frequently, for an entirely different look. Directions for a crochet project will include the hook size and type of yarn you should use for the best results.

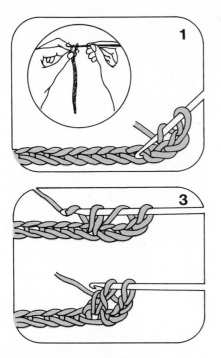

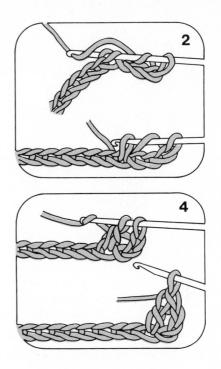

TO MAKE DOUBLE CROCHET STITCHES

1 Wrap the yarn once around the hook (yarn over), and insert it in the fourth chain stitch. Remember, you do not count the stitch on the hook.

2 With the hook through the fourth chain stitch, catch the yarn and pull it through the stitch. Now you have three loops on the hook.

3 Catch the yarn again and draw it through two loops. Now there are two loops on the hook.

4 Catch the yarn a third time and draw it through the two remaining loops. You have just made one double crochet stitch. Continue across the row, making a double crochet stitch in each chain stitch. To get to the next row, chain three, then turn. The chains are counted as the first double crochet stitch of the next row. Work double crochet stitches under the top two yarns of each stitch across the row.

CROCHETING

Terms and Abbreviations

beg—beginning	hdc—half double
lp—loop	crochet
ch—chain	rnd—round
sl st—slip stitch	p—picot
sc—single crochet	sp—space
dc—double crochet	bl—block
st(s)—stitch(es)	sk—skip
tr—treble crochet	inc—increase
dtr—double treble	dec—decrease
tr tr—triple treble	yo—yarn over

To be sure your finished knitted or crocheted project is the correct size, use the needle and yarn recommended in the directions, and check the information concerning the gauge. The gauge refers to the number of stitches per inch [centimeter] and is directly related to the size of your finished project. Make a 3-inch [7.5-centimeter] square and count the number of stitches per inch [centimeter]. If you have more stitches than recommended, they are too small and your end results will be smaller than expected. You can loosen the tension on your stitching, or use larger needles. The opposite is true if you have too few stitches.

Many crafts are also used to make soft, cuddly dolls and toys like these crocheted puppets. *McCall's Needlework & Crafts Magazine*

Knitting and crocheting are the traditional needlework crafts for sweater making. *McCall's Needlework & Crafts Magazine*

WEAVING, HOOKING, AND KNOTTING

Like many of the crafts we have already discussed, weaving, hooking, and knotting have long and diverse histories. They all share some similar skills or techniques and are closely tied to different cultures and civilizations. Weaving, hooking, and knotting all require the interlacing and interlocking of yarns to form a fabric. These fabrics vary greatly in appearance and texture, from the flat, tightly woven loom cloth to the open, airy, knotted macramé to the thickly tufted hooked rug.

WEAVING

The mention of weaving probably brings to mind large looms and yards of fabric. However, weaving has not always been done on such massive equipment nor have large quantities of fabric always been the desired result.

Remember our weaving discussion in Chapter 3? Do you remember how weaving is done?

Bags, bands, and belts are quick, basic projects for beginning weavers. *McCall's Needlework & Crafts Magazine*

Interlacing threads or yarns at right angles to each other is all that is necessary. Usually, weaving is done by working the crosswise yarn over and under the lengthwise yarns.

You can use a picture frame to make a miniature loom or you can build a wooden frame or use a flat piece of plywood. Small headless nails are hammered partly into the wood, close together, along one end and then directly opposite those nails along the other end. Wrap yarn or string around the nails opposite each other to form the lengthwise grain, or warp, of the weave.

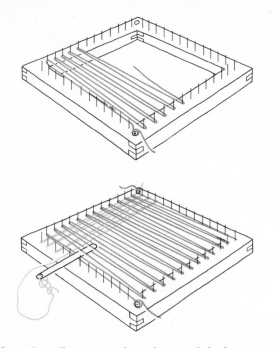

Once the nails are spaced evenly around the frame, you can wrap yarn around one to another, from top to bottom, forming the lengthwise grain. Another yarn is wrapped around the side nails and passed over and under the lengthwise yarns, forming the crosswise grain of the fabric.

Use a large needle, a wooden stick, or your fingers to guide the crosswise filling yarns over and under the warp yarns. Extra yarn, string, strips of fabric, or dried things from nature— twigs, leaves, flowers, nuts, stones, or shells— can then be woven in and out of the warp for an interesting visual and textural effect.

Your woven piece can be removed from the loom and sewn together with other squares to form a larger design. Or it can be left right on the loom and displayed as a decoration.

A cardboard box will also work well as a loom. Just cut notches along opposite edges of the box and string your warp yarn around these. Such things as sticks, a tin can, or even a coat hanger can also serve as a loom. Wind yarn around opposite sides of any of these objects to

The spinning wheel spins fibers into yarns which are used for many crafts. *LeAnn Birch, South Dakota Extension Service*

make the warp, and then weave the filling yarn back and forth. The shape of the loom becomes part of the design. Use your imagination and see what you can find to use as a loom for your weaving project.

You may not have realized it, but *braiding* is another form of simple weaving. The strands of yarn used are both the warp and the filling of the finished project. Braiding, or finger weaving,

Modern geometric designs are easy to follow for the colonial craft of rug making. **McCall's Needlework & Crafts Magazine**

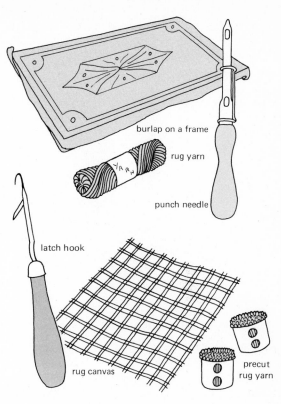

TOOLS FOR RUG MAKING

is usually done to make narrow bands or strips of fabric for belts and trims.

RUG MAKING

Rugs can be made by many methods. Crocheting, knitting, needlepoint, weaving, and braiding all make excellent rugs. However, the method most frequently associated with rug making is *hooking*.

During the period of Colonial America, rugs were needed for warmth—besides being attractive floor coverings or wall hangings. Rug making was also economical since scraps of leftover yarns and worn-out clothing were used.

There are two types of tools used for rug hooking: a *punch needle* and a *latch hook*. When using the punch needle, you should get coarsely woven backing, like burlap, and stretch it over a frame. The frame will hold the backing taut. The punch needle is threaded with the rug yarn, and it is pushed through the burlap. As you hold the yarn with one hand and pull the hook out with the other, a loop is formed. A guide

on the punch needle determines the length of each loop.

The design of your rug might call for different loop lengths for added texture, or for loops of all the same size. The loops are made about ½ inch [12.7 millimeters] apart. When completed, they can be left as they are or cut so that the result is a velvety pile. It is best to work from the center of the design toward the edges. Outline an area with loops and then fill it in.

Making rugs with the latch hook is relatively easy. The yarn is pre-cut to a standard length so that the pile of the rug is even. Instead of loops, you have a cut pile with a shag effect. A heavy rug canvas is used for backing. The canvas looks like a magnified version of the needlepoint canvas. It does not have to be attached to a frame as does the burlap backing for

111

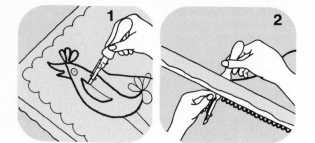

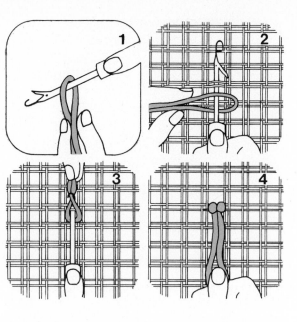

TO USE A PUNCH NEEDLE

1 With the design of the rug facing you, push the threaded needle through the burlap. It is best to begin in the center of the rug and work toward the edges.

2 Pull the needle out while making sure a loop is formed on the underside, which is the right side of the rug.

3 Outline an area of the design; then fill it in. Insert the needle every ¼ inch [6 millimeters].

LATCH-HOOK RUG MAKING

1 Fold the yarn in half around the shank of the latch hook.

2 Slip the hook in one mesh and out the one just above it.

3 Latch into the ends of the yarn and pull them toward you through the loop, forming a knot.

4 Tighten the knot, if necessary, by pulling the ends.

the punch method. The edges of the canvas, though, should be taped so they will not ravel. Rug yarn may be bought in skeins and cut to the length desired, or it can be purchased precut. Each mesh is worked separately and is filled with one precut strand.

MACRAMÉ

Macramé refers to the craft of making fabric by knotting threads. Its origin is primitive. Perhaps it was first done as a means of protection and survival. Knotting vines together to cover and protect bodies or to make nets to catch ani-

mals for food are likely possibilities. As civilization progressed, macramé as a craft became more creative. It is also considered a nautical art. Many sailors claim macramé to be their satisfying pastime while on board ship at sea.

Ponchos, vests, bedspreads, belts, jewelry, placemats, scarves, and wall decorations are just a few of the items that can be made by macramé. The equipment needed is fairly simple. Strands of nonstretchy pliable material, such as yarn, string, rope, cording, or even fine wire, are knotted together to produce various effects.

Some projects require a flat surface for knot-

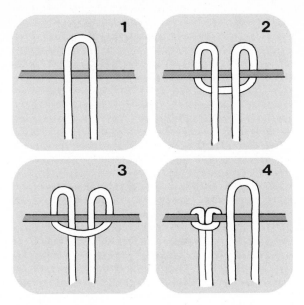

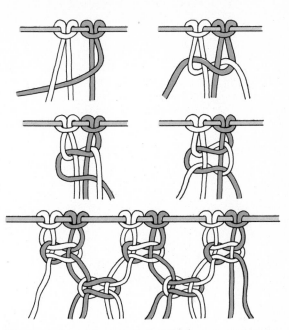

MOUNTING WITH THE LARK'S HEAD KNOT

To begin most macramé, the cords to be knotted are first mounted on a *holding cord.*

1 Fold each strip of cord in half.

2 Bring the top of the loop behind the holding cord.

3 Draw the cord ends through the loop.

4 Pull the knot tight and repeat with each cord to be mounted.

The square knot is one of two basic macramé knots. Various designs can be created by the number of cords used or by the way you combine this and other knots.

Macramé knots can be made into unique-looking accessories, like those shown here. *McCall's Needlework & Crafts Magazine*

ting the rope into specific shapes. Others need to be secured at the beginning for tension. A small pillow, a slab of wood, foam rubber, or a doorknob are just a few items that you might use. You may need pins or small nails to secure the macramé to the working surface or to outline the shape of the item you are going to make. Depending on your project, T-pins, plastic-headed sewing pins, or corsage pins are best suited for this purpose.

The basic knots are the *lark's head, square,* and *half hitch.* Combinations and variations of these produce a limitless number of creative knots.

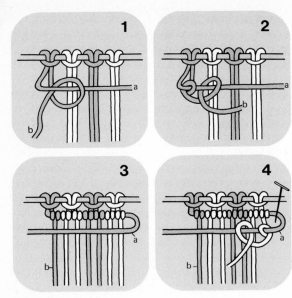

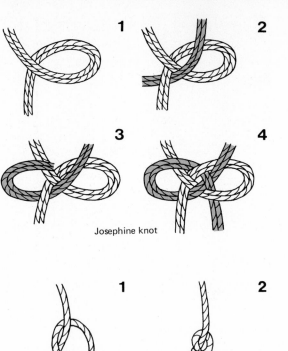

Josephine knot

overhand knot

OTHER MACRAMÉ KNOTS

THE HALF-HITCH KNOT

The half-hitch knot is the first step in the double half hitch, which is one of the two basic knots used in macramé. It consists of one holding cord and one tying cord. Because it is a single loop, the half hitch is rarely used by itself.

1 Bring the outside cord (a) across the other cords to be knotted. Wrap cord (b) around cord (a).

2 Wrap cord (b) around cord (a) again to make a double half-hitch knot.

3 The half-hitch knot can be continued across all or any number of the remaining cords.

4 Use a pin to hold the cord in place for the next row of knots.

QUILTING

When talking about quilts, we usually envision the brightly colored and patterned coverlets used on beds. However, *quilting* refers to stitching through several layers of fabric. The colors, patterns, and textures are the result of appliqué or patchwork. Both of these techniques have been used together with quilting for many centuries. Quilting was originally done to add warmth, since the combined layers of fabric added extra insulation.

Quilts and quilted fabric are made by stitching layers of fabric together to form a pattern or design. The stitching has traditionally been done by hand, but quilting can also be done with the sewing machine.

To make a quilt, you need a top layer of fabric, a filling layer of cotton or polyester batting or an old blanket, and a final layer of fabric that completes the sandwich. The top layer may be embroidered or made from small pieces of fabric to form a patchwork design.

Whether you plan to quilt by hand or by machine, you must first baste the layers together. Beginning in the center of the quilt, make long, running stitches toward each corner and then around the outer edges. After the layers are

In patchwork and appliqué, pieces of fabric are used to make designs and pictures. They are often combined with quilting, which adds design and dimension. *McCall's Needle-work & Crafts Magazine*

loosely basted together, they are permanently stitched according to your planned design.

The quilting design to be followed might depend on the top layer of fabric, or you might prefer to contrast its design with another. Straight lines and diamond shapes are two of the most commonly used patterns. The design should be marked lightly on your fabric before you begin, either with a sharp pencil or with chalk.

For hand quilting a large area, you will find it easier if you have a quilting frame or hoop. When you stitch the layers together, use a short needle and small, fine, running stitches. Begin in the center of the quilt and work toward the edges—following the design. Reinforce the stitching line with a couple of back stitches. Try to keep the stitches evenly spaced. You may be working slow at first, but you will become faster as the project progresses.

If you are quilting by machine, the process is the same—stitching from the center toward the edges. Many machines have a quilting gauge to insure evenly spaced rows of stitching. Since machine quilting is so much faster, a quilting project now is not as overwhelming as it once

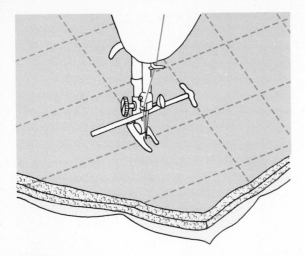

For machine quilting, there is a special presser foot with an adjustable gauge that guides the stitching for straight, even rows.

was. Where it had been used only for things of heirloom quality, quilting is now being used for clothing, accessories, toys, and pillow and chair covers, as well as for the ever popular traditional bed covers.

PATCHWORK

Patchwork and quilting are almost synonymous terms because they are used together so frequently. *Patchwork* refers to the end result of joining small pieces of fabric together to make a design. These pieces are usually square, triangular, or diamond-shaped, but circular, curved, and odd-shaped pieces produce very interesting designs, too.

Choosing a design and combining colors, shapes, and textures is the real fun of patchwork. Museums, books, and magazines on quilting can give you some helpful and creative

Designs on these pillows have been made with patchwork. *McCall's Needlework & Crafts Magazine*

hints. It is a good idea to do a rough plan of your patchwork pattern on paper first.

Once you have decided on the pattern, you then cut each of the patchwork pieces into its specified shape. If your design requires all or some of the fabric pieces to be the same size, a pattern cut from cardboard or heavy paper will make this task easier. Add $\frac{1}{4}$ inch [6 millimeters] around the pattern for the seam allowance.

Start constructing your patchwork from the center and work toward the edges. Sew the pieces together on the sewing machine or by hand. Be sure to secure the threads at the end of each seam. If you follow the patchwork design when you quilt, you will eliminate the need for a separate quilting design.

APPLIQUÉ

Appliqué is the art of applying one piece of material on top of another. Appliqués are usually decorative but can also be used to patch a worn

The schooner is appliquéd to background fabric and is then quilted to give it a raised effect. *McCall's Needlework & Crafts Magazine*

Appliqué and embroidery were used to decorate this jumper. *Butterick Fashion Marketing Co.*

or torn area. While appliqués and patterns to make them are available in stores, your own imagination can find an outlet in this craft.

Almost any fabric can be used to make appliqués. Firmly woven ones are the easiest to handle. To appliqué, cut out various shapes from pieces of fabric; then arrange them in a design you like. Try to let the textures and colors of the different fabrics help in your designing.

When you are happy with the arrangement, you are ready to appliqué. Turn under the raw edges about $\frac{1}{4}$ inch [6 millimeters] around each

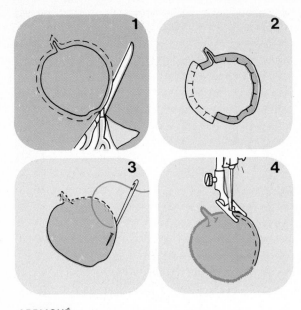

Using graph paper is helpful when enlarging or transferring designs, or when creating your own, for appliqué. *Stacy Fabrics Corp.*

APPLIQUÉ

1 Follow the design of the fabric or use a paper pattern to cut the fabric patch.

2 Fold the cut edges to the wrong side of the fabric.

3 Pin the patch on the fabric to be decorated. Slip stitch the patch in place.

4 When you machine stitch an appliqué in place, you do not have to turn the cut edges under.

shape. Make a crease where you turned the fabric—with your fingers or an iron. Corners and curved areas may turn more easily if a slight clip is made into the seam allowance. You might want to baste the folded edges to keep them in place.

Arrange the appliqués on the background in the design you decided on. You can hand stitch them in place using a short needle and small slip stitches (see page 254). You can also use a sewing machine, but the stitching will be visible on the appliqué.

Should you decide to use the machine, you can completely cover the edges of the appliqué with a satin or zigzag stitch. In this case, it would not be necessary to turn under the raw edges of the appliqué. Just position the design, baste or pin the appliqués in place, and stitch. For a raised or sculptured effect, pad the appliqué with fluffy fibers of polyester or cotton.

Many fusible products are available so you can iron on appliqués rather than sew them in place. The ready-made patches are examples. You can cut out a shape from the patch fabric and iron it onto the background fabric. Since you do not want the fabric around the appliqué to melt due to high temperatures, be sure your fabric can withstand the heat and pressure required to fuse the patch in place.

Another type of fusible material resembles a spider web and is placed between the appliqué and background fabric. Heat from the iron melts the fibers of the web, causing the appliqué to adhere to the background fabric. Again, the fabric must withstand the temperature required to melt the fusible fibers.

Appliqué is one way to dress up or save a favorite pair of jeans. *Talon*

● IDEAS FOR ACTION

1. Set up a display of embroidery stitches. Let everyone in the class contribute two embroidery stitch designs. Assemble these together into a collage or sample. Label the different stitches.

2. Prepare a demonstration of needlepoint stitches. Let your classmates see the back of each design so that they can observe the difference between the continental and half-cross stitches.

3. Most of the needlecrafts need to be pressed or blocked when they are completed. Research to find out what blocking is and why and how it is done. Share this knowledge with your classmates.

4. Visit a local crafts store. Make a list of the types of craft supplies that are available. Report back to your class on your findings.

5. Present a report on the history of macramé to your class. You might also want to demonstrate how to do some of the more unusual knotting techniques.

6. Work together in small groups to create a word game based on crafts. Use the names of stitches and equipment associated with needlecrafts, weaving, hooking and knotting, or quilting. It might be a game like bingo or a card game or a crossword puzzle.

7. Since this chapter only included the basics of each craft, find out where additional information or lessons can be obtained. Check with the local "Y," sewing stores, or community centers. Develop a bulletin board around your findings. If classes are not available in your area, make a list of books in the library which might be helpful for learning new skills.

● DO YOU KNOW

appliqué	knotting
Bargello	latch hook
braiding	macramé
crewel embroidery	needlepoint
crocheting	patchwork
embroidery	punch needle
hooking	quilting
knitting	weaving

PART 2

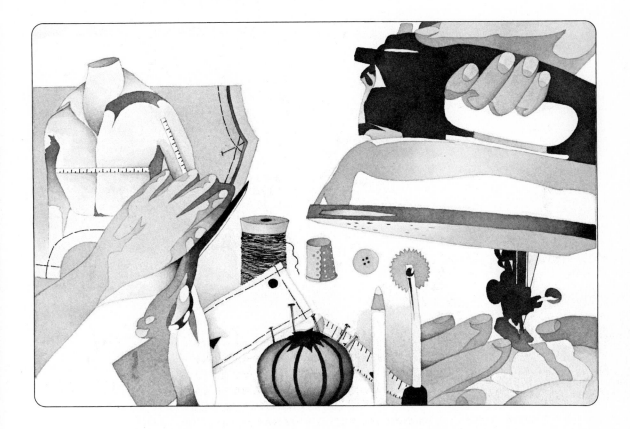

CLOTHING CONSTRUCTION

the sewing machine

After reading this chapter, you should be able to:

- *Recognize the basic parts of the sewing machine and describe how they work.*

- *Insert a needle and thread and operate a sewing machine.*

- *Describe the basic motions of straight-stitch, zigzag-stitch, and stretch-stitch machine models.*

- *Stitch a straight line, a curve, and a sharp corner.*

- *Follow the manufacturer's instructions on how to clean and oil the machine.*

- *Discuss five things to think about when buying a sewing machine.*

LEARNING TO SEW

With a little skill and imagination, you can begin to express your individuality, your tastes, your interests, and your feelings through sewing. You can make clothing for yourself or others. You can also make gifts, crafts, and household items. You might sew a stuffed animal, a pillow, a tie or belt, or a picture or wall hanging.

Once you learn to use the sewing machine and a hand sewing needle, you will be ready to begin. You can remodel clothes and make your own alterations. What better way to continue to use your favorite slacks or dress than by changing the hem length or adding a bit of trim? Holes and tears can be mended with matching fabric and thread so that the repair does not show or with different colors for decoration.

Sewing your own clothes can have many advantages. You can have a one-of-a-kind garment, save money, or feel good that you made the garment yourself. You can even have better made and better fitting clothes than the ones available in a store—for the same price or less.

Being able to sew can help you shop for ready-made clothes. You will be able to look for and recognize quality construction and style.

How do you begin? First, decide that you really want to learn how to sew. There are many sewing skills to master. For example, to make even a simple garment, you will have to know how to:

- Use and care for sewing equipment.
- Measure for pattern size.
- Cut, mark, join, and stitch the fabric pieces to make the garment.
- Finish edges and details.
- Iron and press.

KNOWING THE MACHINE

Before the invention of the sewing machine, it was the responsibility of women to make all the clothes for their families. Young girls were taught to use the sewing needle and made samplers of the stitches they learned. Sewing was not done for enjoyment. It was necessary. It took a lot of time because it was done completely by hand. People had to sew for themselves or pay someone to do it for them. Imagine if you could only have clothes that you made by hand. What would your wardrobe look like?

Today, sewing for enjoyment is directly related to the invention and widespread use of the sewing machine. Changes and improvements have resulted in sewing machines that not only sew straight stitches but also do zigzag and special stitches for sewing hems, attaching buttons, making buttonholes, finishing edges, and adding decoration. Many of today's home sewing machines have features like those of the machines found in modern clothing factories.

CO-ED, SCHOLASTIC MAGAZINES, INC. (both)

Learning to sew can be fun. Wearing what you make can give you a feeling of pride that "you did it yourself."

The sewing machine is not difficult to understand even though there are many models and brands available. Once you learn the basic features and operation of one machine, you can easily apply what you have learned to other makes and models.

There is much more to sewing than simply making and repairing your own clothes. Accessories, toys, crafts, and household items can be made for yourself or for others. *Butterick Fashion Marketing Co.*

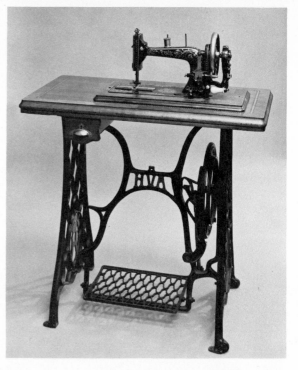

This home sewing machine was made in 1883. It was one of the first machines to be driven by gears and to have all the mechanical parts enclosed. *Viking Sewing Machine Co., Inc.*

Before you operate a machine for the first time, be sure you are familiar with its parts and their uses.

PARTS OF THE MACHINE

- **bobbin**   round plastic or metal spool which holds the bottom thread in the machine
- **bobbin winder**   allows you to fill a bobbin automatically
- **bobbin case**   holds bobbin and regulates bottom thread tension as stitches are formed
- **face plate**   protects the pressure dial and, on some models, contains an upper threading chart
- **feed dogs**   move fabric under the presser foot as the stitches are formed
- **hand wheel**   controls the up-and-down motion of the thread take-up lever and needle

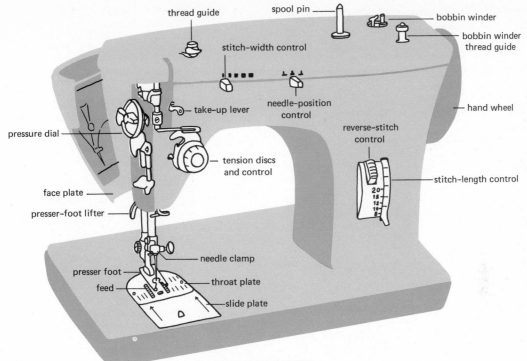

thread guide • spool pin • bobbin winder • bobbin winder thread guide • stitch-width control • take-up lever • needle-position control • hand wheel • pressure dial • tension discs and control • reverse-stitch control • stitch-length control • face plate • presser-foot lifter • needle clamp • presser foot • throat plate • feed • slide plate

PARTS OF THE MACHINE

- **needle clamp** holds the needle in position
- **pressure control** regulates the pressure between the feed dogs and the presser foot
- **presser foot** holds the fabric in the machine
- **presser-foot lifter** raises and lowers the presser foot
- **reverse control** permits the machine to stitch backward
- **slide plate** covers the bobbin case
- **spool pin** holds the upper thread
- **stitch regulator** sets the length of the stitches
- **stitch-width control** sets the width of zigzag and pattern stitches
- **tension control** regulates pressure on the threads
- **thread take-up lever** controls the thread as it flows through the needle
- **throat plate** provides a smooth surface for sewing and is usually marked with stitching guidelines

If you were a sewing machine operator, you would work in a factory where the machines are heavier, faster, and more powerful than home sewing machines. In the clothing industry, you might specialize in the use of attachments for making special seams, sewing and cutting buttonholes, or sewing on sleeves, collars, or buttons. You might make only certain sections of a garment, or you might put all the sections together.

THE MACHINE NEEDLE

Most machine needles range in size from numbers nine to eighteen. A second system of sizing includes needles numbered from 70 to 120. The higher the number, the bigger the needle. The size needle to use depends on the fabric to be

COMBINATIONS FOR MACHINE STITCHING

Fabrics	Thread	Needle	Stitch length
Sheer and delicate chiffon lace organdy fine tricot	fine mercerized cotton polyester nylon	regular ball point 9	15 to 20
Lightweight jersey voile silk crepe plastic film	50 mercerized cotton "A" silk "A" nylon polyester	regular ball point 11	12 to 15 (8 to 10 for plastic)
Medium-weight gingham linen chintz satin velvet suitings double-knit nylon tricot jersey spandex	50 mercerized cotton "A" silk "A" nylon polyester	regular ball point 14	12 to 15
Medium-heavyweight gabardine sailcloth denim coatings deep-pile fabrics	heavy duty mercerized cotton nylon polyester	regular ball point 16	10 to 12
Heavyweight overcoatings upholstery fabrics canvas	heavy duty mercerized cotton polyester	regular ball point 18	6 to 10
Leather suede kidskin calf fake leathers	50 mercerized cotton polyester "A" nylon "A" silk	wedge 11 14 16	8 to 10

sewn. When sewing fine or lightweight fabrics, use a fine needle (low number). For heavy fabrics, use a heavy needle (high number). Needle sizes 11 and 14 (80 and 90) are used for medium-weight fabrics.

Needles can have a sharp point, a ball point, or a wedge point. The regular sharp point needle is used on woven fabrics. The ball point needle was developed especially for knit fabrics. It has a rounded end that slips between the yarns

Regular sharp needle—used with woven fabrics

Ball point needle—used with knitted fabrics

Wedge point needle—used with leather and leatherlike fabrics

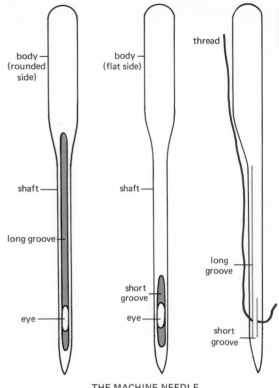

THE MACHINE NEEDLE

without breaking them. The wedge point needle is used for sewing leather and leatherlike fabrics. This special point is strong and sharp enough to make a clean hole through the leather fabric without splitting it.

Sewing machine needles are usually packaged according to type of point. Each package may contain the same-size needles or a combination of sizes. Check the label for the size and type you need. To make selection easier, many manufacturers list on the label the type of fabric for which the needle can be used.

Choosing the correct size and type of needle for the fabric to be sewn is important. The needle affects the quality of your stitching. For example, stitches may skip if you use a fine needle on a heavy fabric. A sharp point needle can break or split the threads of a knit fabric and cause holes or runs in the seams.

Machine needles can bend, break, or get nicked in use. They can also become dull. In all of these cases, they should be replaced right away. Smooth, straight needles give the best results.

The shape of the needle will guide you in positioning it in the machine. Check the needle for the flat and rounded sides. The rounded side has a long groove down the needle shaft. This

long groove helps to hold the thread and prevents the buildup of friction that can break the thread. The flat side of the needle has a short groove around the eye that the thread goes through. This also helps to cut down on friction as the thread moves down into the fabric.

The long-groove side of the needle should be on the same side of the machine as the last thread guide. In this way, the thread goes through the eye of the needle from the long groove and comes out on the short-groove side. If you double-check, you will find that the flat part of the body of the needle faces away from the last thread guide and fits firmly into the needle clamp. Some machines thread from the front to the back, some from left to right, and others from right to left. In all cases, the position of the needle is the same in relation to the thread and thread guide—that is, the long groove of the needle and the last thread guide are on the same side of the machine.

127

machines
of the past

1868
The decorative Leavitt sewing machine

1870
A Howe (Stockwell Brothers) machine

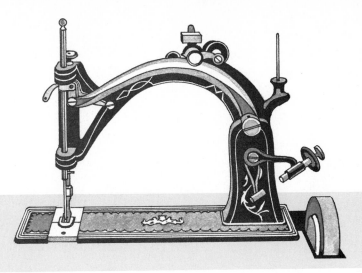

1872
The "catback" sewing machine

1851
Singer's first practical sewing machine

1858
A one-of-a-kind, horse sewing machine

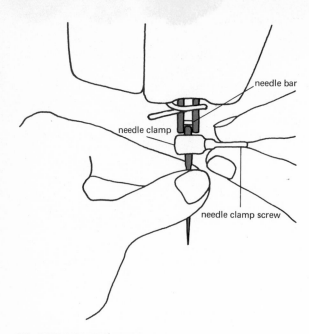

needle bar

needle clamp

needle clamp screw

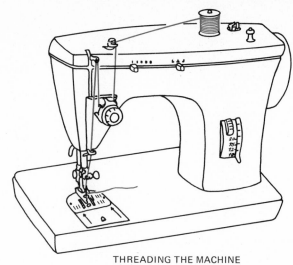

THREADING THE MACHINE

TO REPLACE THE NEEDLE

1 Raise the needle to its highest position.

2 Loosen the needle clamp screw and remove the old needle.

3 Be sure the long groove of the new needle is on the same side of the machine as the last thread guide.

4 Insert the needle into the needle clamp as far as it will go.

5 Tighten the needle clamp screw.

THREADING THE MACHINE

The thread for machine sewing is just as important as the needle. Like the needle, the type and size of thread you choose will depend on the fabric you will be sewing. The weight, construction, and fiber content of the fabric must be considered.

Lightweight fabrics should be sewn with fine threads, and heavy fabrics should be sewn with heavy threads. Stitching with thread that is too heavy or thick can cause pulling and breaking of the fabric yarns. Too thick a thread may also cause puckering of seams and stitching that shows on the right side of the garment. Using thin or lightweight thread on heavy fabric may

result in stitches that are uneven or that skip and pull out. Knit fabrics stretch. The thread that is used on knits should be strong and able to stretch with the fabric.

Thread can be made from different fibers. As a general rule, the thread you use should be made of the same fiber as the fabric to be sewn. For decorative stitching, you may want to use a type of thread different from the one you use for seams.

If you were a sewing machine demonstrator, you would travel around the country, representing the manufacturer. You would demonstrate new machine models and sewing techniques to salespeople of different stores. You would also assist dealers with store events by preparing their staffs for special sales, sewing programs, and fashion shows. You might also help to plan and conduct special sewing and fashion shows for schools, department stores, and sewing centers.

Diagrams for threading machines can be found in the instruction booklets prepared by the manufacturers. On some machines, threading diagrams can also be found on the inside of the face

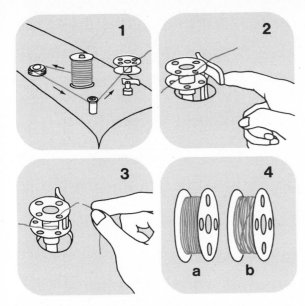

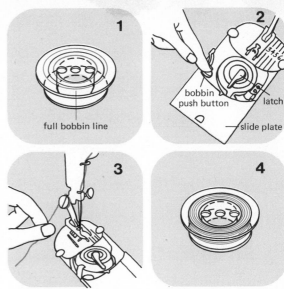

TO WIND THE CONVENTIONAL BOBBIN

1 Stop the motion of the needle. On some models, this is done by loosening the hand wheel. On others, it is done by pressing a special button. Place the thread on the spool pin. Lead the thread from the spool pin, around the thread guides, and through the small hole in the bobbin.

2 Place the bobbin on the spindle and push the latch inward.

3 Hold the thread end and run the machine slowly until the bobbin is filled.

4 a Neatly wound bobbin.
  b Incorrectly wound bobbin.

TO WIND THE TOUCH AND SEW BOBBIN

Thread the machine as if you were going to sew. Keep the presser foot raised.

1 The Touch and Sew bobbin is made of clear plastic. The top side is larger than the bottom side.

2 Place the bobbin in the case, small side down, and push the latch against the bobbin. Press the bobbin push button.

3 Wrap thread around the presser foot screw. Run the machine slowly to fill the bobbin. Close the slide plate to sew.

4 Neatly wound bobbin.

plate. Sewing machines may differ slightly, but they usually thread and work in basically the same way. The following guidelines for threading can be used with most sewing machines.

- Place the thread on the spool pin.
- Turn the hand wheel to raise the take-up lever to its highest position.
- Raise the presser-foot lifter to release the pressure on the tension discs. This opens the discs to allow you to insert the thread.

- Pass the thread through each guide and the tension discs from the spool pin to the needle.
- Thread the needle through the long-groove side.

How bobbins are filled with thread and placed in the machine varies with different machine models, but bobbins all do the same job. They hold and distribute the bottom thread needed to make complete stitches. Before you begin to sew, you must pull the bobbin thread from the

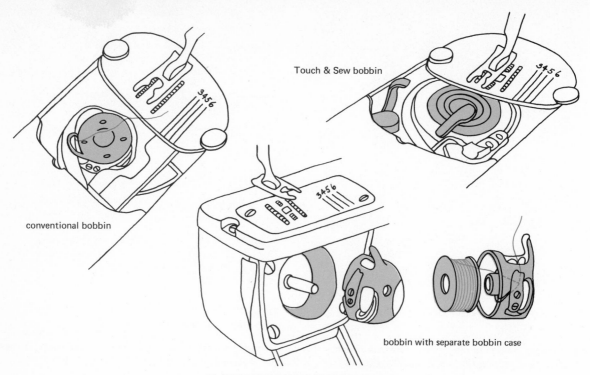

conventional bobbin

Touch & Sew bobbin

bobbin with separate bobbin case

PLACING THE BOBBIN IN THE MACHINE

bobbin case through the hole in the throat plate. To do this, hold the end of the upper thread with one hand and turn the hand wheel with the other. The bobbin thread will loop around the upper thread and come up through the throat plate opening. Pull the looped bobbin thread up and out of the bobbin case (see page 133).

HOW STITCHES ARE MADE

As the needle goes down, it carries thread through the fabric into the bobbin case. As the needle rises, the upper thread forms a loop in the bobbin case. This loop catches the bobbin thread and a stitch is formed.

Both upper and bobbin threads are regulated by tension controls which keep the threads from becoming slack. When the tension is correct, the needle and bobbin threads meet at the center of the fabric to make even stitches on both sides of the fabric. If the tension is too loose or too tight, the stitches will be loose or tight. (See

page 133.) The upper tension is easily adjusted by the control outside of the machine. The bobbin tension control is located in the bobbin case and is sometimes difficult to reach. It should be adjusted only by someone with a thorough knowledge of the machine. Often, what seems to be a tension problem proves to be a threading problem. Before changing the tension, check to be sure that the machine is threaded correctly.

If you were a sewing machine repair person, you would fix and maintain machines. You would need a complete knowledge of the basic mechanics of sewing machines. You might work in a local store that sells machines or travel to several different areas. You may be licensed to work on one or several brands of sewing machines.

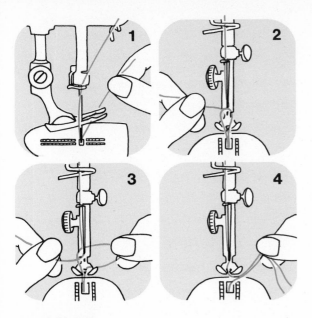

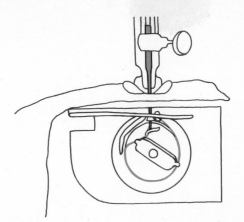

Stitches are formed as the upper thread loops around the bobbin case and locks the bobbin thread in place.

TO RAISE THE BOBBIN THREAD

1 Hold the needle thread and slowly turn the hand wheel so that the needle enters the throat plate.

2 Keep turning the hand wheel and holding the thread until the needle rises out of the throat plate. Pull the needle thread to bring up the bobbin thread loop.

3 Open the loop.

4 Place both threads under the presser foot and to the back and right of the needle.

The fabric moves under the presser foot as the stitches are formed. The feed dogs drop and rise to move the fabric into position for each stitch.

Pressure settings on the machine control the hold on the fabric between the presser foot and the feed dogs. Heavy pressure is used on heavy fabrics, and light pressure is used on light fabrics. If the pressure is too great, the upper fabric will be pushed forward faster than the under piece. If the pressure is too light, the material will slide under the foot and the stitches will not be even.

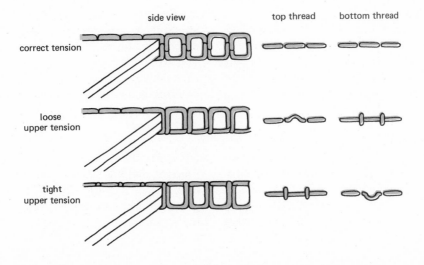

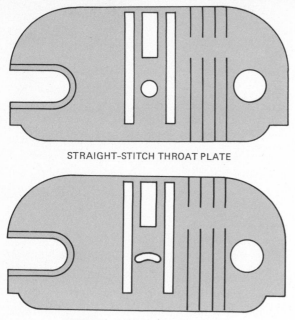

STRAIGHT-STITCH THROAT PLATE

GENERAL-PURPOSE THROAT PLATE

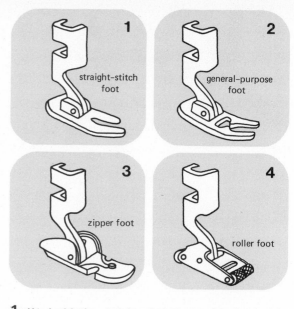

1 straight-stitch foot

2 general-purpose foot

3 zipper foot

4 roller foot

1 Used with the straight-stitch throat plate for straight stitching and for sewing lightweight or delicate fabrics.

2 Used with the general-purpose throat plate for zigzag stitching and straight stitching on medium- to heavy-weight fabrics.

3 Used with either throat plate for sewing on zippers and for stitching close to a bulky or raised edge.

4 Used with either plate for sewing on bulky, knit, or stretch fabrics, as well as imitation leathers and plastic fabrics.

There are different kinds of presser feet available for a variety of sewing needs. The most common are the regular presser foot for straight stitching, the general-purpose foot for doing zigzag and straight stitching, and the zipper foot for sewing on zippers. Some other presser feet include the special foot for decorative stitching, the button foot for sewing on buttons, the buttonhole foot for making buttonholes, and the roller foot for sewing knits and bulky fabrics.

The stitch regulator controls the number of stitches per inch the machine sews. Longer stitches are are used for any basting and sewing bulky fabrics, and shorter stitches are used for sewing fine and lightweight fabrics.

USING THE MACHINE

You can learn to control machine stitching without threading the machine. Begin by sewing along straight lines drawn on paper. Try to keep your stitching right on the lines. Practice sewing at different speeds. Once you have mastered stitching in straight lines, try stitching corners and curved lines. This simple practice will teach you to control the machine at different speeds to make straight, even stitching. When you are comfortable with the machine and can control your stitching line and speed, you are ready to start sewing.

STITCHING A SEAM

Practice making seams with two straight pieces of fabric. Place the right sides of the fabric together and line up the cut edges. Pin and baste the stitching line $5/8$ inch [15 millimeters] from

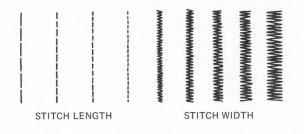

STITCH LENGTH   STITCH WIDTH

The length of straight stitching can be changed for different sewing jobs. Longer stitches are used for basting and for sewing on bulky and heavy fabrics. Shorter stitches are used on lightweight fabrics.

The width of zigzag stitches can also be controlled. Narrow width zigzag stitches can be used to make stretchable seams. Wider stitches are used for edge finishing, mending, and for decoration.

the straight edge. Remove the pins. Place the fabric under the presser foot. The cut edge will be on the ⅝-inch [15-millimeter] stitching guideline, which is located on the throat plate and just to the right of the presser foot. The bulk of the fabric will be to the left of the stitching line and out of the way while sewing. Both the needle and bobbin threads should be pulled out straight a few inches behind the needle. Turn the hand wheel until the needle is lowered into the beginning of the stitching line. Lower the presser foot.

Place your left hand lightly on the fabric to the left and slightly behind the machine needle. Hold the fabric with your right hand in front of the needle. Your hands will help guide the fabric as you sew. Be careful to keep your fingers away from the needle. Begin stitching. Start slowly and increase your speed as you gain control.

Keep your eye on the seam guideline. If you watch the needle, you will have trouble controlling the fabric. When you finish stitching the seam, lift the presser foot and raise the needle to its highest position. Slide the fabric from under the foot and cut the threads.

What does the seam look like? Is it straight? Are the stitches even? Are the tension and stitch length right for your fabric?

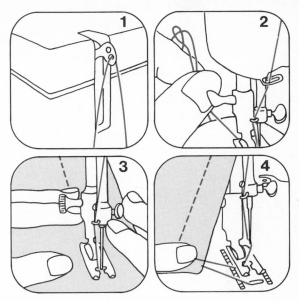

TO STITCH A STRAIGHT SEAM

1 Always begin and end sewing with the thread take-up lever in its highest position. This will prevent the threads from slipping out of the needle or jamming in the bobbin case.

2 Place the fabric under the presser foot. Hold the thread ends three to four inches behind the presser foot. Position the needle into the fabric. Lower the presser foot.

3 Guide the fabric with your hands as you sew.

4 When you have finished sewing, again, put the take-up lever in its highest position and raise the presser foot. Pull the fabric back and out from under the foot. Cut the threads.

REINFORCING A SEAM
At the beginning and end of a stitching line, you can reinforce the stitches so they will not pull out. To begin a seam, position the needle in the fabric several stitches in from the fabric edge. Put the machine in reverse and stitch to the edge. Return to the forward position to sew. At the end of the seam, repeat the process by stitching in reverse.

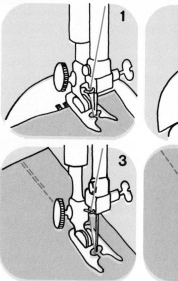
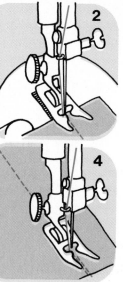

TO MACHINE-FASTEN
YOUR STITCHES

1 Position the needle into the fabric—on the seamline and about ½ inch from the edge.

2 Lower the presser foot and set the machine for reverse stitching. Sew back to the edge of the fabric.

3 Set the machine in forward position and sew to the end of the seam.

4 Reverse-stitch to reinforce the end of the seam.

TO HAND-FASTEN
YOUR STITCHES

1 Pull the top thread up to loosen the bottom thread. Pull the loop until the end of the thread is on the top side.

2 Tie both threads in a double knot. Pull the threads so that the knot is close to the fabric.

3 For added strength and a neater finish, put the ends of both threads through the eye of a needle and make a small stitch beside the knot.

You might prefer to tie the thread ends by hand to lock the stitches. This is done after the fabric is removed from the machine. Simply take the top thread of the seam and pull it up until a loop appears. With a pin, pull the loop until the end of the bottom thread is on the top side of the stitching. Tie the two threads in a double knot close to the fabric. Cut off the thread ends.

STITCHING A CURVE
When you stitch a curved seam, follow the directions for stitching a straight one. However, you must stitch and guide your fabric under the presser foot more slowly. This will help you to control the fabric and to make an even seam. Remember to watch the guideline, not the needle when stitching.

STITCHING A SHARP CORNER
When you want a pointed corner rather than a curved one, you use a technique called *pivoting*. To pivot, stitch to within ⅝ inch [15 millimeters] of the cut seam edge. Keep the needle in the fabric and raise the presser foot. Turn the fabric until the next edge is lined up on the stitching guide. Lower the presser foot and continue to stitch on the seam line.

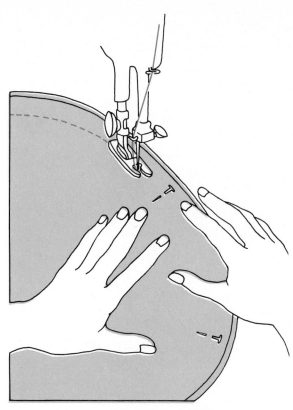

STITCHING A CURVE

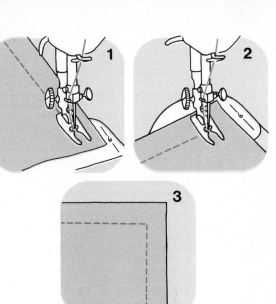

TO PIVOT A CORNER

1 Stitch to the end of the seam allowance on the first edge of the fabric.

2 Keep the needle down in the fabric and raise the presser foot. Turn the fabric until the second edge is on the stitching guideline. Continue sewing to the end of the seam.

3 The result is a sharp corner.

CARING FOR THE SEWING MACHINE

A sewing machine is an investment. It has many working parts that will run smoothly and trouble-free if cared for correctly. Check the instruction booklet for the kind and amount of special care your machine may need. Basic care for all machines includes keeping them clean and well lubricated.

Lint from thread and fabric that collects in the bobbin case, feed dogs, and tension control can cause uneven stitching. In humid weather, lint absorbs moisture that can cause rusting. Lint should be removed with a brush specially designed for this purpose. The bobbin case and the throat plate of some machines can be removed for cleaning. You may be surprised to see the quantity of lint fibers the machine has

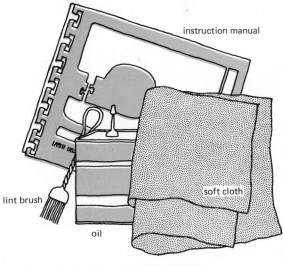

MACHINE CARE EQUIPMENT

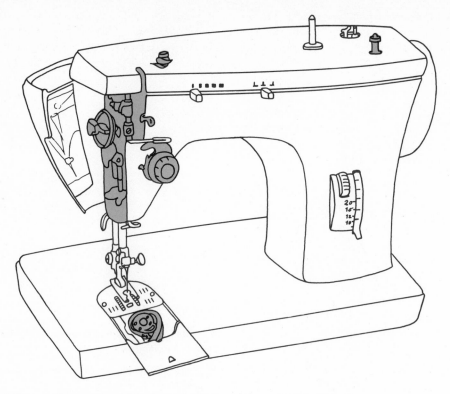

Some areas of the machine need special care to keep them clean and free from lint.

collected. As you brush away the lint, turn the hand wheel. This will help to remove any fibers caught in or under the moving parts of the machine. To clean lint from the tension discs, run a piece of gauze fabric or cheesecloth gently between the discs.

You avoid soiling garments as you sew them by keeping the outside of the machine clean and free of dust. Use a soft cloth and a gentle hand. Again, check the instruction booklet to see what type of soap or cleaner can be used. Some machine and cabinet finishes can be damaged by strong cleaning solutions.

Sewing machines need to be lubricated to keep the moving parts running smoothly and quietly. Some machines are permanently lubricated when they are made. This type of machine should never have to be oiled unless it is repaired.

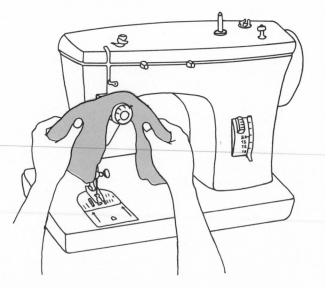

Use a lightweight, lint-free cloth and a gentle hand to clean between the tension discs.

Many machines *do* have to be oiled. The instruction booklet will show how to oil the machine and tell how often to do so. Oil only when necessary.

When you are finished oiling, place a piece of cloth in the unthreaded machine, lower the presser foot, and stitch back and forth over the cloth. Then leave the needle in the cloth to help absorb excess oil. It is best to oil the machine when it will not be used for several hours.

If you were a sewing machine salesperson, you would need to understand the mechanics of the sewing machine. You would demonstrate how to operate machines and answer questions about them for interested customers. You might work in a store selling several brands of sewing machines or only one brand. You might also travel as a manufacturer's representative to obtain contracts for selling machines in stores.

CHOOSING A SEWING MACHINE

Today sewing machines are available with a variety of features at a variety of prices. With all these differences, there are only three basic types of machine models: the straight stitch, the zigzag, and the stretch stitch.

The straight stitch machine is used for basic sewing. This machine stitches in forward and reverse (backward). It may be purchased with a variety of sewing attachments, including ones for zigzag stitching and making buttonholes.

The zigzag machine has three basic motions. It stitches forward, backward, and from side to side. These motions can be used for straight stitching, finishing edges, decorative stitching, sewing on buttons, making buttonholes, and embroidering. This type of machine may offer only one zigzag stitch or many different zigzag stitches and combinations of stitches.

The stretch stitch machine works in the same forward, backward, and side-to-side motions as the zigzag machine. Its special feature is the stretch stitch for knit fabrics. The machine moves the fabric back, forward, and back again to form each stretch stitch.

A sewing machine may cost from less than $100 to more than $600. The price is related to the number of decorative stitches and features available. The style of case or cabinet will also affect the price.

Cost is not the only or best indication of which machine is for you. Before you buy, decide which features are best suited to your present and future needs. Have a salesperson demonstrate how to use the model you are interested in and try it yourself. Consider the following when you are shopping for a machine:

- Do you want a portable machine, which can be set up on a regular desk or table? Do you prefer a model in a cabinet that also serves as your sewing table?
- Is the machine easy to thread and operate? Does the bobbin wind evenly?
- Is the stitching area well lighted? Is the light located so you will not accidentally touch the hot bulb?
- Does the machine run quietly? Is it free from vibration?
- Is the speed control easy to use?
- Does it sew equally well on lightweight fabrics, stretch fabrics, and bulky fabrics? (Take a variety of fabrics along to test the machines.)
- Is there a written guarantee? Read it carefully. How long is the guarantee effective? Does it cover parts and labor? Are parts available? Who will perform the service?
- Do you want a new or used machine?
- Can you use the machine as a trade-in for a future purchase?

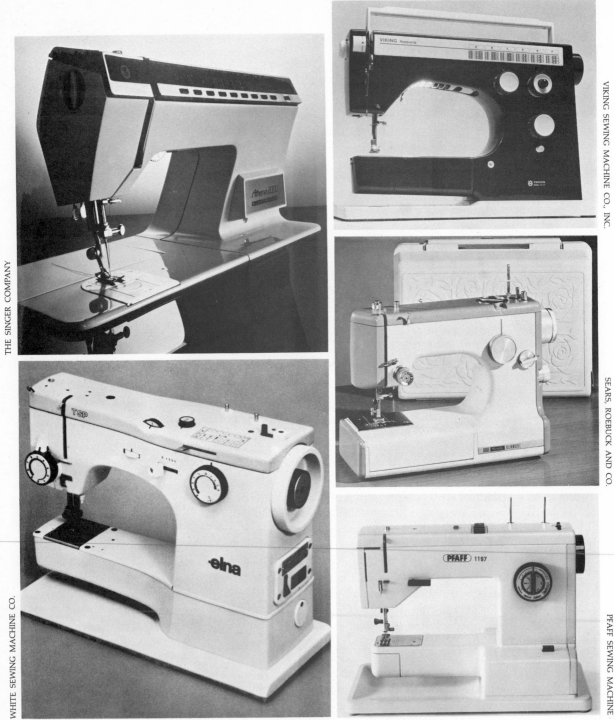

Among the many makes and models of sewing machines, there is one especially for you. Select, with care, a machine that suits your sewing needs.

MACHINE STITCHES

straight stitch	seaming and machine basting
straight stretch stitch	triple lock stitch that combines strength and stretch
zigzag	general purpose stretch sewing, buttonholes, buttons, applique, and seam finish
multistitch zigzag	sewing elastic, mending, and darning
blind stitch	hem stitch that does not show on right side of garment; also for inserting laces
feather stitch	makes stretchable seams for knits, fagoting, and embroidery
rick rack stitch	stretch sewing on heavy fabrics and topstitching and seam finish
overedge stretch stitch	joins and finishes seams in one step
slant overedge stitch	joins and finishes seams, provides flexibility for woven and knit fabrics

SOME DECORATIVE MACHINE STITCHES

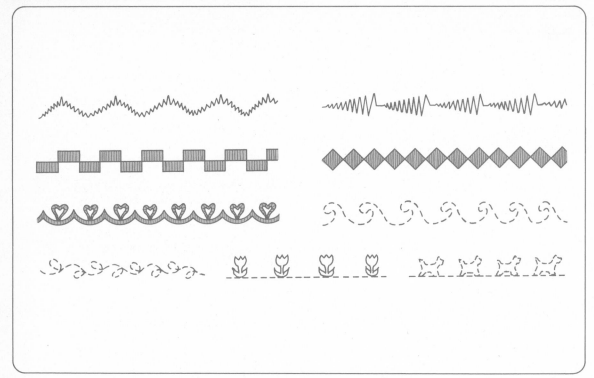

COMMON MACHINE PROBLEMS

If the machine does not start, check to see that . . .	machine is plugged into electrical supply power and light switches are on hand wheel is in position for sewing needle is down into fabric
If stitches skip or are not formed, check to see that . . .	machine and needle are correctly threaded needle is straight needle size and style and thread are correct for the fabric you are using bobbin is correctly placed in machine bobbin contains thread bobbin case area is free of lint and loose thread ends

If fabric puckers, . . .	thread tension may be too tight presser-foot pressure may need adjusting needle, thread, or both, may be too heavy for fabric stitch length may be too short for fabric
If stitching is irregular, or needle thread breaks, check to see that . . .	machine is correctly threaded needle is placed correctly in machine thread is even and free of knots needle is straight and correct size for thread and fabric upper thread unwinds smoothly from spool thread tension is not too tight thread is not caught in tension discs presser foot is raised for bobbin winding bobbin case is correctly threaded and placed threads are behind presser foot when you start to sew bobbin case area is free of lint and loose thread ends bobbin is not damaged
If fabric does not move, check to see that . . .	presser foot is down and pressure is correct for the weight and texture of your fabric presser foot is correctly attached stitch length is correct the feed is clear of lint
If needle breaks, . . .	needle may have been bent needle may be the wrong size and style for your machine or fabric needle may not be fully inserted in needle clamp needle may be hitting presser foot, throat plate, or pins presser-foot shank may not be securely fastened to presser bar you may be pulling the fabric as you guide it
If the machine jams, . . .	threading may be incorrect take-up lever may not have been at its highest point or thread ends may not have been held tightly when you began stitching bobbin thread may not have been raised through the hole in the throat plate lint buildup may be in the bobbin case thread may be knotted in bobbin case tension may be incorrect

1. Plan and sew a sampler of machine stitches. You can get ideas and directions for your stitches from the sewing-machine instruction booklet and your teacher. Use different-colored threads to complete your design. Frame your sampler or use it to make a book cover or pillow.

2. Prepare samples of a straight seam, a curved seam, and a pivoted corner.

3. Visit local stores or check store catalogs to find out what kinds of sewing machines are sold in your area. Compare different models and brands. What are the highest and lowest prices? Compare the features and services you get with a low-priced machine, a medium-priced machine, and a high-priced machine.

4. Ask friends and classmates who sew what sewing machine problems they may have. Keep a record of their answers. What are the most common complaints? Why do you think they have these problems? How might you help to solve some of these problems?

5. Make a bulletin board entitled "Sewing . . . Then and Now." Illustrate "Then" with a pair of hands, a sewing needle, a thimble, and thread. Use pictures or descriptions of the kinds of clothes people sewed completely by hand in this group. Use a picture of a modern sewing machine as a symbol for the "Now" group. Include pictures and descriptions of clothes and accessories made with home sewing machines.

6. Research the history of the sewing machine. The library and sewing machine manufacturers may be helpful. Present your information to the class. Use drawings or pictures to illustrate your story.

7. Design your "dream machine." What features would you include on the sewing machine of the future? What will it look like? Why? Let your imagination run wild, but remember the machine has to work for you.

8. Make samples of long, short, and medium stitches. Stitch a seam on long, narrow pieces of lightweight fabrics. Every two inches [5 centimeters], change the stitch size. Begin with 5 stitches to the inch [2.5 centimeters]. Then increase to 9, 12, 15, and 20 stitches to the inch [2.5 centimeters]. Repeat, using a heavy fabric. Look at the finished seams. Which stitch sizes are best for your sample fabrics?

● DO YOU KNOW

bobbin	reinforce
bobbin case	sampler
curve	seam
machine attachments	stitch length
machine care	stitching guides
machine features	straight stitch
machine needles	stretch stitch
parts of the machine	tension
pivot	thread
pressure	zigzag stitch

small sewing equipment

After reading this chapter, you should be able to:

- *Identify different pieces of small equipment that are used in sewing.*

- *Recognize the difference between scissors and shears.*

- *List three different measuring devices.*

- *List three means of marking your pattern or garment.*

- *Select appropriate pins and needles for marking and hand sewing different fabrics.*

- *Explain how pressing and ironing differ.*

- *Describe five aids for pressing and ironing.*

- *Select the equipment needed for a sewing project.*

- *Know the use and care of the equipment you select.*

There are tools for every craft. This is true for sewing, too, to make certain jobs easier and to give professional results. There are a variety of tools for cutting, measuring, marking, sewing, and caring for the finished product. Some of these tools are necessary for every project you work on. You will need others rarely, if ever. Special tools for sewing are called *small sewing equipment*.

CUTTING TOOLS

There is a large variety of tools for cutting fabric and thread. Knowing which tools to use and when to use them will help to prevent damage to fabric, thread, the finished garment, and yourself.

Scissors are probably the first thing you think of as a cutting tool for a sewing project. A pair of scissors has two blades with cutting edges that slide past each other. You control the opening and closing of the blades with the handle.

Shears are large scissors. There are different types of both scissors and shears used for different purposes. You will need shears for cutting out your pattern or trimming and cutting large areas of fabric. You will need scissors for working in small areas, where shears would be awkward.

Some general information to guide you as you select scissors and shears for your sewing projects follows:

- Right- and left-hand models are available.
- The length of scissors and shears determines their balance in your hand and your control while cutting. Shorter shears may be better for small hands than longer shears.
- The tension screw regulates the ease of opening and closing the blades. You should be able to adjust the tension when necessary.
- Always try out the scissors and shears before you cut fabric to be sure they are in good working order and comfortable for you.
- Use your cutting tools only on sewing projects. The blades are made especially for fabric. Cutting heavy paper, cardboard, or hair will dull them, causing them to chew and chop the fabric.

Using dull scissors can cause you to make mistakes that cannot be fixed and that show in the finished product. For example, you could tear a buttonhole or cut through a seam where you mean only to clip the allowance. Some manufacturers claim that their brands of scissors or shears never need sharpening if cared for properly. However, most scissors and shears do become dull after long use. You will know your scissors are dull if they chop and tear at fabric instead of cutting it cleanly and easily. Sharpening should be done by a professional who knows how to handle different kinds of blades and metals. Many fabric stores and sewing centers, as well as manufacturers of scissors and shears, offer sharpening service for a fee.

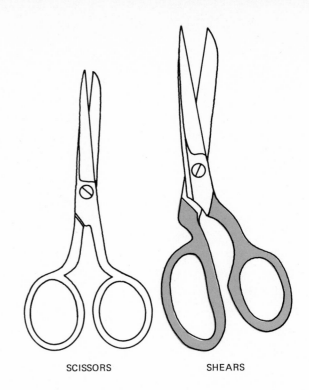

SCISSORS   SHEARS

Sewing scissors are also known as embroidery scissors. They are 4 and 5 inches [10.2 and 12.7 centimeters] long. The two handles are small and round and of equal size. The blades are thin and come to sharp points. They can be used for clipping threads, cutting and trimming small areas, and opening buttonholes.

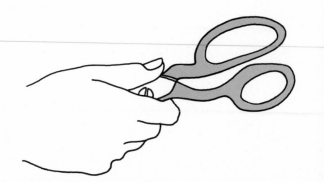

For safety, always pass shears, or any sharp object, with the handles toward the person to receive them.

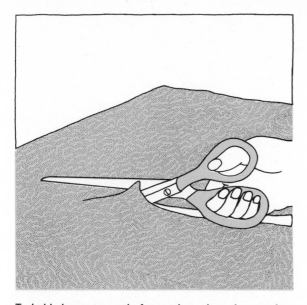

To hold shears correctly for cutting, place three or four fingers in the large handle and your thumb in the smaller, round handle. As you move your thumb up and down, the blades will open and close.

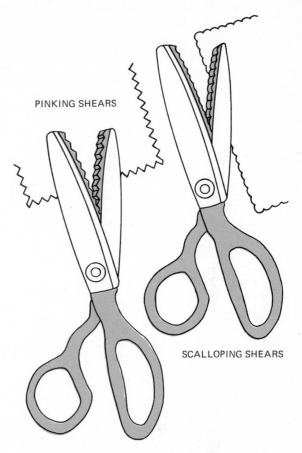

PINKING SHEARS

SCALLOPING SHEARS

Dressmaker shears are usually 7 or 8 inches [17.3 or 20.3 centimeters] long. The handles are shaped to fit comfortably in the hand. The large handle is for the fingers and the small handle for the thumb. The handles are also bent, allowing fabric to rest on a flat surface as the blades cut.

Pinking shears and **scalloping shears** are used for trimming seam edges to keep them from raveling. Pinking shears create a pointed zigzag edge, while scalloping shears create a rounded zigzag edge. Never use either to cut out a pattern. If you do, the seam allowance will be distorted, and it will be difficult to follow the guide while you stitch.

Electric scissors do not look or operate like regular scissors, but they do perform the same job. They are sold under several brand names and with a variety of features. Some have fast and slow speeds and a small light to brighten the path of the blades as you cut. Some are battery operated; others must be plugged into a socket.

It takes practice to use electric scissors effectively. Since the blades have a continuous cutting action, you need to learn how to control them. Practice on scrap fabric before you attempt to cut out your pattern.

Electric scissors are used only to cut out patterns, unlike regular shears, which are used for a variety of sewing tasks. When the blades become dull, they can be replaced. Always check the guarantee when you buy any type of electrical or battery-operated equipment.

Seam rippers are designed to cut and remove machine stitching. A ripper has a metal point and a thin, sharp cutting edge. The point slips easily under a stitch as the cutting edge lifts and cuts it. A fine scissors with sharp points or a pin can be used instead of a ripper.

some
small
equipment

Pins for attaching garment pieces together . . .
and for fitting

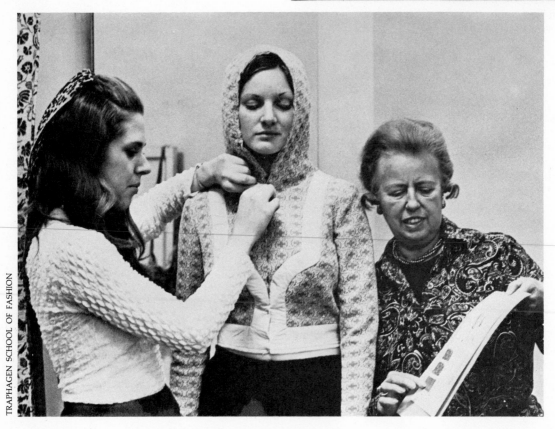

Tape measure for checking width for fit and alignment of seam before pressing

Needle, thread, thimble for hand sewing

Shears for cutting out your pattern

Yardstick or meterstick for measuring hem length

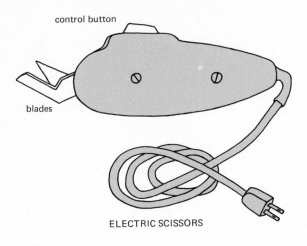

control button

blades

ELECTRIC SCISSORS

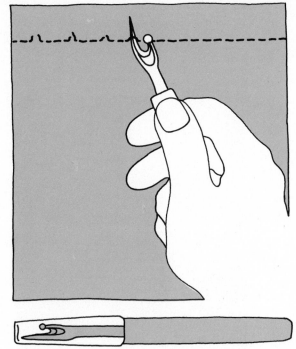

USING A SEAM RIPPER

MEASURING AIDS

In a short time, the United States will be changing to the metric system of weights and measures, which is the standard measuring system elsewhere in the world. You are all familiar with inches, feet, and yards to measure certain distances. Using the metric system to measure the same distances, you will be working with centimeters and meters. To obtain correct measurements, you should know the different measuring devices and how to handle them. Many of the measuring aids used in sewing are marked with both our customary measuring units and metric units. Using equipment with both units will help you get used to the conversion.

The **tape measure** is a narrow, flexible piece of material marked off in inches or centimeters. It is usually 60 inches [150 centimeters] long. Select a tape measure which is made of material that will not tear or stretch. Metal ends protect the accuracy of the tape by preventing raveling. Tape measures are usually marked with measurements on both sides. Sometimes the numbers run in opposite directions. Tapes are available with centimeters on one side and inches on the other.

The **yardstick** or **meterstick** is a long ruler made of wood, plastic, or metal. It is convenient to use when placing patterns on the straight grain of the cloth, measuring fabric length, and marking long, straight lines. A yardstick is divided into inches and feet. Thirty-six inches or three feet equal one yard. A meterstick is slightly longer than a yardstick and is divided into centimeters. There are 100 centimeters in a meter.

The **sewing gauge** is a 6-inch [15.2-centimeter] ruler with a sliding pointer. It is used to measure short distances, such as the width of hems and the placement of buttonholes and pockets. Six- and twelve-inch [15.2- and 30.4-centimeter] rulers could serve the same purpose.

The **skirt marker** is used to measure and mark. It is a ruler that stands upright on a base. It has an adjustable gauge and is used to measure and mark points on the hemline that are equal distances from the floor. There are two types of hem markers: pin and chalk. The pin marker requires a second person to place the pins. The chalk marker can be used alone.

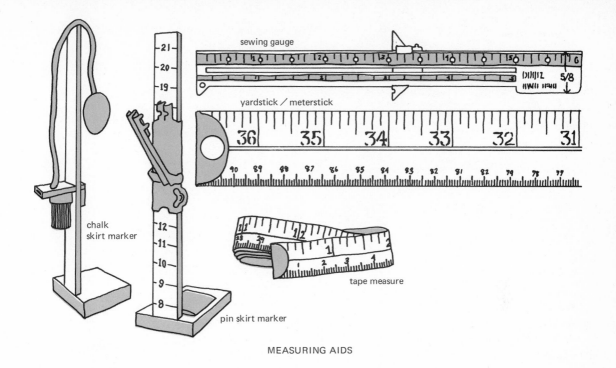

sewing gauge

yardstick / meterstick

chalk
skirt marker

pin skirt marker

tape measure

MEASURING AIDS

MARKING SUPPLIES

Marking is done when you transfer symbols from the paper pattern to your fabric and when you fit or alter your garment. You can use thread, pins, chalk, or a tracing wheel and tracing paper. Not all methods can be used on all fabrics or are used at all times. The appropriate method is determined by what the color, weight, and texture of the fabric are, as well as how permanent you want these markings to be.

Tracing wheels are available in two styles. The smooth-edge wheel makes a continuous line on the cloth. The serrated-edge wheel makes a broken line. It is wise to place a magazine or

piece of cardboard under the fabric you are marking. This helps to get clear lines and prevents marking the surface you are working on.

Tracing paper is used in combination with the wheel to transfer accurate markings to the wrong side of the fabric. It comes in white and different colors. Select a color that is as close as possible to the color of your fabric but is still visible. Tracing paper may be chalky or waxy. The chalky markings fade with handling and ironing. The waxy markings may require many washings before they begin to disappear.

Tailor's chalk is available in 2-inch squares or in pencils. It is soft and powdery and can be used for marking all fabrics. Chalk makes a

When you know	Multiply by	To find
inches	2.5	centimeters
feet	30	centimeters
yards	0.9	meters

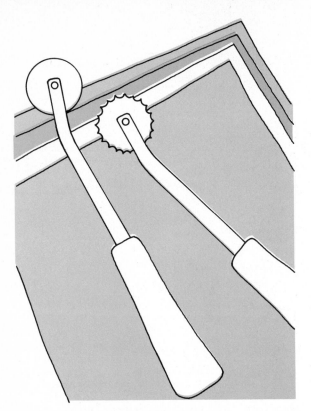

TRACING WHEELS AND TRACING PAPER

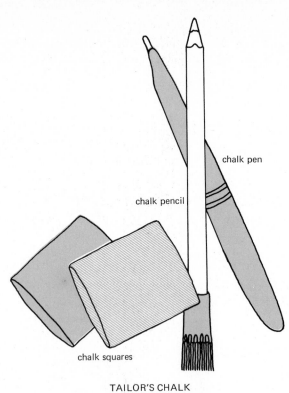

chalk pen

chalk pencil

chalk squares

TAILOR'S CHALK

temporary mark. It is available in a limited number of contrasting colors. Chalk may be difficult to remove from some fabric, so always test a scrap first.

Tailor's wax looks like tailor's chalk and is used in the same way. It is more oily than chalk. It should be used only on soft wool fabrics that will not hold chalk. It usually cannot be removed, so be careful when you use it.

Dressmaker or **silk pins** are the best pins for many types of fabric. They are used to mark symbols, hold darts and seams together while being stitched, and to fit and alter garments. Most brands are sold by weight in boxes, but some are available in paper packages. Select a fine, nonrusting, sharp pin. Size 16 or 17 is best for general use. Be sure to check the number or inspect the size of the pin before buying. Heavy pins can damage tightly woven and knit fabrics. Some pins have round, colored heads, which make them easy to find in most fabrics. They, too, are available in various sizes.

Ballpoint pins are used on knit or stretch fabric. The point is rounded so it separates rather than cuts the fibers.

Needle and thread are used to make markings that can be removed easily but will not pull out accidentally. Thread markings are used on fabrics that do not hold or that could be damaged by tracing paper, chalk, or wax. When you mark with thread, choose a color that will be easy to see.

Hand-sewing needles vary in size from a number 1, the coarsest, to a number 10, the finest. A medium-length needle with a small, round eye is called a *sharp*. A *milliner's* or a *between* needle

PINS

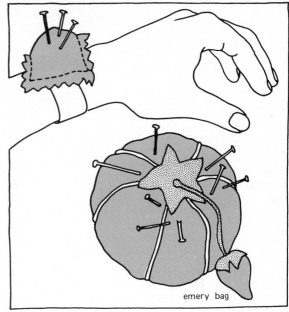

PIN CUSHIONS

emery bag

that polishes and cleans needles and pins. You can buy one separately or attached to a pin cushion.

A **thimble** is an aid worn for hand sewing. It protects the middle finger as it pushes the

has the same round eye as a sharp; a milliner's needle is slightly longer than a sharp, and a between, shorter. A *crewel,* or *embroidery,* needle has a long, narrow eye. Select the type of needle that has the easiest eye to thread. Remember, the body of the needle must be fine enough to slip easily through the cloth.

You can use a size-7 or a size-8 crewel or sharp for most sewing purposes. Short needles are used for making short, fine stitches. Long needles are best for hand basting.

Needles are sold in packages of one size or assorted sizes. Most are treated to prevent rusting. You may want to have an assortment of sizes and types on hand for your sewing needs.

You can keep needles sharp and clean by occasionally pushing them in and out of an *emery bag.* An emery bag is filled with a coarse grain

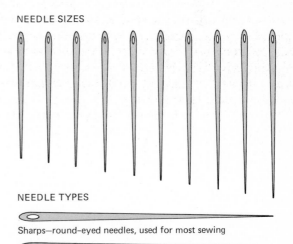

NEEDLE SIZES

NEEDLE TYPES

Sharps—round-eyed needles, used for most sewing

Embroidery (Crewel)—same length as sharps but have a special long eye for easy threading

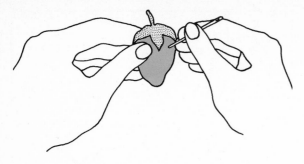

CLEANING NEEDLES IN AN EMERY BAG

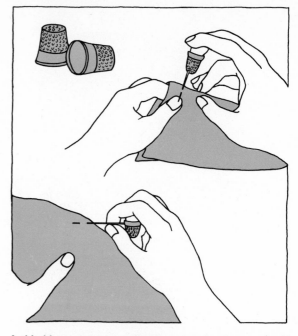

A thimble protects your finger as you hand sew. Push the needle through the fabric with the top or side of the thimble—whichever is more comfortable for you.

needle through the layers of fabric. The beginner often finds a thimble difficult to use, but as you progress, you will discover that some fabric cannot be sewn without one. A thimble will help you to make neat stitches. It also helps to increase your hand-sewing speed.

A thimble should fit comfortably on the middle finger of the hand that holds the needle. If it is too tight or too loose, it will hinder your ability to sew.

If you are interested in a career in the small-sewing-equipment industry, there are numerous opportunities for you to explore. The development of new sewing aids and improvement of those that have already been established are only a beginning. Every new idea has to be introduced, designed, and tested. Instructions for use and care of equipment have to be written. Jobs exist in all stages of designing, manufacturing, testing, advertising, and selling of home sewing equipment.

PRESSING EQUIPMENT

Pressing is essential to produce a garment that looks professionally made. It is also necessary for caring for store-bought clothes. Your sewing projects will have a professional appearance if you follow a few simple rules and learn to use pressing equipment correctly.

- Know the name, use, and care of each piece of equipment.
- Press as you sew.
- Never cross one line of stitching with another without pressing first.

The **iron** is used for pressing and ironing. *Pressing* involves the use of steam with an up-and-down motion. You press by lifting and lowering the iron on the fabric to smooth and shape the garment. After you sew a seam or dart, you should press it. This will eliminate bulk, help seams lie open and flat, and make further sewing easier. *Ironing* is the back-and-forth motion of an iron on the fabric to remove wrinkles and improve its appearance. You iron when a garment is complete and when you care for it later.

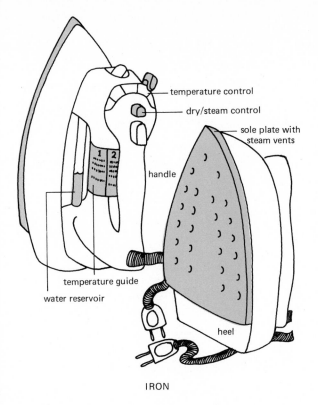

temperature control

dry/steam control

sole plate with
steam vents

handle

1 2

temperature guide

water reservoir

heel

IRON

Combination steam-and-dry irons can be used on all fabrics. They have temperature settings for synthetics as well as for wool, cotton, and linen. The care label you get when you purchase fabric or the permanent care label on ready-made garments will give you the necessary information for selecting the correct temperature for ironing.

Allow an iron a few minutes to reach the desired temperature before it is used. Test a heated iron on a piece of scrap fabric or inside the hem of a finished garment. If the temperature is too hot, the fabric can be discolored or melted. If it is too cool, the fabric will not press. Turn the iron off when you are not using it and stand it on its heel. *Never leave an iron on when it is not in use,* even if you plan to use it again in a few minutes.

Water and a hot iron temperature must be present for steam to form. If the temperature is not hot enough, water will run out of the holes in the soleplate.

Before you fill a steam iron, you must unplug it or set the dial on the "off" position. If there is a "steam-dry" switch, it should be in the "dry" position. Pour water into the iron from a container with a spout or use a funnel to prevent spillage. Be careful not to overfill the iron with water. If you do, the excess water will spill out. Empty the iron each time you are finished using it and before you put it away. Water remaining inside may cause rusting which may stain your fabric the next time you use the iron.

Most synthetics must be ironed on dry settings which are cooler than those used for steam ironing. An iron that is too hot can melt synthetic fibers, leaving a hole in the fabric and a mess on the soleplate.

There are commercial preparations available to clean the water reservoir of an iron. You can use them when the holes in the soleplate become clogged with calcium deposits, which build up from hard water.

The soleplate can become dirty from ironing fabrics with different finishes or from using spray starch. When it is dirty, it does not slide easily. It may also leave a film on the items you press and iron. Clean the soleplate with a damp cloth.

The **ironing board** was designed for pressing and ironing different parts of a garment. Select an ironing board that is a convenient height for you. Many are adjustable for use in a sitting or standing position.

Pad the top of the board to make pressing more effective. You can use old blankets or sheets or a commercial pad made to fit the board. The pad should be covered with smooth, fitted material. Wrinkles in the pad cover may cause wrinkles or shine to appear in the fabric as you press.

Most ready-made covers are fastened with a drawstring or elastic to allow them to be removed easily for washing. Some covers are available with a special finish which will not scorch or burn. These can also be cleaned easily to remove soil that sticks to the surface.

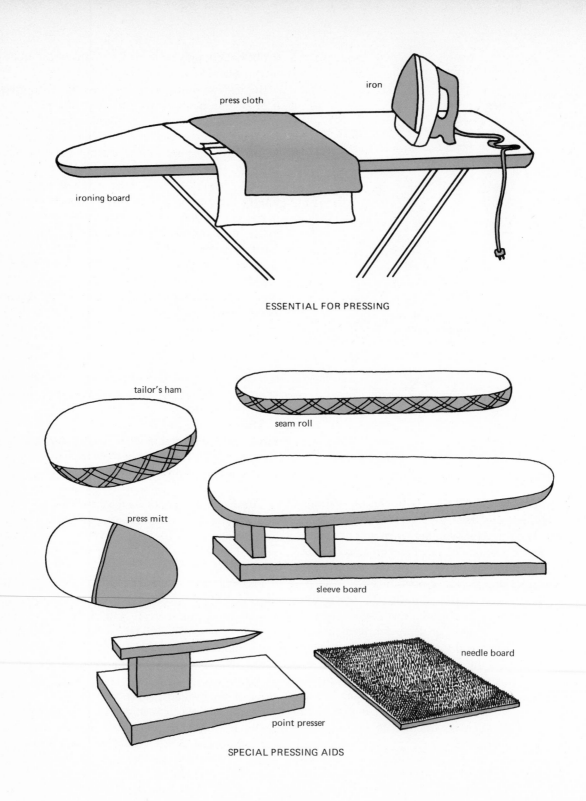

press cloth

iron

ironing board

ESSENTIAL FOR PRESSING

tailor's ham

seam roll

press mitt

sleeve board

point presser

needle board

SPECIAL PRESSING AIDS

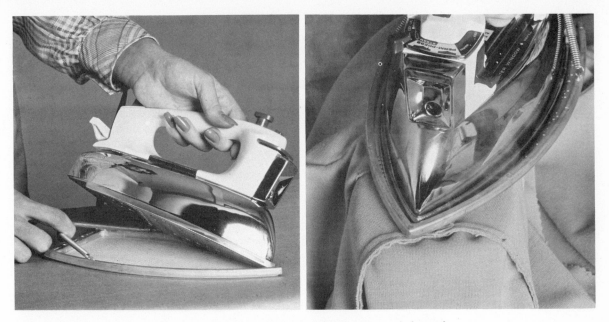

Another pressing aid is an attachment that covers the soleplate of an iron. It is used in place of a press cloth and can be used with or without steam. *Stacy Fabrics Corp.*

A **press cloth** is placed on top of the fabric being ironed. A press cloth will protect the fabric and prevent it from scorching or becoming shiny. The cloth can be used dry or damp. A damp cloth adds moisture to make sharp creases and flatten bulky edges. It can also be used to make steam when you do not have a steam iron.

A see-through press cloth is suitable for lightweight fabrics. Wool, canvas, and cotton press cloths are used with woolen and heavy fabrics.

You can buy various types of press cloths at most fabric stores or make your own from sheets or leftover pieces of fabric. They all must be laundered periodically so that soil will not be transferred to the garment while it is being pressed.

Special pressing aids are available to help produce professional-looking garments. They include:

· The tailor's ham and the press mitt used for pressing curved areas such as darts, sleeve caps, and hip seams. The press mitt is padded on one side and is worn over the hand as you press curved areas. A ham is larger and fully padded.
· The sleeve board looks like a small ironing board. It is used for pressing sleeves, shoulders, and other hard-to-reach places.
· The seam roll is best used for pressing long, narrow seams and zipper plackets. It helps prevent the outlines of the seam allowances from showing on the right side of the fabric.
· The point presser is made of hard wood. It is most often used for advanced sewing projects and tailoring to open seams in the points of collars, lapels, and other hard-to-reach places.
· The needle board is used for pressing napped fabrics such as velvet or corduroy. The pile of the fabric is placed facedown on the needles. The fabric is then pressed on the wrong side. The needles in the board prevent the pile from flattening when it is ironed. A terry cloth towel can be used as a substitute.

● IDEAS FOR ACTION

1. Make a list of all the pieces of equipment you need for a sewing project. They should be items that you could not sew without. Visit a local fabric store or sewing center and price these items. How much would it cost to assemble the necessary items for your own sewing box?

2. Explain why the correct iron temperature is important for any type of fabric.

3. What safety rules would you follow in using small sewing equipment? Make a list of these rules.

4. Choose one group of small equipment: cutting tools, measuring aids, marking supplies, or pressing equipment. Prepare a bulletin board on their use, proper storage, and general care.

5. Collect several pieces of scrap fabric. For each piece of fabric, answer the following questions: What would be the best method of marking the pattern symbols? What color chalk, tracing paper, or thread would you use for marking? What temperature would you iron with? Is there any special ironing equipment you would need to press and protect the fabric?

6. Research our customary system of measuring. Where did it come from? How long has it been in practice? Does conversion to the metric system seem practical? Why?

● DO YOU KNOW

crewel needle
dressmaker pins
emery bag
hem gauge
iron
ironing board
meterstick
metric system
needle board
pinking shears
press cloth

pressing
scissors
seam ripper
sharps
shears
tailor's chalk
tailor's ham
thimble
tracing paper
tracing wheel
yardstick

the pattern
and fabric

After reading this chapter, you should be able to:

- *Take body measurements for correct pattern size.*

- *Use the pattern-book measurement chart to determine pattern type and size.*

- *Discuss five important features on the back of the pattern envelope.*

- *Use information on the back of the pattern envelope to select fabric and yardage.*

- *Consider the style and use of a garment when purchasing fabric.*

- *Explain some ways to test fabric in stores.*

To change a flat piece of fabric into a garment or accessory, you need a plan. This plan is known as a pattern. A pattern is a guide for cutting fabric into shaped pieces, marking them, matching one piece to another, and sewing them together. Pattern sizes in the United States have been standardized. This means your pattern size should be the same, no matter what company has made the pattern.

Your pattern size is determined by your body measurements, and you buy patterns according to them. Patterns, however, are not cut to exact body measurements. If they were, they would fit skin-tight. Each of the styles in any size has *ease,* additional width allowed for comfort and movement.

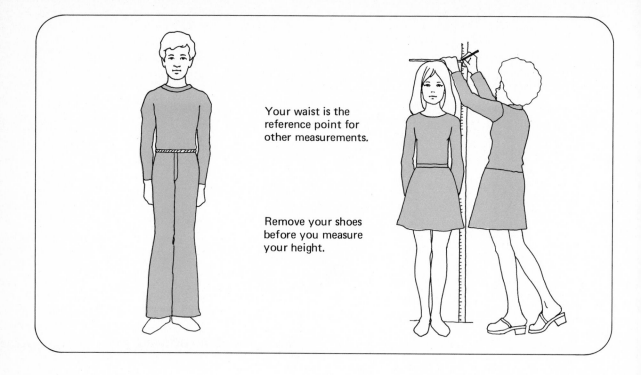

Your waist is the reference point for other measurements.

Remove your shoes before you measure your height.

MEASURING FOR PATTERN SIZE

To select your correct pattern size, you will have to know your measurements. You will use a tape measure to find them. When you take your measurements, you will need a partner to help adjust the tape and read it accurately. After your measurements have been taken, you can switch roles and help your partner.

Before you begin, remove bulky articles of clothing that would add inches to your results. Next, tie a piece of string securely, but not tightly, around your waist. The string will define your natural waistline and give you a reference point for taking several measurements.

TAKING MEASUREMENTS

Check the tape to see that it has not been cut, stretched, or knotted. While your measurements are being taken, stand or sit straight, but relaxed. If you slouch, you will change the shape

of your body and distort your measurements. When you are taking someone else's measurements, hold the tape straight and even as it goes from one side of the body to the other or up and down. Be careful not to twist it as you wrap it around the body. If you pull the tape too tight or not tight enough, you will not get true measurements.

As each measurement is taken, record it on a piece of paper. The record of your measurements should be used as a reference when you purchase a pattern or have to alter it. Some guides for taking measurements follow.

Height: Remove your shoes and stand straight with your back against a wall. Your partner will mark (with chalk or tape) a spot on the wall level with the top of your head. Measure the distance from the mark to the floor.

Back waist length: While standing straight, bend your head forward to find the prominent bone at the base of the back of your neck. Place

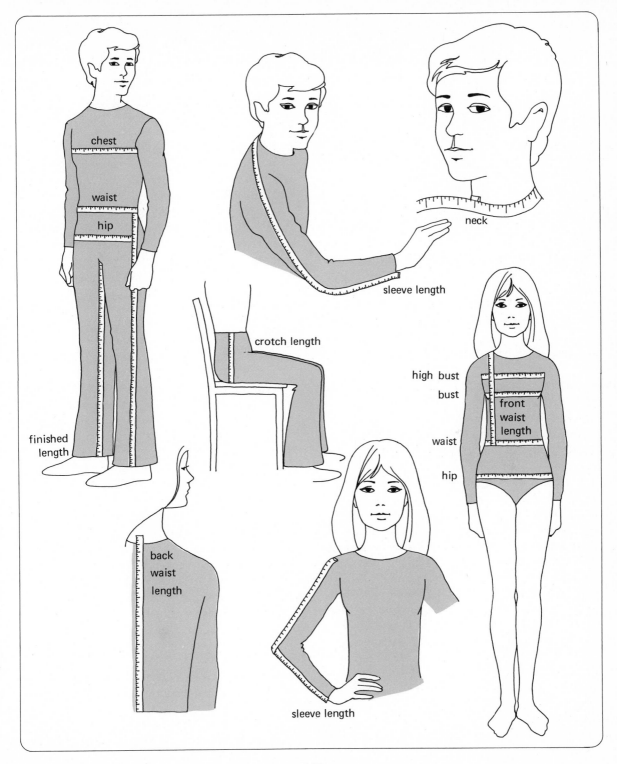

chest

waist

hip

finished
length

sleeve length

crotch length

neck

high bust

bust

front
waist
length

waist

hip

back
waist
length

sleeve length

the end of the tape on this bone and lift your head. Hold the tape on the bone. Have your partner measure straight down the middle of your back to the string tied around your waist.

Neck: Place the tape on the bone found for the back waist length. Have your partner measure around the base of your neck. Add $\frac{1}{2}$ inch [12.7 millimeters] and record the total on your chart.

Chest: Measure the fullest part of your chest by placing the tape across the back, under the arms, and around the front. While you hold the tape in front, your partner can check that it is straight and even around your body.

Waist: Wrap the tape comfortably around your waist (over the string). Do not pull the tape too tight or hold your breath while taking this measurement.

Hip: The hip measurement is taken around the fullest part of your body—usually 6 to 9 inches [15 to 23 centimeters] below the natural waistline.

Front waist length: Begin at the base of your neck at the shoulder seam. Extend the tape over the chest to your natural waistline, where you have tied the string.

Sleeve length: Sleeve measurements are taken with the elbow bent. For women and girls, the tape is placed at the curve of the shoulder where the seam of the sleeve would be. Measure from this point straight down to the elbow. Bend the tape at the elbow and continue to the wristbone.

For men and boys, the tape is placed on the bone at the back of the neck. Measure over to the shoulder, down to the elbow, and then to the wristbone.

Crotch length: Sit straight but comfortably on a hard chair. Measure from your waist to the seat of the chair and add $\frac{3}{4}$ inch [19 millimeters] for ease. Record the total on your chart.

Finished length: Begin at your waist and hold the tape (along the outside of your leg) down to the desired length. This measurement will change, depending on the garment you are making. Remember to wear the type of shoe that you will wear with the finished garment. Differ-

ent heel heights can affect the desired length of a skirt or slacks.

YOUR PATTERN TYPE AND SIZE

Some of the measurements you have recorded are guides for choosing your pattern size. Others are guides for altering your pattern. Pattern sizes are grouped according to different types, or classifications. The correct type for you depends on your height, not on your age. You will find these types listed in the back of pattern catalogs and magazines.

For girls and women, there are six classifications. They are: *girls'*, *junior*, *junior petite*, *miss petite*, *misses'*, and *half-size*. The variety exists so that you will be able to choose a size that is very close to your own body proportions.

For boys and men, there are three pattern types. They are: *boys'*, *teen boys'*, and *men's*.

If you were a pattern grader, you would work with the master pattern, adapting it to all the different pattern types and sizes. You would need a knowledge of drafting to measure and alter the different pieces. If you worked for any of the larger fashion houses or pattern companies, you might use a computer for greater accuracy and speed in grading.

Once you know your pattern type, refer to it on the measuring chart for your size. Compare your measurements with those on the chart. Select the pattern size with measurements closest to your own. For women and girls, the important measurements are: bust, waist, hip, and back waist length. For men and boys, they are: chest, waist, hip, neck, and sleeve length.

If your measurements are halfway between two pattern sizes, you can use your bone structure to help you choose the correct size. Select the smaller size if you are small-boned. If you are large-boned, choose the larger.

Use your hip measurement to select pants and skirt patterns; your bust or chest and neck mea-

Refer to your record of measurements as you read the charts to find out the pattern type and size best for you.

Photos and drawings for each pattern in the catalog give you an accurate idea of what the finished project will look like.

surements, for shirts and tops. It is not unusual for a person to have one size pattern for shirts and vests and another size pattern for slacks and skirts.

If your chest and hip measurements put you in two different sizes, purchase the pattern by the chest size. It is easier to alter the hips of a pattern than the chest.

It is a good idea to take your measurements each time you want to purchase a new pattern. As you mature, gain or lose weight, or grow taller, your body changes. Often, the change will result in a new size for you.

SELECTING A PATTERN

You can buy patterns in fabric stores, in the sewing sections of large department stores, and in variety (five-and-ten) stores. They can be ordered through the mail from home catalogs and magazines. No matter where or how you buy, you have to know what you want.

Catalogs and magazines are published by pattern companies and are distributed to the stores where you can buy their patterns. You might have school catalogs and magazines available to you in the classroom. The catalogs are divided into sections according to pattern types and styles, so you can go directly to the part of the book you need. Each pattern has detailed artwork or photographs representing the different ways the garment can be made. For example, a shirt may be made with long or short sleeves; a suit, with slacks or a skirt. These variations of the pattern are called *views*. Simple back views are drawn. The size and yardage chart is also there for your information.

MEASUREMENT CHART
Approved by the Measurement Standard Committee of the Pattern Industry
m—meters   cm—centimeters

MISSES'

Misses' patterns are designed for a well-proportioned, developed figure; about 5'5" to 5'6" without shoes.

Size	6	8	10	12	14	16	18	20
Bust	30½	31½	32½	34	36	38	40	42
Waist	23	24	25	26½	28	30	32	34
Hip	32½	33½	34½	36	38	40	42	44
Back Waist Length	15½	15¾	16	16¼	16½	16¾	17	17¼

MISSES'

Misses' patterns are designed for a well-proportioned, developed figure; about 1.65 m to 1.68 m without shoes.

Size	6	8	10	12	14	16	18	20	
Bust	78	80	83	87	92	97	102	107	cm
Waist	58	61	64	67	71	76	81	87	cm
Hip	83	85	88	92	97	102	107	112	cm
Back Waist Length	39.5	40	40.5	41.5	42	42.5	43	44	cm

JUNIOR PETITE

Junior Petite patterns are designed for a well-proportioned, petite figure; about 5' to 5'1" without shoes.

Size	3jp	5jp	7jp	9jp	11jp	13jp
Bust	30½	31	32	33	34	35
Waist	22½	23	24	25	26	27
Hip	31½	32	33	34	35	36
Back Waist Length	14	14¼	14½	14¾	15	15¼

JUNIOR PETITE

Junior Petite patterns are designed for a well-proportioned, petite figure; about 1.52 m to 1.55 m without shoes.

Size	3jp	5jp	7jp	9jp	11jp	13jp	
Bust	78	79	81	84	87	89	cm
Waist	57	58	61	64	66	69	cm
Hip	80	81	84	87	89	92	cm
Back Waist Length	35.5	36	37	37.5	38	39	cm

JUNIOR

Junior patterns are designed for a well-proportioned, shorter-waisted figure; about 5'4" to 5'5" without shoes.

Size	5	7	9	11	13	15
Bust	30	31	32	33½	35	37
Waist	22½	23½	24½	25½	27	29
Hip	32	33	34	35½	37	39
Back Waist Length	15	15¼	15½	15¾	16	16¼

JUNIOR

Junior patterns are designed for a well-proportioned, shorter-waisted figure; about 1.63 m to 1.65 m without shoes.

Size	5	7	9	11	13	15	
Bust	76	79	81	85	89	94	cm
Waist	57	60	62	65	69	74	cm
Hip	81	84	87	90	94	99	cm
Back Waist Length	38	39	39.5	40	40.5	41.5	cm

YOUNG JUNIOR/TEEN

This size range is designed for the developing preteen and teen figures; about 5'1" to 5'3" without shoes.

Size	5/6	7/8	9/10	11/12	13/14	15/16
Bust	28	29	30½	32	33½	35
Waist	22	23	24	25	26	27
Hip	31	32	33½	35	36½	38
Back Waist Length	13½	14	14½	15	15⅜	15¾

YOUNG JUNIOR/TEEN

This size range is designed for the developing preteen and teen figures; about 1.55 m to 1.60 m without shoes.

Size	5/6	7/8	9/10	11/12	13/14	15/16	
Bust	71	74	78	81	85	89	cm
Waist	56	58	61	64	66	69	cm
Hip	79	81	85	89	93	97	cm
Back Waist Length	34.5	35.5	37	38	39	40	cm

BOYS' AND TEEN BOYS'

These size ranges are for growing boys and young men who have not yet reached full adult stature.

Size	BOYS'				TEEN BOYS'			
	7	8	10	12	14	16	18	20
Chest	26	27	28	30	32	33½	35	36½
Waist	23	24	25	26	27	28	29	30
Hip (Seat) . . .	27	28	29½	31	32½	34	35½	37
Neckband . . .	11¾	12	12½	13	13½	14	14½	15
Approx. Height	48	50	54	58	61	64	66	68

MEN'S

Men's patterns are sized for men of average build; about 5′10″ without shoes.

Size	34	36	38	40	42	44	46	48
Chest	34	36	38	40	42	44	46	48
Waist	28	30	32	34	36	39	42	44
Hip (Seat) . . .	35	37	39	41	43	45	47	49
Neckband . . .	14	14½	15	15½	16	16½	17	17½
Shirt Sleeve . .	32	32	33	33	34	34	35	35

BOYS' AND TEEN BOYS'

These size ranges are for growing boys and young men who have not yet reached full adult stature.

Size	BOYS'				TEEN BOYS'				
	7	8	10	12	14	16	18	20	
Chest	66	69	71	76	81	85	89	93	cm
Waist	58	61	64	66	69	71	74	76	cm
Hip (Seat) .	69	71	75	79	83	87	90	94	cm
Neckband .	30	31	32	33	34.5	35.5	37	38	cm
Approx. Height . .	122	127	137	147	155	163	168	173	cm

MEN'S

Men's patterns are sized for men of average build; about 1.78 m without shoes.

Size	34	36	38	40	42	44	46	48	
Chest . . .	87	92	97	102	107	112	117	122	cm
Waist	71	76	81	87	92	99	107	112	cm
Hip (Seat) .	89	94	99	104	109	114	119	124	cm
Neckband .	35.5	37	38	39.5	40.5	42	43	44.5	cm
Shirt Sleeve	81	81	84	84	87	87	89	89	cm

3778 SWEATSHIRT

Loose-fitting sweatshirt, eased into ribbed knit band at waist and wrist has attached hood with purchased cording drawstring, full length raglan sleeves, patch pockets, and separating front zipper closing. Purchased turtleneck.

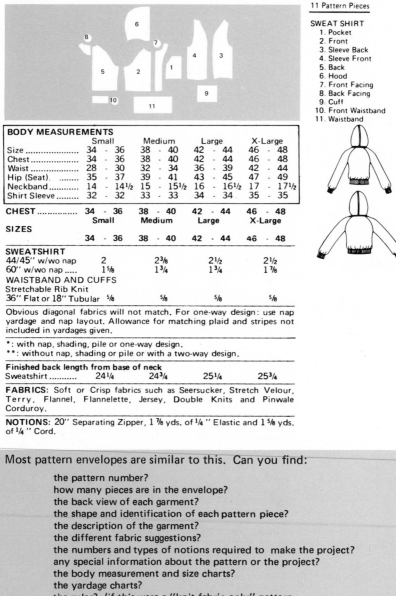

11 Pattern Pieces

SWEAT SHIRT
1. Pocket
2. Front
3. Sleeve Back
4. Sleeve Front
5. Back
6. Hood
7. Front Facing
8. Back Facing
9. Cuff
10. Front Waistband
11. Waistband

BODY MEASUREMENTS

	Small	Medium	Large	X-Large
Size	34 - 36	38 - 40	42 - 44	46 - 48
Chest	34 - 36	38 - 40	42 - 44	46 - 48
Waist	28 - 30	32 - 34	36 - 39	42 - 44
Hip (Seat)	35 - 37	39 - 41	43 - 45	47 - 49
Neckband	14 - 14½	15 - 15½	16 - 16½	17 - 17½
Shirt Sleeve	32 - 32	33 - 33	34 - 34	35 - 35

CHEST	34 - 36	38 - 40	42 - 44	46 - 48
	Small	Medium	Large	X-Large
SIZES				
	34 - 36	38 - 40	42 - 44	46 - 48
SWEATSHIRT				
44/45'' w/wo nap	2	2⅜	2½	2½
60'' w/wo nap	1⅝	1¾	1¾	1⅞
WAISTBAND AND CUFFS				
Stretchable Rib Knit				
36'' Flat or 18'' Tubular	⅝	⅝	⅝	⅝

Obvious diagonal fabrics will not match. For one-way design: use nap yardage and nap layout. Allowance for matching plaid and stripes not included in yardages given.

*: with nap, shading, pile or one-way design.
**: without nap, shading or pile or with a two-way design.

Finished back length from base of neck				
Sweatshirt	24¼	24¾	25¼	25¾

FABRICS: Soft or Crisp fabrics such as Seersucker, Stretch Velour, Terry, Flannel, Flannelette, Jersey, Double Knits and Pinwale Corduroy.

NOTIONS: 20'' Separating Zipper, 1⅞ yds. of ¼'' Elastic and 1⅝ yds. of ¼'' Cord.

Most pattern envelopes are similar to this. Can you find:

the pattern number?
how many pieces are in the envelope?
the back view of each garment?
the shape and identification of each pattern piece?
the description of the garment?
the different fabric suggestions?
the numbers and types of notions required to make the project?
any special information about the pattern or the project?
the body measurement and size charts?
the yardage charts?
the ruler? (if this were a "knit fabric only" pattern,
    there would be a stretch gauge instead)

Butterick Fashion Marketing Co.

Some patterns, labeled "easy," are designed to eliminate difficult steps. Patterns with a few pieces are usually easier to sew than patterns with many pieces. For your first project, try to avoid styles with shirt-type collars, plackets, cuffs, fly-front zippers, and pleats or tucks. Make something simple. It will give you confidence and enthusiasm for future projects.

Look through the different catalogs and select the pattern you like best. When you have made your choice, write down the number and size you need so you will remember them. Patterns are filed numerically according to company. Some stores have them arranged so you can get your own pattern. In other stores, you will have to tell the salesperson the name of the pattern company, and the number, type, and size of pattern that you need. Never settle for a different size if the one you want is not available. You may have to order the pattern you want, or try another store, or choose another pattern. Buying the correct size eliminates unnecessary fitting problems later. Check to be sure you are given the pattern you asked for. Once you buy it, it cannot be returned.

If you were a patternmaker, you would make the first, or master, pattern from the designer's drawing or sample garment. You would work closely with the designer to put every detail of the design, such as pleats, tucks, darts, pockets, and cuffs, into the pattern. You might work for a fashion house, factory, or home-sewing pattern company. You would need knowledge and experience in design and sewing.

THE PATTERN ENVELOPE

Everything you need to know about the pattern, the project, and the finished garment is listed on the pattern envelope. It tells you how many pieces you will be working with and shows you what they look like. It has a detailed description of the garment. It gives suggestions to help you decide on the type of fabric to buy. There is also a chart to tell you how much fabric to buy and other valuable information for your reference.

The suggested fabrics on the envelope are part of the designer's plan for the finished garment. These suggestions serve as a guide for choosing fabric that is suitable for the style of the garment. There is usually quite a variety for your selection. Some patterns recommend knit fabrics only. Using a woven fabric for these projects would be a mistake. Since woven fabrics do not stretch the way knits do, your finished garment would probably not fit. Other patterns may recommend lightweight fabrics. In these cases, heavy-weight fabrics may be too bulky for comfort and may spoil the style.

The pattern envelope also gives special instructions for different types of fabric. For example, there may be a note about pile fabrics, such as corduroy and velvet, telling you to buy them according to the "with nap" yardages. Special instructions may also be given for fabrics with plaids, stripes, and diagonals. You will have to buy enough of these fabrics to match the designs at the seams. A pattern envelope may tell you to avoid fabrics and designs that are not suitable for a pattern. For example, some garments would not look good or wear well if made with a napped fabric. Others would not look good made up in a small print, or a large print, or a plaid, or stripes, or diagonals.

Sewing notions are the items, in addition to a pattern and fabric, that you will need for sewing and finishing your project. These are specified by the pattern envelope, too. Thread, the number and size buttons, length and type zippers, binding, and snaps are a few examples of the notions that might be listed. It is best to select your notions when you buy your fabric. Often, the color, type, and size you choose will depend upon the fabric.

clothing careers

Making the sample pattern

Designing

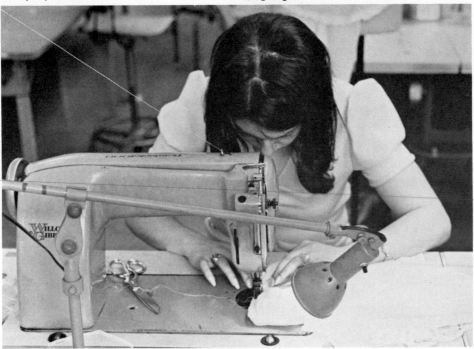

Sewing sample garments

Draping

Sketching

Grading the pattern

169

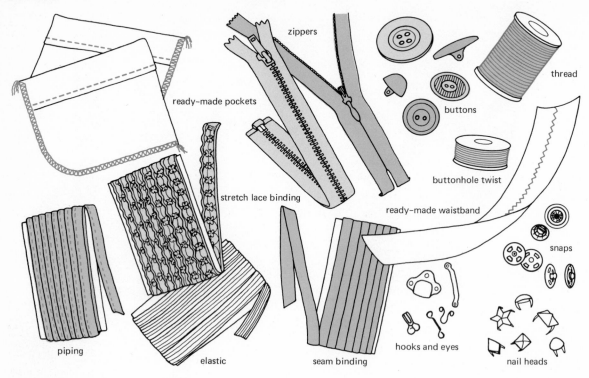

ready-made pockets

zippers

buttons

thread

buttonhole twist

stretch lace binding

ready-made waistband

snaps

piping

elastic

seam binding

hooks and eyes

nail heads

BUYING FABRIC

Buying fabrics is very much like buying anything else. You have choices to consider and decisions to make. Having a knowledge of what you are looking for and where you can get it will be helpful. Often you will be able to buy fabric in the same place you buy your pattern and sewing notions and equipment. There are specialty stores that sell only a certain type of fabric, such as knits, cottons, men's suiting, or imports. Some stores sell fabrics at discount rates. There are stores that buy fabrics directly from the mill where they were made. There are other stores that buy remnants from clothing manufacturers. A large fabric store may house all these types under one roof.

Explore the stores in your shopping area to find suitable, reasonably priced fabric. Price is

not always the best way to determine quality. Your knowledge of textiles will help you to choose the best quality fabric for your money.

BOLT OR PRECUT—BY THE YARD

Most fabric is displayed on bolts. Manufacturers roll several yards of fabric into bolts for easy shipping, storing, displaying, and selling. The ends of the bolts are labeled with the manufacturer's name, fiber content, fabric width, and care instructions. When you buy fabric, be sure you get the care label that matches the information on the bolt. Fabric not on bolts is known as *precut fabric*.

Remnants are short lengths of fabric that were left on the bolt after the last sale. Stores often sell remnant pieces at reduced prices. Fabric not on bolts might also be irregulars, or seconds, and factory cuts. These, too, are sold at lower prices. These fabrics may have defective weaves, holes, irregular grainlines, or imperfect printing or dyeing. Before you choose one of these fabrics, you should inspect it carefully. Sometimes the defect will not show in the product you plan.

Often, precut fabric is not properly labeled. Always ask a reliable person when you have a question about a fabric's fiber content. Remember that fiber content relates to correct care procedures. Proper washing, drying, and ironing are necessary to prevent shrinkage and to promote long garment life.

Fabric is bought by the yard and fractions of the yard, and in meters and tenths of meters. The amount you will need depends on the width of your fabric and the view of the pattern you would like to make. You will notice that on the back of the pattern envelope under the view or item you are making, there is a list of numbers: 35 or 36 inches [90 centimeters], 44 or 45 inches [115 centimeters], 54 inches [135 centimeters], and 60 inches [150 centimeters]. These numbers represent standard widths of fabric:

- **35–36** silk, fine cottons, linen
- **44–45** cottons, blends, woven synthetics
- **54–60** wools, knits, woven synthetics

To find the correct amount of fabric for your project, look at the chart under the view or item you are making. Follow the line that has the width of your fabric across the chart to your size column. If you select a fabric that is narrow, you will need more of it than if you select a wider fabric.

Fabrics are draped over bolts so you can see more of their print and design and can easily feel their texture, weight, and crispness.

COMBINING PATTERN AND FABRIC

The style of your pattern and your reason for making it often help you decide on the type of fabric to buy. While fabric choice does not have to be limited to the list on the pattern envelope, it is wise to follow the suggestions. Read the list and ask the salesperson to point out which fabrics are available in that store. Use your knowledge of clothing selection to help you choose fabric. Consider what colors and textures look best on you and suit the line and shape of your pattern.

- Large-patterned, plaid, or bulky, textured fabrics are best for styles with few seam lines.
- Solid-color fabrics emphasize the style, design, and detail of a garment.
- Lightweight fabrics give a soft look to full and loose-fitting garments.
- Some pattern styles are labeled "for knits only." This means that the garment must be made with a stretch-knit fabric. A stretch gauge on the pattern envelope shows the amount of give a fabric must have if it is to be made into that style. The "knit only" pattern is sized with less ease to allow the garment to fit closely but give with the body. If nonstretch fabric is used, the garment will be uncomfortably tight.

Consider the wear of the garment and the care of the fabric. What are your plans for this garment? Will you wear it often or only for special occasions? Durable fabrics that can be cared for at home are best suited for garments that will be worn frequently. Fabric that needs special cleaning is better for something that will not be worn too often. Even if a garment is worn only occasionally, dry-cleaning bills must be considered part of the real cost of the garment.

Will you need to know special methods of sewing and handling for the fabric you select? When you are in the store and can see and feel the fabric, remember the following:

- Plain or small-patterned fabrics are easier to work with than plaids or stripes, which require the knowledge and skill to match the design.

Before she makes a decision, what do you think this girl will consider as she looks at, and touches, each fabric? *American Thread*

- Is the cloth preshrunk? If it is not, how much shrinkage can be expected? Will you need to buy extra fabric to allow for this?
- Is the fabric colorfast (does it keep its dyed color during normal wear and care)? Will you have to care for the garment you make separately or differently from your other clothes?
- Look closely at the grainline. The yarns should meet at right angles for the material to be grain-perfect. If the cloth is printed, woven, or cut off-grain, the hang of the garment will be affected. Never buy material that is obviously off-grain. In most fabrics, it cannot be corrected.
- Be sure any woven fabric you buy has at least one *selvage*. The selvages are the finished lengthwise edges of the cloth. If both edges are trimmed off, it is difficult to determine the

grainline and to place your pattern pieces for cutting.
- The stretchiness of a knit fabric is important to the fit and appearance of the finished garment. The amount of stretch a fabric should have for a project is indicated on the "knit fabric only" pattern envelope. Be sure to use the stretch gauge when choosing knit fabrics.
- Check the cut edge of the cloth. Does it ravel or fray easily? If it does, special sewing techniques will be required to finish seams.
- Test to see how the fabric will stand up to wear. Crush a corner of it in your hand for several seconds; then release it. Does the fabric hold the wrinkles, or does it spring back to its original shape? Cloth that wrinkles easily will need frequent touch-up ironing to keep it looking fresh.

- Is the weight of the fabric suitable for your pattern? Let some of the fabric fall from the bolt. Does it fall into loose folds, or does it seem stiff? Sheer and lightweight fabrics are ideal for making ruffles, gathers, and loose-fitting, full garments. They are best used in garments with few seams, since the seam allowances may be seen on the outside of the garment. Stiff fabrics are used for styles that have tailored, straight lines or where soft fullness is not required.
- Is the fabric soft or rough against your skin? If you choose a rough fabric, it may require a lining, something better left to a more advanced sewer.
- Hold a piece of cloth between the thumb and first finger of each hand and stretch it. If the fibers separate easily as you pull, the slippage

You will often find threads, zippers, tapes, trims, and other notions displayed similarly to these.

is great. Tightly woven fabrics have little or no slippage. A garment made of cloth with a tight weave will not pull at the seams. Fabric which pulls apart easily is best used for loose-fitting clothing.

Use your knowledge of textiles. The more care you take in selecting fabric appropriate for you and your pattern, the more satisfied you will be with the finished garment.

SELECTING THREAD AND OTHER NOTIONS

The thread you choose for your sewing project is directly related to the fabric you select.

The label on the thread spool contains important information. It indicates the fiber content, manufacturer's name, color name and code number, and amount and size of the thread.

Size numbers tell you the fineness or coarseness of the thread. Thread varies from a coarse number 8 to a very fine number 100. For most sewing, sizes 40, 50, and 60 are used. Silk thread is available in sizes A and D. Size A is the fine thread which is used on silk and wool fabrics. Size D is the heavy thread used for handmade buttonholes, decorative topstitching, and thread loops.

Select a color thread that is a shade darker than your fabric. The darker color blends better when sewn. If your fabric contains many colors, select the dominant one for thread.

Different finishes are applied to threads to make them more suitable for sewing. Mercerization improves cotton thread. It adds strength and luster to the thread and gives it greater ability to absorb dyes. Mercerized thread is preshrunk. Glazing is the finish on polyester, quilting, and button threads that makes them smooth and glossy. It makes the thread more slippery and easier to pull through the fabric. Wax and silicone finishes also give a smooth surface.

Cotton thread is most often used for general sewing with cotton and linen fabrics.

Polyester thread was originally recommended for use only with synthetic fabrics. Its strength gives it an elastic quality, making it a good choice

Check the fiber content to select notions and fabric that not only look good together, but can also be laundered and handled as one.

for all knitted fabrics. It can also be used for most types of sewing with almost all fabrics.

Silk thread produces a fine stitching line. It may be used with fine woolens and silk fabrics.

Nylon thread is used with nylons and nylon blends. Nylon thread usually requires a loose upper and lower tension on the machine, and a fine needle.

Elastic thread is used for gathering or for shirred effects. It is used only as the bobbin thread for machine stitching.

Buttonhole twist is a heavy silk thread. It is used for decorative stitching, handworking buttonholes and sewing on buttons, and as the bobbin thread when gathering large sections of fabric. It is a strong, smooth thread and slips easily through fabric, making gathering an easier task.

Since each project requires different sewing notions, be sure to read your pattern envelope. It is a good idea to purchase zippers and seam bindings at the same time you buy fabric and thread. Sometimes they are all displayed together in color families to make selection easy.

METRIC EQUIVALENCY CHARTS

mm—millimeters   cm—centimeters   m—meters   (metric equivalents may be rounded off)

inches	mm		cm
1/8	3		
1/4	6		
3/8	10	or	1
1/2	13	or	1.3
5/8	15	or	1.5
3/4	20	or	2
7/8	22	or	2.2
1	25	or	2.5

inches	cm	inches	cm
1	2.5	26	66
2	5	27	68.5
3	7.5	28	71
4	10	29	73.5
5	12.5	30	76
6	15	31	79
7	18	32	81.5
8	20.5	33	84
9	23	34	86.5
10	25.5	35	89
11	28	36	91.5
12	30.5	37	94
13	33	38	96.5
14	35.5	39	99
15	38	40	101.5
16	40.5	41	104
17	43	42	106.5
18	46	43	109
19	48.5	44	112
20	51	45	114.5
21	53.5	46	117
22	56	47	119.5
23	58.5	48	122
24	61	49	124.5
25	63.5	50	127

METRIC EQUIVALENCY CHARTS

mm—millimeters   cm—centimeters   m—meters

Available Fabric Widths

25″	65 cm
27″	70 cm
35″/36″	90 cm
39″	100 cm
44″/45″	115 cm
48″	122 cm
50″	127 cm
54″/56″	140 cm
58″/60″	150 cm
68″/70″	175 cm
72″	180 cm

yards	meters	yards	meters	yards	meters
$\frac{1}{8}$	0.15	$2\frac{1}{8}$	1.95	$4\frac{1}{8}$	3.80
$\frac{1}{4}$	0.25	$2\frac{1}{4}$	2.10	$4\frac{1}{4}$	3.90
$\frac{3}{8}$	0.35	$2\frac{3}{8}$	2.20	$4\frac{3}{8}$	4.00
$\frac{1}{2}$	0.50	$2\frac{1}{2}$	2.30	$4\frac{1}{2}$	4.15
$\frac{5}{8}$	0.60	$2\frac{5}{8}$	2.40	$4\frac{5}{8}$	4.25
$\frac{3}{4}$	0.70	$2\frac{3}{4}$	2.55	$4\frac{3}{4}$	4.35
$\frac{7}{8}$	0.80	$2\frac{7}{8}$	2.65	$4\frac{7}{8}$	4.50
1	0.95	3	2.75	5	4.60
$1\frac{1}{8}$	1.05	$3\frac{1}{8}$	2.90	$5\frac{1}{8}$	4.70
$1\frac{1}{4}$	1.15	$3\frac{1}{4}$	3.00	$5\frac{1}{4}$	4.80
$1\frac{3}{8}$	1.30	$3\frac{3}{8}$	3.10	$5\frac{3}{8}$	4.95
$1\frac{1}{2}$	1.40	$3\frac{1}{2}$	3.20	$5\frac{1}{2}$	5.05
$1\frac{5}{8}$	1.50	$3\frac{5}{8}$	3.35	$5\frac{5}{8}$	5.15
$1\frac{3}{4}$	1.60	$3\frac{3}{4}$	3.45	$5\frac{3}{4}$	5.30
$1\frac{7}{8}$	1.75	$3\frac{7}{8}$	3.55	$5\frac{7}{8}$	5.40
2	1.85	4	3.70	6	5.50

1. Plan a "metric" bulletin board. Show body measurements and the amount of fabric needed for a particular sewing project in both customary and metric units.

2. Compare the information found on the backs of two pattern envelopes. Select one view on each envelope and make a list of the fabric you would choose, notions you would need, and any special sewing techniques you would have to know to make each garment.

3. Collect samples of three different fabrics. Test each sample for slippage, crush resistance, and grain. Staple each sample to a larger piece of paper and record the results of your findings.

What garments would you use each fabric for? What special construction or care techniques would you need to know?

4. Visit two or three fabric stores in your area. List what company's patterns they carry and what types of fabric they sell. Check to see if the bolts of fabric are labeled and if care labels are available. Is there a precut table? Are the precut fabrics remnants or seconds or factory cuts? Do the stores give discounts to students? Report your findings to the class.

5. Discuss what you should know and consider to select the right pattern for you and the right fabric for your pattern.

● DO YOU KNOW

bolt	precut fabric
catalog	remnant
ease	selvage
"knits only"	size
measurements	stretch gauge
notions	style
pattern	suggested fabrics
pattern envelope	thread
pattern type	view

getting ready to sew

After reading this chapter, you should be able to:

- *Tell what a guidesheet is and describe the information it contains.*

- *Identify pattern markings.*

- *Discuss how to alter patterns to increase or decrease length or width.*

- *Explain how to prepare fabric for the pattern layout.*

- *Find the lengthwise and crosswise grains of a piece of fabric.*

- *Identify the correct layout for the pattern size and view and fabric width.*

- *Follow basic instructions for pinning and cutting pattern pieces.*

- *Select a suitable method of marking a piece of fabric.*

THE GUIDESHEET

Inside the pattern envelope are the tissue pattern pieces and guidesheet. The guidesheet contains general information about the pattern and how to use it, as well as instructions for cutting and sewing your garment. On the guidesheet, you will find:

· Sketches of the different pattern views.
· Labeled sketches of all the pattern pieces.
· Lists of the pattern pieces needed to complete each view.
· A metric conversion chart for body measurements and fabric.
· General notes to help you understand the pattern pieces, the symbols on them, and the sewing instructions.
· Layouts or guides for placing the pattern pieces on fabric.
· Step-by-step directions for completing each phase of the garment construction.

Butterick 3638
Page 1 (of 3 Pages)
TOTAL PATTERN PIECES · 9

How to Use Butterick Patterns

Butterick's **easy-to-follow** guide combines a fashion sketch and pattern pieces with cutting layouts and sewing instructions for each view.

Ready

Select pattern pieces needed. Disregard perforations.

Butterick patterns are made to body measurements with added allowance for wearing comfort and for style.

If body measurements differ from envelope measurements, make necessary adjustments before cutting.

Lengthen or **Shorten** pattern at adjustment lines (▭▭▭▭) or where indicated on pattern.

TO LENGTHEN - Slash between adjustment lines. Place on paper - spread pattern amount needed.

TO SHORTEN - Crease along adjustment line. Make a fold, half the amount needed to shorten.

For further alterations, see Butterick's Basic Fitting Patterns or Sewing Book; "**Ready Set Sew**".

Cut

Press fabric (pre-shrink if necessary).

Choose layout for garment, fabric width and size. For fabrics with nap, pile, shading or one-way design, use "with nap layout".

PATTERN MARKINGS

Grainline: Place line on fabric, an even distance from selvage or straight thread.

Fold: Indicates edge that is placed on fold of fabric.

Cutting Line: Scissors indicate exact cutting line.

Follow layouts for arranging fabric and placement of pattern pieces (occasionally the same piece may be used more than once).

When **Fold** is indicated on layout, fold fabric with right sides together. For single thickness of fabric, place fabric right side up.

Pattern pieces shaded (\\\\) in layouts are placed printed side down. White pieces are placed printed side up.

Pin pattern pieces to fabric. Cut along heavy outline, cutting multiple notches as a group or individually.

Markings indicate placement, length and size of buttonhole and button.

TRANSFER MARKINGS

Before removing pattern from fabric, transfer all construction lines and symbols (●, ●, ■, ▲) to fabric with tracing wheel and dressmaker's tracing paper, chalk or tailor's tacks.

5/8" (15mm) seam allowances on all patterns, unless otherwise indicated. Presser foot ( ) indicates exact stitching line.

Sew

Construct garment following **Sewing Instructions**. Pin seams, matching notches with corresponding numbers and match symbols. Baste with pins or thread. Stitch seams in direction of fabric grain to prevent stretching (generally from the widest part to the narrowest part of each piece). **PRESS** as you sew.

PRESS SEAMS OPEN, unless otherwise indicated, clipping where necessary so seams will lie flat.

For additional sewing details, see the Butterick Sewing Book, "**READY SET SEW**".

SHADING on sewing illustrations denote:

RIGHT SIDE	WRONG SIDE	INTERFACING	LINING

Bolder lines on sewing illustrations, highlight construction procedure.

(Conversion of inches to millimeters)

Inches	1/8"	1/4"	3/8"	1/2"	5/8"	1"
Metric	3mm	6mm	10mm	13mm	15mm	25mm

NOTE: Conversions not listed above will appear (within parenthesis) where required.

NOTE: USE THE SELECT-A-KNIT GAUGE BEFORE CUTTING. PATTERN IS SIZED FOR STRETCH KNIT FABRICS ONLY.

Pants
2 PATTERN PIECES

2 BACK **1** FRONT

Cut USE PIECES 1 and 2

44/45" (115 cm) FABRIC WITHOUT NAP FOR SIZES 8-10-12

44/45" (115 cm) FABRIC WITHOUT NAP FOR SIZES 14-16

60" (150 cm) FABRIC WITHOUT NAP FOR SIZES 8-10-12-14

60" (150 cm) FABRIC WITHOUT NAP FOR SIZE 16

SELVAGES

FOLD

Sew

STEP 1—FRONT AND BACK

Stitch FRONT 1 sections together along center front.

Stitch BACK 2 sections together along center back.

Stitch front to back at sides and inner leg edge.

STEP 2—CASING

Turn upper edge of pants to inside along foldline; press. Stitch 1" from upper edge, through all thicknesses, leaving an opening, as shown.

Cut elastic the measurement of waist, plus 1".

Insert elastic through casing. Lap ends. Adjust to fit. Stitch ends securely.

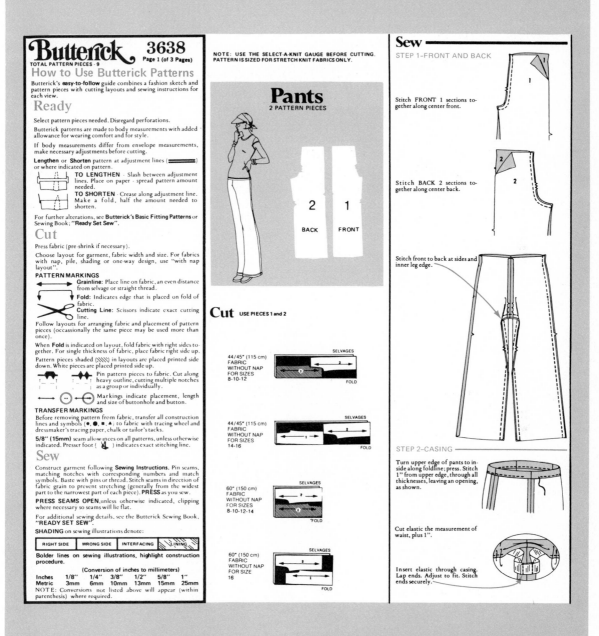

Before you work with your pattern pieces and fabric, read the guidesheet carefully. Understanding the directions before you have to apply them will make following them easy and logical.

PREPARING THE PATTERN

As you remove the pattern pieces from the envelope, you will notice that they are labeled with the name of the pattern company, pattern number, size, name of the pattern piece, and, sometimes, special instructions such as to cut only one piece. Some of this information may be printed in more than one language. They are also numbered or lettered as a means of identifying which view and garment they are part of. Refer to the guidesheet for the pattern pieces you will need for the view you are making. The different

pattern companies have different ways of labeling the views and pattern pieces. When the views are numbered, the pattern pieces are lettered. When the views are lettered, the pattern pieces are numbered. Often many small pattern pieces are printed on one large sheet. You will have to cut them apart to select the pieces needed.

Some patterns have pieces for only one garment, for example, slacks. Some patterns have the pieces needed for making different views of the same basic garment, for example, a shirt with a choice of two different collars or types of sleeves. Other patterns include pieces for making more than one garment, for example, a jacket, vest, and slacks or skirt.

Since the pattern pieces have been folded to fit in the envelope, they might be crushed and very wrinkled. Sometimes, carefully smoothing

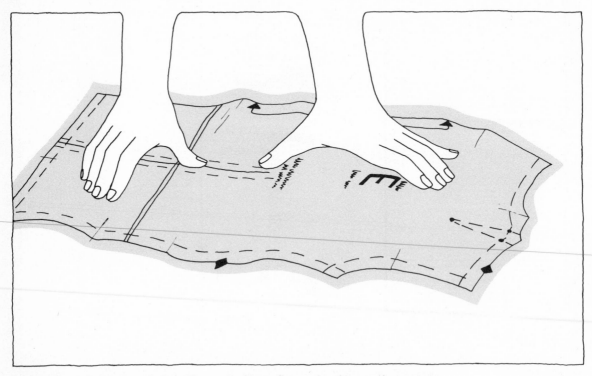

Gently smooth the pattern pieces with your hands, to flatten the pieces and to remove wrinkles.

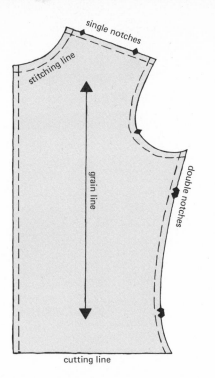

single notches

stitching line

grain line

double notches

cutting line

times, a pair of shears is printed on the cutting lines to help identify those lines. It is important to cut directly on the cutting lines—cutting to either side will change the size of the garment piece.

Stitching lines, or **seam lines,** are the broken lines usually $\frac{5}{8}$ inch [1.5 centimeters] inside the cutting line. Arrows on the seam lines show the direction for stitching. Sometimes, a machine presser foot is printed on the stitching lines to help identify them. The amount of fabric between the cutting line and stitching line is the *seam allowance.* Most seam allowances are $\frac{5}{8}$ inch [1.5 centimeters], but some are $\frac{1}{2}$ inch [1.27 centimeters] or less.

Grain line markings are indicated by long, straight lines with arrows at each end and are used to place the pattern pieces on the straight grain of the fabric. The words "place on the straight grain of fabric" are usually printed on or above the marking.

A grain line marking with the ends curved toward the edge of the pattern piece means the outer line must be placed on the fold of the fabric, which should also be the straight grain. The fold eliminates the need for a seam to join the two sides. When this marking is used, *never* cut the fabric along the fold. A seam has not been allowed for, and having to stitch one would make the garment too small. The fold line is usually found at the center front or back of garments.

Notches are the diamond-shaped markings that cross and point out from the cutting lines. Single, double, and triple notches are all used to show where and how pattern pieces are joined. Notches are also numbered to help you match one pattern piece to another. Always cut around notches. If you cut the notches off as you cut out the pattern, you will have difficulty lining up seams correctly.

There are a variety of other pattern symbols and markings. They include markings for darts, tucks, ease and gathering, buttonholes, buttons, and zippers. There may be still other markings

the pieces with your hands will flatten them enough for easy and accurate handling. If not, you may want to press the pattern pieces you plan to use with a warm iron.

PATTERN MARKINGS

Patterns have special symbols or markings to guide you in working with them. These symbols show which pattern pieces will be joined; where to make seams, darts, tucks, or pleats; and where to place pockets, zippers, buttonholes, and buttons. Most of these markings are transferred to the fabric after the pattern pieces have been cut out.

Some patterns have many markings, others only a few. The number and types of markings on the pattern depend on the detail and style of the garment. However, markings such as cutting lines, stitching lines, grain lines, and notches are on all patterns.

Cutting lines are the thick, solid lines outlining the shape of the pattern pieces. Some-

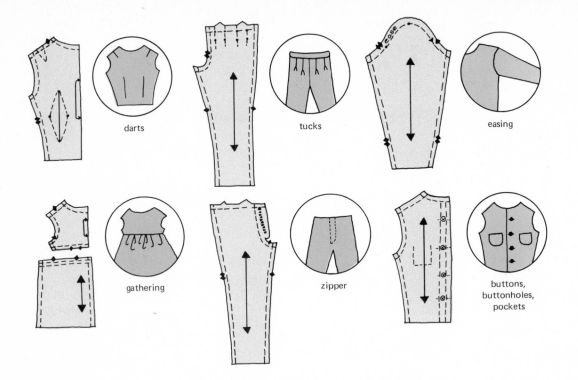

darts

tucks

easing

gathering

zipper

buttons,
buttonholes,
pockets

that are special to a particular pattern because of its style and detail.

Darts are folds of fabric that give shape to a garment. The folds are tapered to a point at one or both ends. Darts are found where fit and shape are important to the style of the garment. They are represented by broken lines (like the stitching lines) that outline the shape of the dart. Sometimes a solid line runs through the center as the fold line.

Tucks are folds of fabric that also give shape to garments, but they do not come to a point. They are represented by two broken lines parallel to each other. A solid line for folding may be between the two broken lines.

Easing is done to fit one seam line to another seam line that is slightly shorter. It is represented by a stitching line with smaller broken lines between two dots or arrows. The area to be eased is also labeled. Easing is done for com-

fort and fit when attaching sleeves, waistbands, collars, and other slightly curved areas.

Gathering is basically very much like easing but is done where there is a large difference in lengths of seam lines. It is a part of the garment's design. Gathering is represented by two or more rows of broken lines. One row is on the stitching line, and at least one row is in the seam allowance. The area is also labeled for gathering.

Pockets, buttonholes, buttons, zippers, and other additions to the garment are represented on the pattern pieces by simple sketches or drawings. The sketches indicate the size and placement of the details and are usually labeled.

Dots, squares, and **triangles** are shown in different sizes to indicate a variety of construction details. All the markings and symbols on patterns are clearly defined and often referred to in the guidesheets. They are on the patterns to make the step-by-step instructions easy to follow.

PATTERN ALTERATIONS

When you change the length or width of a pattern, you are *altering* that pattern. Certain alterations can be made after a garment is constructed. These should be limited to minor adjustments which help make the garment fit perfectly. Shortening the length and taking in seams are examples of this type of adjustment.

Some alterations cannot be made after the fabric is cut. For instance, adding length or width to the pattern must be done before the pieces are cut from the fabric. When you alter one pattern piece, you must consider the fit of all the pattern pieces. For example, if you change the length of one pattern piece, you will have to change all the pieces that will be joined to it, so that seams will match and the garment will be balanced.

When you purchase your pattern according to your body measurements, the alterations are usually minor. However, patterns are made for an "average" figure within the size range. Variations in body builds sometimes make alterations necessary. In order to determine the amount and type of adjustment needed, you must compare your measurements as you recorded them with those on the pattern envelope. Differences of more than $\frac{1}{2}$ inch [12.7 millimeters] should be recorded next to your actual measurements. Use a (+) to add if you have to increase the pattern because your measurements are larger, or a (−) to subtract if you have to decrease the pattern because your measurements are smaller.

Some measurements may not be listed on the pattern envelope. These measurements, such as high bust, sleeve length, and crotch length, can be very important for individual alterations. You will have to measure the corresponding parts of the pattern and compare those measurements with your own. Mark to add or subtract differences of more than $\frac{1}{2}$ inch [12.7 millimeters]. Remember, your measurements do not include

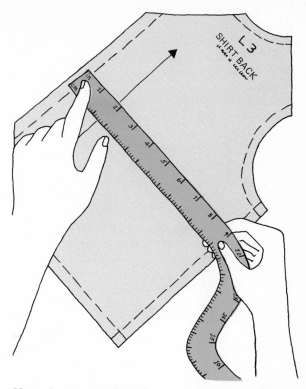

Measuring pattern pieces from seam line to seam line is sometimes done to determine if any alterations need to be made.

seam allowances or hems, so measure from one seam line to the other. Your measurements do not include the style of the pattern or your fabric, so take these into consideration. If your pattern is very full, it will be quite a bit wider than you are; if you are using a stretch pattern, the pattern may be smaller to allow for snug fitting of knit fabric.

You can also fit the pattern by holding the tissue pieces up to your body or by pinning them together and trying them on as you would a garment. The pattern usually represents only half of the finished garment, and you will be fitting it to half your body.

Fitting the tissue pattern will be easier if you work with one section of the garment at a time. For example, if you were trying on a shirt pattern,

Trying on the tissue pattern can also help you determine what alterations have to be made. Whether you fit the pattern on yourself or have someone help you, work gently with the pieces to prevent them from tearing.

you would join the front and back pieces together and fit them as one section and then fit the sleeve. To do this accurately, pin shape details, such as darts and tucks, and join the front and back pieces at stitching lines. Slip on the pattern over undergarments or the clothes you will wear under the completed garment. Pin the center front and center back lines to your clothing or undergarments. The pattern will probably be tight because the tissue does not give the way fabric does. If the pattern is too tight, it will not comfortably reach the center front and back for pinning in place. In this case, remove the pins from the side seams and gently move the pattern until the center front and back lines are correctly placed. You will need someone to help you repin the side seams and draw a line connecting the pins. This will be your new stitching line. When you let out a side seam, remember to add

this same amount to the seam allowances when cutting. If the pattern is slightly too big, you can simply take in the seam allowance when sewing. If the pattern piece is very long or short, or wide, or narrow, you will have to make further alterations.

It is often necessary to make pattern pieces longer or shorter. A line labeled "lengthen or shorten here" is printed across the pattern as a guide for this alteration. It is there so you will not change the style line and shape of the pattern if you do have to alter its length. If there is no alteration line, you can add to or subtract from the bottom edge without disturbing the pattern's style line or shape.

To lengthen the pattern, add a paper patch to the tissue. The patch has to be longer than the alteration needed and about 1 inch [2.5 centimeters] wider than the pattern piece. Cut the pat-

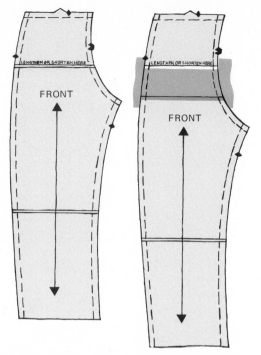

Lengthen the tissue pattern by adding a paper patch to the adjustment line.

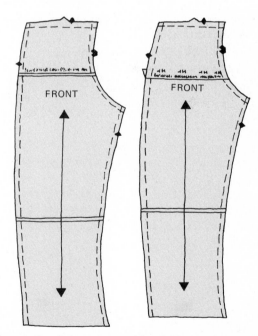

Some patterns can be made longer by adding the necessary amount to the bottom edge.

tern along the alteration line. Pin the patch in place along one of the pattern edges. Measure the desired increase in length and pin or tape the remaining pattern piece in place. Remember to consider seam allowances and hems where necessary. Be sure both ends of the adjustment are straight and even. Join the cutting and stitching lines with a pencil and ruler. If you have cut through the grain line marking, check to be sure it is still straight. Remember, if you add to the length of the pattern front, it is necessary to make the same adjustment to the pattern back.

To shorten a pattern, simply make a fold or tuck in the tissue paper along the alteration line. If there is no line, make one of your own across the pattern or take the pattern up at the bottom. A fold or tuck decreases the length of the pattern piece twice as much as the width of that fold. If you want to shorten your pattern 1 inch [2.5

Shorten the tissue pattern with a fold or tuck along the adjustment line.

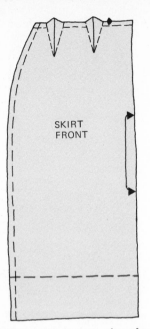

You might fold or cut the bottom edge of some patterns to make them shorter.

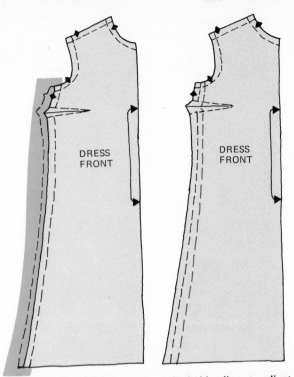

When you change the cutting and stitching lines to adjust the width of the garment, be sure the seam allowance is at least ⅝ inch [15 millimeters] after the alteration.

centimeters], you should make a ½-inch [12.7 millimeter] tuck straight across the pattern. Pin the fold in place. Redraw the cutting, stitching, and grain lines, if necessary.

Altering width is most often necessary in the chest, waist, and hip areas of a garment. It may also be necessary to change the fullness of shirt sleeves or pant legs.

You can increase or decrease the width of a pattern piece the same way you lengthen or shorten a pattern piece—by cutting and adding to the tissue or by folding the tissue. You can also change width by moving the cutting lines to add to or take away from the lengthwise seam allowances.

PREPARING THE FABRIC

There are several steps you may have to take to prepare the fabric before you can pin and cut the pattern. This preparation includes preshrinking, straightening the grain, and ironing.

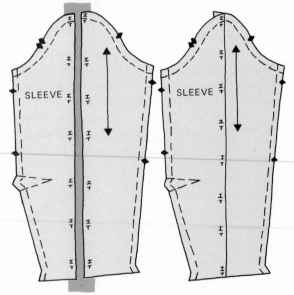

To make a pattern wider or narrower, add a paper patch or make a tuck along the length of the pattern.

PRESHRINKING

Preshrinking may have to be done to avoid the disappointment of having your garment shrink after it is made. Many fabrics are preshrunk by the manufacturer. Some you have to preshrink yourself. Other fabrics do not need to be pre-shrunk at all. Whether the fabric will shrink and how much it will shrink is related to the fabric's fiber content, weave, and finish. Always check the label to see if a fabric has been preshrunk.

You can preshrink your fabric by washing or cleaning it. For example, if the fabric can be machine washed and dried, washing and drying it in automatic machines will preshrink the fabric. Hand washing will preshrink fabrics that cannot be machine washed. Fabrics which must be dry-cleaned should be preshrunk by dry cleaning. Some fabrics, especially woolens and some blends and knits, may be preshrunk by steam pressing.

STRAIGHTENING THE GRAIN

Straightening the grain of your fabric is necessary if your fabric is *off-grain,* or not straight. Should you try to lay out your pattern on off-grain material, you will have difficulty placing the pieces because the fabric will not lie flat. You may also have difficulty when you sew the off-grain pieces together: A print or design may look lopsided or may not match at the seams. When your garment is completed, off-grain fabric can cause a real disappointment. It might gradually begin to hang or sag on one side, and side seams may edge their way towards the front or back. To avoid these problems and disappointments, al-ways be sure your fabric is on grain, that is, the grain is straight.

To check the straight grain of the fabric, first find the lengthwise and crosswise threads. The selvages mark the lengthwise grain of most woven and double-knit fabrics. The threads that run parallel to the selvage are the lengthwise threads. To find the crosswise grain of a woven fabric, look closely at the crosswise threads along the cut edge of the fabric. If you cannot see the

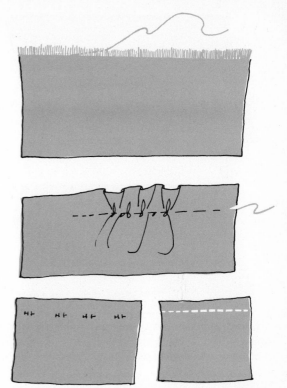

The selvage shows the lengthwise grain on woven fabrics. You can find the crosswise grain by unraveling the cut edge until a thread pulls continuously across the fabric without breaking; by pulling a thread across the width of the fabric and cutting off the uneven edge above it; or by following a prominent thread across and marking it with pins or chalk.

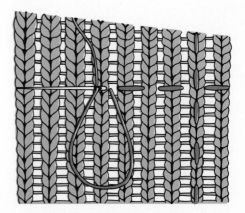

To find the grain of a knit fabric, mark a row of stitches across and down the fabric near the edges.

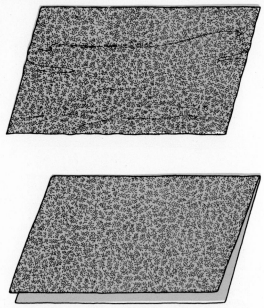

threads on the right side of the fabric, look on the wrong side. Pick out a single thread and follow it from one selvage to the other. This thread marks the crosswise grain. You can cut along the thread to make the edge straight or use pins, chalk, or basting to mark the thread line. To find the grain lines on knit fabrics, follow a single row of stitches. Mark across the top of the stitches for the crosswise grain and down the sides for the lengthwise grain.

Once you have found both grainlines, fold the fabric in half lengthwise. The lengthwise (selvages on woven fabric) and the crosswise grains

If fabric is not grain perfect, it will pucker when you try to fold it in half. Straight grain fabric lies flat when folded with corners at right angles.

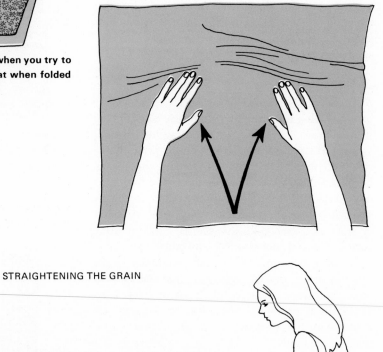

STRAIGHTENING THE GRAIN

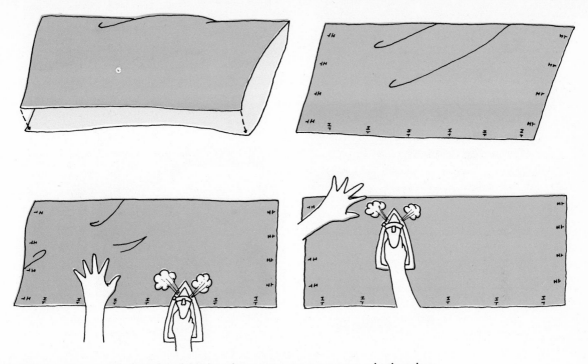

If the fabric does not lie flat when folded or the corners are not square, pin the edges together. Begin pressing, with steam, from the cut edge and work toward the fold. Smooth the fabric with your hands while the fabric is still hot. Continue pressing toward the fold, smoothing the hot fabric as you go along. Avoid pressing directly on the fold.

should meet at right angles. If the corners will not meet without wrinkling, the fabric is off-grain. Many woven fabrics and some stable knits can be straightened by pulling to move the crosswise and lengthwise threads into position.

Pulling to straighten grain can be done by one person alone but is easier when done with the help of a second person. Two people, each holding the fabric at opposite ends, pull against each other, first with the left hands and then with the right hands, until the crosswise grain is even and straight. This technique usually works well with unfinished and unbonded fabrics.

Some woven fabrics that are off-grain cannot be straightened. These include fabrics that have been treated with special stabilizing finishes, such as permanent press and waterproofing, or those that are bonded to another fabric.

Pressing can be used to straighten fabrics. This is the same procedure that is used for preshrinking. After pressing, allow the fabric to completely dry on a flat surface before pinning the pattern to it.

IRONING
Ironing will remove any wrinkles in preshrunk and straightened fabric. Iron with the grain to keep the fabric straight. Avoid ironing or pressing on the fold line, since a pressed crease could be difficult to remove in the finished garment.

THE LAYOUT

How each pattern piece is placed on the fabric for pinning and cutting is called a *layout*. The width of the fabric, whether the fabric has a nap

189

THE LAYOUT

Pants   USE PIECES 1,2,3 and 4

★ Open fabric right side up and cut one

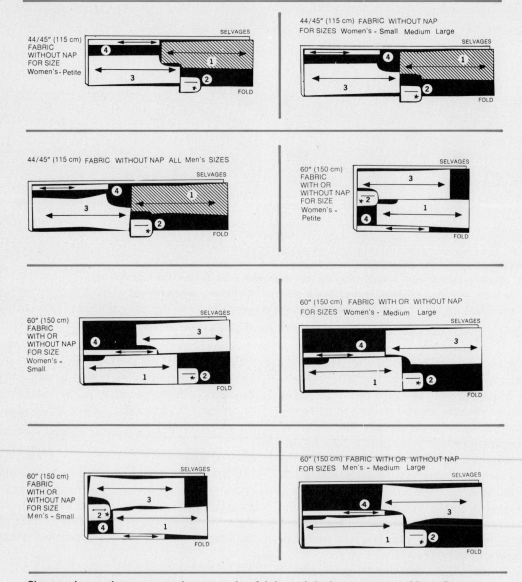

Choose a layout that corresponds to your size, fabric, and the item you are making.   Be sure that your layout looks like the one you chose on the guidesheet. *Butterick Fashion Marketing Co.*

or one-way design, and the pattern size and view are all taken into consideration when the layouts are planned. Different layouts are illustrated on the guidesheet. When you purchase fabric according to the pattern envelope, it is necessary to select the layout that goes with the amount of fabric you have.

As you look at all the layouts, you will note the views, the fabric widths, and the sizes for each. The layout that shows the view you are making, with your fabric's width and your size, is the one you should follow. Circle it so you can easily refer to it later. Check the layout to see how the fabric is folded. Some layouts require a fold along the length of the fabric with the two selvages together. Others require a fold across the width of the fabric with the cut ends together. Sometimes the fabric is folded diagonally, on the bias. Still other times, the fabric is not folded at all, and the layout is done on a single layer of cloth. Some layouts will also indicate whether the fabric should be folded with the right or wrong sides together.

It is often easier to keep the fabric clean and to pin, cut, mark, and join pieces with the right sides of the fabric together. However, the fabric is usually folded right side out when matching a pattern such as a plaid, stripe, or large print, and when using fabric with a nap or one-way design.

Place your fabric on a flat surface that is large enough to support it. Do not let your fabric hang over the sides. The weight of the overhanging fabric could cause it to slide or move, and knit fabrics, especially, could stretch. To prevent this, keep the fabric folded at one end, and work in small sections at a time. Gather all the supplies you will need to measure and pin the pattern. These are a tape measure, ruler or yardstick, pins, and cutting shears.

Before you begin to place the pattern on the fabric, see that you have all the pieces needed for the view you are making. Double-check the layout you circled on the guidesheet to be sure it is the correct one. Arrange the pattern pieces on the fabric as shown on the guidesheet. Note whether the pieces on the layout are placed printed side up or printed side down, which pieces are placed on the fold, and in which direction the pieces are placed. Once the pieces are arranged on the fabric, check them again against the layout before you begin pinning.

PINNING THE PATTERN

The pattern pieces are pinned to the fabric to keep them straight and in place while you are cutting. To anchor the pattern pieces to the fabric, push the pin down through the tissue pattern and all the layers of fabric and then up again about $\frac{1}{2}$ inch [12.7 millimeters] away, just as if you were making a stitch. There are some

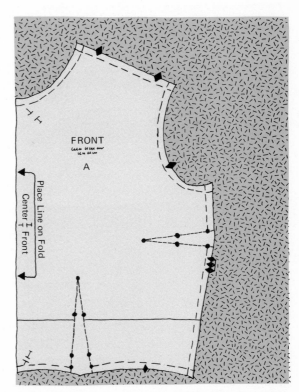

Begin pinning your pattern to the fabric with those pieces placed on the fold line.

general rules to follow to help make pinning easy and accurate.

- Place the pins at right angles to the stitching, cutting, and fold lines and diagonally toward the corners.
- Work with one pattern piece at a time and start by pinning the grain line.
- Space pins 4 to 6 inches [10.2 to 15.2 centimeters] apart around the entire pattern piece, but closer where there are curves.
- Smooth the tissue gently from the secured grain line as you pin the opposite sides of the pattern.
- Place a pin inside each notch to prevent yourself from cutting it off.
- Keep pins from extending over the cutting line so they will not be in your way as you cut.

If your particular pattern has pieces that are placed on the fold, pin them first. Be sure the fold line on the pattern is directly on the fold in the fabric. An error here will either increase the width of the garment if the pattern is placed inside the fold or decrease the width if placed outside the fold. Begin by pinning one end of the fold, then the center, then the other end. Place more pins where needed in the fold line. Now, gently smooth the tissue pattern and place pins in each corner. Continue around the entire pattern.

Pattern pieces with the straight grain lines must be placed on the straight grain of the fabric. Measuring the distance from the grain line to the selvage or fold of the fabric will help you be accurate. Place a pin at the center of the grain line and measure to the edge of the fabric. The

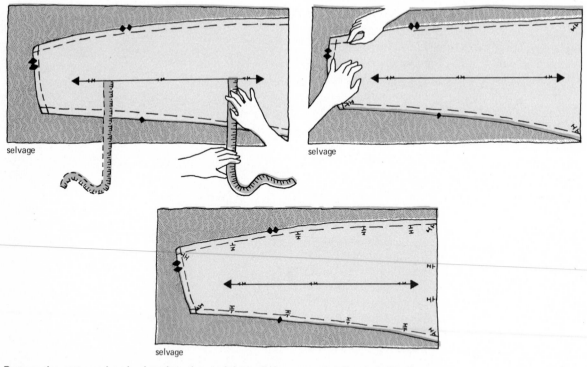

Be sure the pattern piece is placed on the straight grain by measuring the grain line from the fabric's edge. After pinning the grain line, smooth the tissue and place pins diagonally toward the corners of the pattern. Then place pins where necessary to keep the pattern pieces flat for cutting.

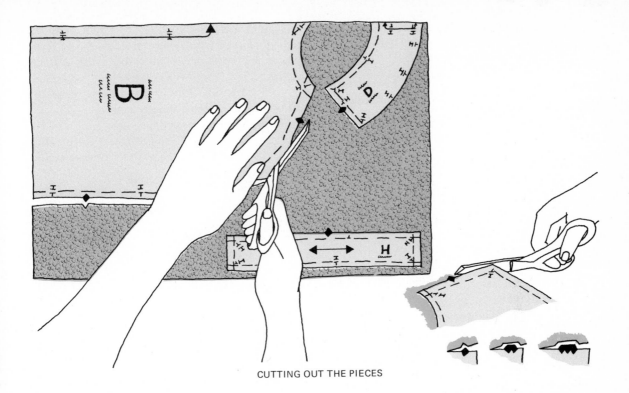

CUTTING OUT THE PIECES

arrows at each end of the grain line must be that same distance from the edge of the material. Measure both ends, before you pin and again afterwards, to be sure that they are even.

For each pattern piece, the procedure is the same. Pin as much as necessary to ensure accuracy when cutting.

CUTTING

Cutting out your pattern is actually the first step you take to change the flat fabric into a shaped garment. Take care each step of the way to follow the cutting lines accurately. As you cut, hold the shears with one hand and rest the other gently on the fabric to keep it flat and even. First, cut the pieces that are pinned to the edges of the fabric and work your way toward the pieces in the center. Some general information about cutting will help you as you cut out your pattern.

- Cut with the grain by following the arrows on the pattern. Cutting against the grain can cause the fabric edges to stretch and begin to ravel.
- Keep the fabric flat on the table or cutting surface and open the shears wide to make long, even strokes with them. This will result in smooth cut edges without stretching or chopping the fabric.
- Walk around the fabric to reach the pattern pieces, rather than move them toward you. If you pull the fabric or pattern when cutting, you may cause wrinkling or puckering that can change the shape and size of the garment pieces.
- Cut around notches outside the cutting line, *not* into the seam allowance. Cut across the tops of double and triple notches to make one large notch. This will make the notches easier to cut and identify.

· Use the full length of the blades to cut long, straight areas and the points to cut corners, curves, and small details.

Neatly fold the pattern pieces as they are cut. Save the small fabric scraps for test-marking and stitching.

MARKING

After you cut, you must transfer the pattern markings to the fabric. Leave the pattern pieces pinned on the fabric until all the marking is completed. Check each pattern piece for construction details. Darts, tucks, center front and center back lines, and button and buttonhole placement all have to be marked. Large and small dots, squares, and triangles on the pattern and guidesheet show where to match seams and also details such as where the top of the sleeve meets the shoulder seam, where the collar is centered on the neck seam, and where the pockets are placed. Seam lines, especially straight ones, are not usually marked. However, you may want to mark seam lines that could be difficult to follow. Small curved areas, sharp corners, and places where seam lines cross are examples.

There is a variety of marking techniques. Each has its own advantages, and no one method is best for all fabrics. You will have to learn to select the method of marking most suitable for the fabric you are working with.

TRACING WHEEL AND TRACING PAPER
The tracing method of marking is fast and easy to do. Remove enough of the pins from your

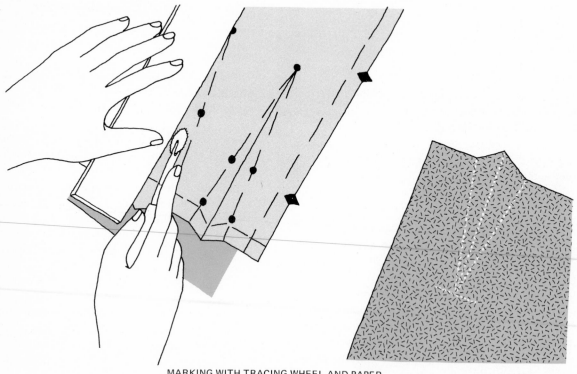

MARKING WITH TRACING WHEEL AND PAPER

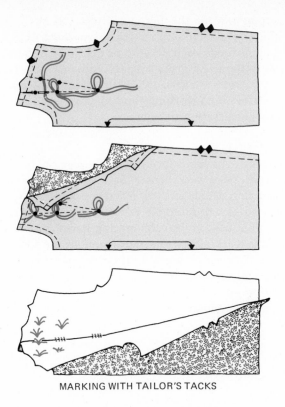

make a stitch about $\frac{1}{4}$ inch long [6 millimeters] through the pattern and all the thicknesses of fabric. Leave the thread ends about 1 inch [2.5 centimeters] long. Make a second stitch in the same place as the first, leaving the threads in a loop about 1 inch [2.5 centimeters] long. Repeat at each point to be marked, using a continuous thread. When all points have been marked, clip the threads between each marking. Remove the pattern piece and gently begin to separate the layers of fabric. As you reach each stitch (tailor's tack), clip the threads between the layers of fabric. The small thread ends remain as markings. Tailor's tacks show on the right and wrong sides of the fabric and are easily removed after machine stitching.

PINS
At each point to be marked, push a pin through the tissue paper and both layers of fabric. Turn

MARKING WITH TAILOR'S TACKS

pattern so you can slip in the tracing paper. Make sure the colored sides of the paper are against the wrong sides of the fabric. Roll the tracing wheel over all the symbols and lines to be marked. Use just enough pressure to leave the marks. If you press too hard, the markings may show through to the right side of the fabric. When marking straight lines, use a ruler to guide the wheel. Always test-mark a scrap of fabric to find out which color and amount of pressure to use. It is often difficult to mark very heavy fabrics with this method, and markings may show through white or sheer fabrics.

TAILOR'S TACKS
Tailor's tacks are simple hand stitches made with loose loops of thread. Use a long, unknotted double thread. At each point to be marked,

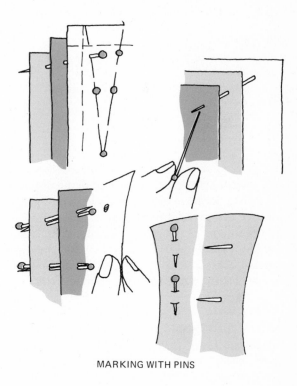

MARKING WITH PINS

wrong side of the fabric. Chalk can be used alone or in combination with pin marking. Place a pin through each point to be marked. Remove the pattern and make a small chalk mark at each pin. You may also use chalk to draw stitching lines between markings and to show seam lines and construction details.

BASTING

Machine or hand basting can be used to mark center front and center back lines and construction details such as where a pocket is to be placed or a buttonhole is to be sewn. Basting is often used to transfer tracing paper, pin, and chalk markings to the right sides of the fabric. It is also used to mark fitting lines. Basting may take longer than other marking methods, but it shows on both sides of the fabric and will not slip out accidentally.

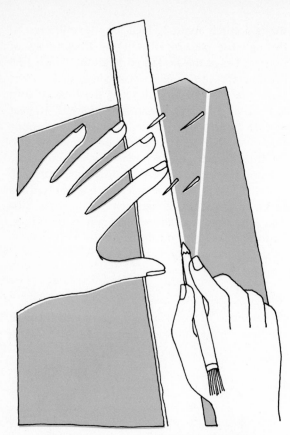

MARKING WITH TAILOR'S CHALK AND PINS

the garment section over and insert a second pin where each of the others come out in the opposite direction. Remove the paper pattern, and gently pull the two garment pieces apart so that the pins do not slip out of the fabric. Then, carefully slip the pins in and out of the fabric so that they will not fall out. The advantage of the pin method is that it does not leave a permanent mark.

CHALK

Tailor's chalk is quick and easy to use in both pencil and block form. Disadvantages are that chalk marks may not show or may easily rub off some fabrics and that they show only on the

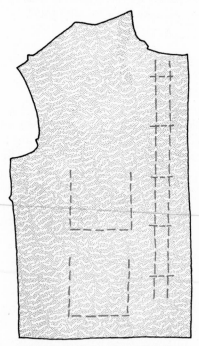

MARKING WITH BASTING STITCHES

1. Study each of the pattern pieces you will need to construct your garment. Identify the markings and make a display to compare the markings on your pattern with those on your classmates' patterns. Draw, label, and describe what each mark or symbol represents.

2. Prepare a class demonstration on simple pattern alterations. Include how to lengthen and shorten basic pattern pieces.

3. Make a list of all the things you have to know to select the proper cutting layout on the pattern guidesheet. Explain how to use the pattern layout.

4. Discuss the advantages of preparing your fabric before pinning and cutting the pattern pieces. Bring the fabric for your project into class. Decide if preshrinking, straightening the grain, or ironing are necessary. If so, which techniques would you choose to prepare your fabric and why?

5. Prepare a bulletin board on either the guidesheet, pinning the pattern, or cutting the fabric. Include all the important information and use of, or directions for, each.

6. Make a comparison study of the different methods of marking. Gather sewing scraps of a few different types of fabric. Mark each with tracing wheel and paper, tailor's tacks, pins, chalk, and basting. Which method or methods work best for each fabric? Do you like any one method best? If so, why?

● DO YOU KNOW

alteration	off-grain
construction details	pattern markings
cutting	pattern pieces
cutting lines	pinning
easing and gathering	preshrinking
guidesheet	seam allowance
layout	stitching lines
marking	straight grain line
notches	straightening fabric

sewing:
other times,
other places

la couture

basic
techniques—
the
shapemakers

After reading this chapter you should be able to:

- *Staystitch the curved areas of each garment piece to preserve their shape and grain.*

- *Select the weight and type of interfacing that goes with your garment's style and fabric.*

- *Demonstrate the difference between gathering and ease stitching.*

- *Fit and adjust your garment before and after the seams are sewn.*

- *Stitch and press darts, tucks, and seams.*

- *Determine the type of seam and seam finish most appropriate for the fabric and garment style you have selected.*

The basic shape of a garment is determined by the grain and shape of the pieces of fabric. More shape is added by seams and other construction details. Each step in fitting and stitching the fabric contributes to the finished shape and look of the garment.

STAYSTITCHING

Staystitching is a simple but important way to maintain the size and shape of garment pieces as you work with them. It is done along the curved areas of each garment piece to keep the edges from stretching and to hold the grain in place. Use a regular machine stitch on a single layer of fabric. Sew directly on the seam line of very curved areas or just inside the seam allowance (toward the cut edge) of slightly

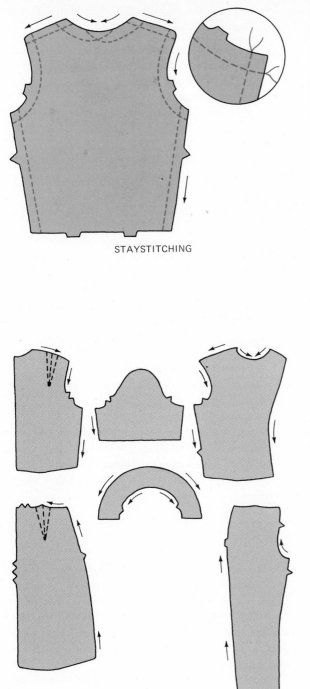

STAYSTITCHING

DIRECTIONAL STITCHING

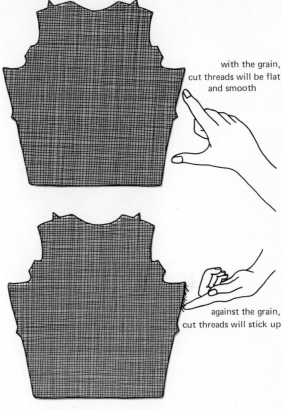

with the grain,
cut threads will be flat
and smooth

against the grain,
cut threads will stick up

FINDING THE GRAIN FOR DIRECTIONAL STITCHING

curved areas. Never staystitch more than ⅛ inch [3 millimeters] into the seam allowance. Stitch with the grain.

The arrows on each pattern piece indicate the direction of the grain, for stitching. You can also find the direction of the grain by running your finger along the cut edge of a curved or slanted piece of the fabric. If the yarn ends lie flat, you are moving in the direction of the grain. If the yarn ends lift up, you are moving against the grain. When you stitch in the direction which keeps the fabric grain perfect, you are *directional stitching*. All machine sewing, as well as cutting and pressing, should be directional.

Interfacing can add crispness to collars or body to capped sleeves. *Butterick Fashion Marketing Co.*

INTERFACING

Interfacings help to shape and add body and strength to necklines, collars, lapels, waistbands, cuffs, and button and buttonhole closings. Like other fabrics, interfacings are made from a variety of natural and synthetic fibers in light, medium, and heavy weights.

There are woven interfacings with grainlines to consider when cutting and sewing, and bonded interfacings with no grain at all. Some interfacings can be machine-washed, and others must be dry-cleaned. Some woven interfacings may have to be preshrunk. Most interfacings are sewn into the garment. Some, however, have a special backing that allows them to be held in place simply by ironing them onto the fabric. These iron-on, or fusible, interfacings are popular because they are easy to apply and work well

with many lightweight and knit fabrics. When selecting interfacings, remember:

- The pattern envelope will tell whether interfacing is needed and how much to buy. The envelope may also have information on what type of interfacing to choose.
- Directions for cutting and applying the interfacing can be found on the pattern pieces and guidesheet.
- Directions for applying fusible interfacings are often included with the interfacing fabric or printed along the edges of it.
- Read the labels carefully. Know the fiber content, width, and care of the interfacing. Cleaning and pressing instructions for the interfacing and garment fabric should be the same.
- Consider the intended use and weight of the interfacing. Lightweight interfacings add strength and body to lightweight and medium fabrics. Heavy interfacings can be used with heavy fabrics or to add extreme shape or stiffness to a fabric.
- To test the effect of an interfacing on your fabric, place the interfacing over your hand and drape the garment fabric over the interfacing. Check the feel and look of the two fabrics.
- In most cases, you will want to use interfacing that is the same weight as, or lighter than, the garment fabric.

FITTING

The fit of a garment has a lot to do with its style, but whether the style of a garment is loose and baggy or slim and body hugging, proper fit is necessary. Well-fitted clothes are comfortable and easy to move in. They do not pull, wrinkle, or ride up as you wear them, and they do not bag or hang off the body.

Usually a garment is fitted before the seams are sewn and again afterwards to double-check the fit and to place the collar, sleeves, or waistband. You will need someone to help you pin

Well-fitted clothing complements you—helps you look your best. *Simplicity Pattern Co.*

and fit the garment. A full-length mirror is also helpful for viewing the overall look and fit of the garment.

- Make any necessary gathering, and pin darts, tucks, and seams. Place the pins horizontally on the stitching lines, so that you will be able to slip the garment on easily.
- Wear the type of undergarments or clothes you will be wearing with the finished garment.
- Wear the same height shoes you will wear with the finished garment.
- Try the garment on right side out. Pin the outside seams on the stitching lines.
- As the garment is being pinned, stand natu-

rally with your hands at your sides and look straight ahead.
- When altering seams, adjust an even distance on both sides.
- If you have to change the size or placement of darts, be sure that corresponding darts are the same length and width and are positioned evenly.
- When you finish the first fitting, remove the garment carefully so that pins marking the adjustments do not fall out. Transfer the pin markings to the wrong side of the garment and pin or baste the garment together.
- Try on the garment once more. If you are satisfied with the alterations, you are ready for machine stitching.

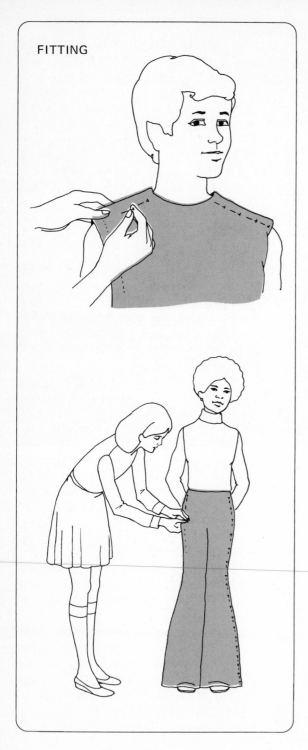

FITTING

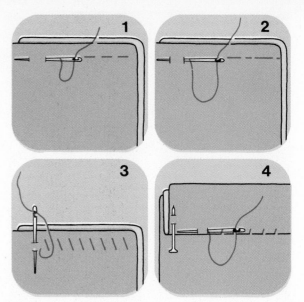

HAND BASTING STITCHES

1 Even basting is used for fitting and stitching curves and areas to be eased.

2 Uneven basting is used to make sewing guidelines, to hold a hem in position, to mark center lines, and to indicate the location of pockets and trimmings.

3 Diagonal basting is used to hold two pieces of fabric together so that they cannot shift or move.

4 Slip basting is used when it is necessary to baste from the right side of the garment.

DARTS AND TUCKS

Darts are used to shape the style and fit of a garment. If you look at various patterns or items of clothing, you will find darts at the elbows of sleeves; at the waists of slacks, shorts, skirts, and dresses; at the bustline of blouses and dresses; and at the shoulders of shirts, blouses, and jackets. Darts can be short, long, narrow, wide, curved, or straight. They may come to a point at one or both ends.

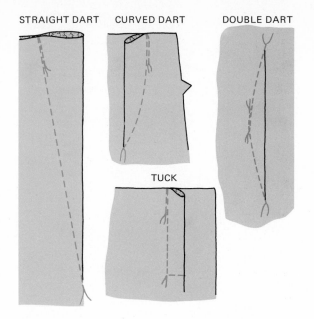

STRAIGHT DART   CURVED DART   DOUBLE DART

TUCK

PRESSING

Press darts and tucks as shown on the pattern guidesheet. Horizontal darts, for bustline and sleeve, are usually pressed downward. Vertical darts, for shoulder and waistline, are pressed toward the center of the garment. To begin, position the dart or tuck on the ironing board so that the folded edge and the stitching line are flat; then press. Do not press beyond the end of the dart or tuck. Since darts create curves or shape, it is best to press them on a curved surface, such as the tailor's ham or press mitt. Press the dart or tuck again on the right side of the fabric. (Remember, for some fabrics you will have to use a press cloth.)

When making simple garments, like a skirt or slacks, you can organize your work and save time by pinning, sewing, and pressing all the darts and tucks of a garment at one time.

STITCHING

To make a single or one-pointed dart, fold the fabric with right sides together to match the stitching lines and then pin. Place each pin so that the head is toward the folded edge of the fabric. Put the first pin at the point and the second pin at the cut edge. Continue pinning as necessary. Be sure there are no folds or wrinkles in the material. Begin stitching at the wide end of the dart and continue to the point, removing the pins as you sew. Follow the stitching line carefully to get a clean, sharp point. If you do not stitch to the point, the dart will pucker or wrinkle. Secure the thread ends.

To make a double or two-pointed dart, fold, pin, and stitch the same as for the single dart. Handle the widest part of the dart like the edge of a single dart. Again, follow the stitching line carefully. You may have to clip the center of the dart so that it will lie flat. (See page 210.)

Tucks, like darts, are used for shape and fit and can vary in length and width. The difference is that darts have points and tucks do not. When sewing tucks, follow the pattern stitching lines.

GATHERS AND EASE

The style and design of a garment determine when and where gathering or ease is needed. For example, set-in sleeves of a shirt can be smooth and curved or full and puffed. The look depends upon the amount of fabric at the top of the sleeve, or *sleeve cap*. The narrow sleeve cap would be eased to fit smoothly into the armhole seam, and the wider sleeve cap, gathered.

The technique for gathering and ease stitching are the same. The difference is in the amount of fullness desired. Gathering gives more fullness than ease stitching. Both gathering and ease stitching help to control the amount and placement of fullness created. The pattern will show where to ease or gather.

Start by setting the stitch regulator to the longest stitch. On the right side of the fabric, make two rows of stitching. Sew the first row directly on the seam line, and the second row $\frac{1}{8}$ inch [3 millimeters] from the seam line toward the cut edge. Leave long thread ends at the beginning and at the end of each row of stitching.

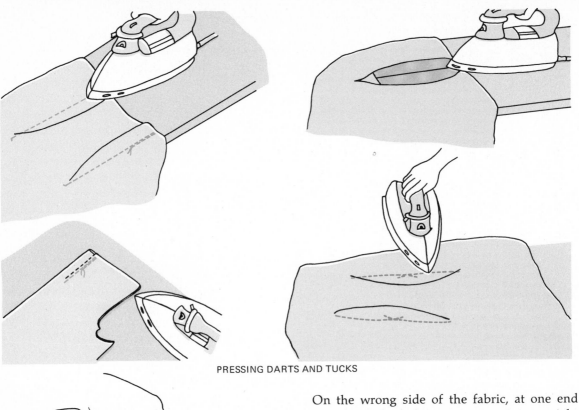

PRESSING DARTS AND TUCKS

On the wrong side of the fabric, at one end of the rows of stitching, insert a pin at a right angle to the stitches. Wrap the thread ends around the pin in a figure eight to keep them from slipping out. Hold the fabric securely over the stitching line with one hand. With the other hand, grasp the loose bobbin threads firmly between your thumb and first finger, and pull the threads gently. The fabric will begin to gather in small bunches along the stitching line. Do not pull too hard; the thread might break.

When the cloth is gathered the desired amount, secure the threads by wrapping them around a pin as previously described. Now that the threads are anchored at each end, distribute the fabric evenly along the line of stitching.

JOINING SEAMS

Before you begin to sew a garment together, check the pattern pieces to see which ones have

GATHERING

Gathering is used to create fullness. The amount of fullness depends upon the fabric, where the gathering is placed, the style of the garment, and the effect you want. *Simplicity Pattern Co.*

corresponding markings. Look for single, double, and triple notches. You may find that notches are numbered to help you match them. To join seams and assemble the garment correctly, match notches, other pattern symbols, and cut edges.

Match and pin the notches and the cut edges. Then divide the distance between pins and pin again. Repeat this "divide and pin" technique until the seam is firmly in place for stitching. Place the pins at right angles to the stitching line with the pin heads in the seam allowance. It is easy to match and pin straight seams with no easing to be done.

When one seam edge is slightly longer than the other, the longer edge must be eased to fit without making gathers or tucks. The longer edge can be machine stitched and eased to fit the shorter one. Stitch eased seams with the shorter seam edge on top. The feed dogs will help to distribute the fullness in the longer seam edge underneath. This type of seam is commonly found at the shoulder or waist or elbow. The area to be eased is indicated on the tissue pattern.

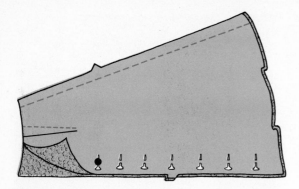

Match notches by numbers and other construction details as you pin the pattern pieces together. Be sure to place enough pins to keep the pieces even.

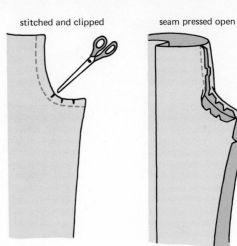

stitched and clipped   seam pressed open

OUTSIDE CURVE

Curved seams are often found in the shoulder, sleeve, chest, waist, and hip areas of garments. The same basic steps for making straight seams are also used to make curved seams. However, because it is sometimes more difficult to control a curved edge when stitching, place the pins more closely together. In some cases, you may want to baste the seam before making permanent stitching. Sew slowly, keeping the seam allowance at an even width.

An inside curve seam will pull if it is not clipped toward the stitching line before it is pressed. Inside curves can be found in necklines, armholes, and waistlines. Be careful to use only the points of a very sharp scissors. Cut about halfway toward the stitching. The seam allowance will spread and lie flat when pressed.

An outside curve will bunch along the seam allowance unless it is clipped. Outside curves can be found along the outer edges of rounded collars, cuffs, and pockets. Instead of clipping straight toward the seam line, cut small wedges out of the fabric. When the seam allowance is opened and pressed, the cut wedges will close to make an even, flat edge.

Things to remember when making seams:

· Reinforce the beginning and end of each seam. (See page 136.)

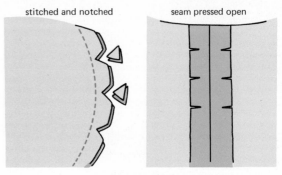

stitched and notched   seam pressed open

INSIDE CURVE

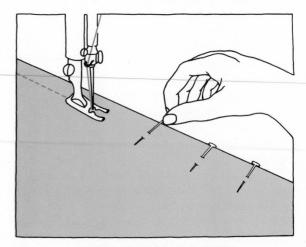

REMOVING PINS AS YOU STITCH

- Do not sew over pins. Remove them as you stitch.
- Keep the two cut edges even as you stitch.
- Sew slowly to keep the stitching straight and even.
- Press seams carefully. First press the seam allowances together flat. Then press them open or to one side according to the directions for your pattern.
- Curved seams must be clipped before they are pressed so they will lie flat.

TYPES OF SEAMS

Most clothing is sewn with the plain seam. A variety of other seams can be made by using a combination of simple sewing techniques.

PLAIN SEAMS

Plain seams are used in all areas of a garment. Begin by pinning the right sides of the fabric together. Adjust the stitch regulator and sew a $\frac{5}{8}$-inch [15-millimeter] seam. Back stitch at each

When you sew seams with the sewing machine, guide the fabric slowly and remove pins before they reach the presser foot. *Massey Junior College.*

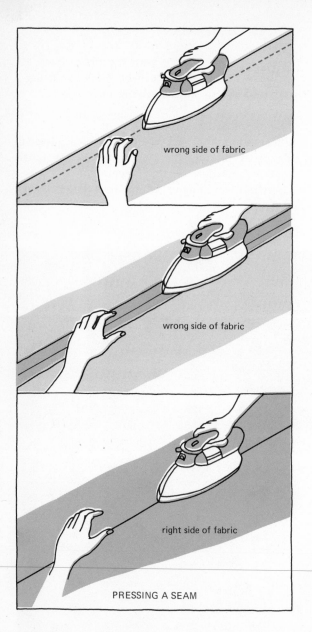

wrong side of fabric

wrong side of fabric

right side of fabric

PRESSING A SEAM

TOPSTITCHED SEAMS

Topstitched seams are plain seams with one or more rows of extra stitching made to decorate the outside of the garment. Topstitching is practical as well as decorative. Topstitched seams remain flat and usually do not fray because the seam allowances are stitched in place. Most topstitching is done about $\frac{1}{4}$ inch [6 millimeters] from the seam line. Topstitching can be done through two layers of fabric (seam pressed open) or through three layers of fabric (seam pressed to one side).

WELT SEAMS

Welt seams also start as plain seams. Both seam allowances are pressed to one side. The under seam allowance is trimmed to $\frac{1}{4}$ inch [6 millimeters]. The seam is then topstitched through the outer layer and wider seam allowance. The trimming helps to eliminate bulk on heavy fabric and to give a padded look to the seam line.

FLAT-FELL SEAMS

Flat-fell seams are commonly used on jeans, sportswear, and tailored shirts. This is a strong seam because the seam allowances are enclosed and the seam is double-stitched. One or two rows of stitching show on the right side of the fabric, making the flat-fell seam decorative as well as strong.

To get a single line of stitching on the outside, begin by sewing a plain seam with the right sides of the fabric together. Sew a plain seam with the wrong sides together to get a double row of stitching on the outside. Press the seam allowances open, and then to one side. Trim the under seam allowance to $\frac{1}{8}$ inch [3 millimeters]. Fold the upper seam allowance under and pin it to cover the trimmed one. Topstitch close to the folded edge and press.

FRENCH SEAMS

French seams are used on sheer or lightweight fabrics where raw edges might show through. Because the seam edges are enclosed, fraying is

end to lock the stitches. Finish the seam by pressing it in three steps. Begin on the wrong side and press both edges flat along the seam line, in one direction. Next, open the seam allowance and press. Then turn the garment to the right side and press along the seam crease using a press cloth to protect the fabric.

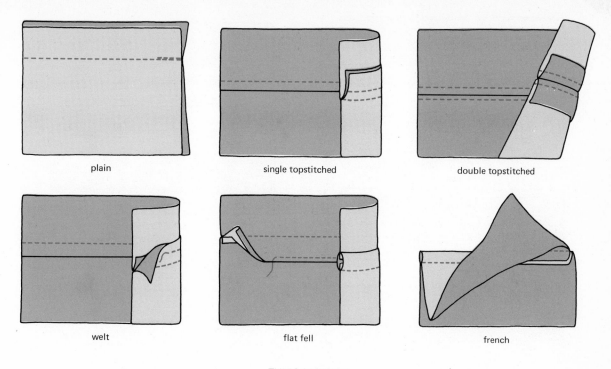

plain

single topstitched

double topstitched

welt

flat fell

french

TYPES OF SEAMS

prevented here, too. With the wrong sides to-gether, sew a 3/8-inch [9-millimeter] seam. Trim the seam allowances to 1/8 inch [3 millimeters]. Fold the garment on the stitching line to bring the right sides of the fabric together and press, if necessary. Sew 1/4 inch [6 millimeters] from the fold. The bulk of the seam will be inside the fin-ished garment. Press the enclosed seam allow-ances to one side.

SEAM FINISHES

Some double-knit and bonded fabrics do not stretch or fray and do not have to be finished. However, most fabrics do require seam finishes to prevent fraying and stretching and to give a finished look to the inside of the garment. There are a variety of finishes suitable for use on differ-ent fabrics. Select a seam finish according to the weight of the fabric, how much the fabric gives or stretches, and how much the fabric frays.

The pattern directions cannot recommend one particular seam finish since different people will use different fabrics to make the garment. Guidesheets, therefore, usually have brief direc-tions for more than one type finish. You must choose the finish best suited to your needs.

PINKED AND SCALLOPED

Pinking and scalloping shears create a simple but effective finish on firmly woven fabrics. The cut of the shears increases the surface edge of the fabric and helps keep it from fraying. Do not use a pinked finish on sheer fabrics; the cut edge will show through to the right side of the gar-ment. When using pinking or scalloping shears, be careful to trim only the edges of the fabric. The wider the remaining seam allowance, the flatter the seam will stay.

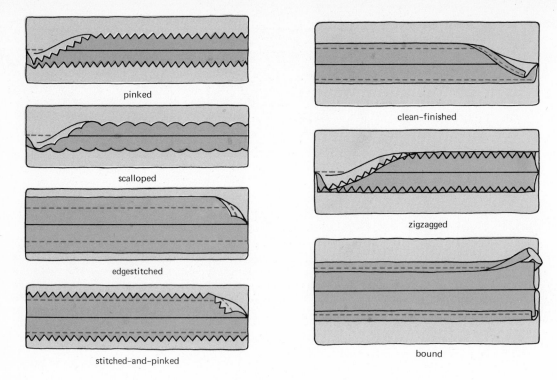

pinked

scalloped

edgestitched

stitched-and-pinked

clean-finished

zigzagged

bound

SEAM FINISHES

EDGESTITCHED
Firmly woven and knit fabrics are often edge-stitched to prevent stretching. Wools and polyester knits are good examples of the types of materials on which this method is used. This finish is done by stitching $\frac{1}{4}$ inch [6 millimeters] from each raw seam edge of a single seam allowance.

STITCHED-AND-PINKED
The techniques of edge stitching and pinking are combined to produce this finish. The stitching prevents stretching, and the pinking provides a neat edge that will not fray.

CLEAN-FINISHED
The clean-finished method is also called *turned and stitched*. It is used on light- to medium-weight materials that fray. It is not used on heavy fabrics because it would be too bulky. Stitch

through a single thickness $\frac{1}{8}$ inch [3 millimeters] from the raw edge. Fold the edge under on the first row of stitching and make a second row of stitching close to the fold.

ZIGZAG
Seams that ravel easily can be finished with a machine zigzag stitch. This works best on medium- to heavyweight fabrics. Feed the fabric carefully so that the stitch comes near but not over the seam edge, to keep thread from jamming and to make a neat finish.

BOUND
The bound seam edge is covered with bias binding. This is a common finish on unlined jackets. Fold the binding over the edge of each seam allowance. Stitch so that the top and bottom of the binding and the seam allowance are held together with one line of stitching.

1. Discuss the advantages of staystitching. What may happen to a garment that is not staystitched before construction?

2. Visit a fabric store. Make a list of the different kinds and weights of interfacings in the store. Note the care instructions for each. Compare your findings with others in your class. Discuss how interfacing can be used.

3. Demonstrate or explain how darts, tucks, gathers, and ease give a garment shape and style.

4. Prepare a bulletin board on the different types of seams: plain, flat-fell, french, topstitched, and welt seams. Include examples of each type of seam. You could also list how each type of seam is used in clothing.

5. Select samples of four different types of fabric. Select an appropriate seam finish for each fabric and explain why you selected it.

6. Demonstrate how to check the fit of a simple garment before permanent stitching.

● DO YOU KNOW

curved seams	seam finishes
darts	seam variations
directional stitching	shape makers
ease	staystitching
fitting	topstitching
gathers	tucks
interfacings	welt seam

12

more on construction techniques

After reading this chapter, you should be able to:

- *Identify different zipper applications in ready-made and home-sewn clothing.*

- *List three different ways a facing is used to finish the edge of a garment.*

- *Explain the difference between trimming a seam and grading a seam.*

- *Apply a simple collar to a garment.*

- *Set a sleeve into a garment.*

- *Describe the basic steps in making a patch pocket.*

- *List the similarities and differences of an edge casing and an applied casing.*

- *Describe some methods of sewing knit and stretch fabrics.*

ZIPPERS

Zippers of various types, lengths, and colors are available for use in jackets, coats, dresses, pants, skirts, and shirts. The zipper needed for your project is listed on the back of the pattern envelope with the other notions. The pattern information includes both the type and length zipper most suitable for the garment being made. For example, if you are making pants or a skirt, you may need a 7-inch [17.8-centimeter] skirt zipper. For a dress, you may need a 14-inch [35.5-centimeter] neck zipper. A separating zipper might be suggested for a jacket.

While zippers are functional, some are also decorative and are sewn with teeth and slide in full view. Other zippers are carefully concealed in a seam or under a lap. The type of application should be considered when you choose the zipper for your project. If a pants pattern calls for

216

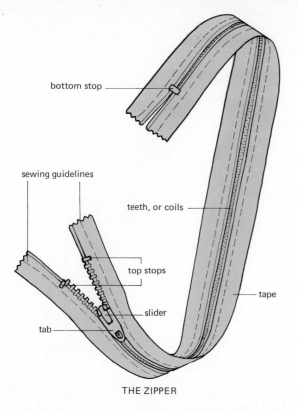

bottom stop

sewing guidelines

teeth, or coils

top stops

tape

slider

tab

THE ZIPPER

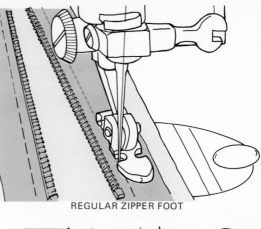

REGULAR ZIPPER FOOT

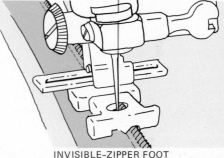

INVISIBLE-ZIPPER FOOT

a fly front, an invisible zipper could not be used. However, if you are making a skirt or dress, either the conventional or invisible zipper may be suitable.

The design of the garment often determines how the zipper is applied. The most popular zipper applications are: lapped with one flap, as seen on fly-front slacks and sides of skirts; slot, or centered, with two flaps, as seen in center front or back of garments; and invisible, which looks like part of the seam on dresses, skirts, pants, and shirts.

ZIPPER FOOT

Zippers are usually inserted by machine, although it is also possible to stitch some in place by hand. You need a zipper foot to insert the zipper by machine. This is a one-sided presser foot that can be used to stitch to the left or right of the zipper teeth. A conventional presser foot cannot be used since one side of it would ride

on the zipper teeth, making close, even stitching impossible. The regular zipper foot is used with all but invisible-type zippers. A special foot that is placed over the zipper teeth instead of next to them is used for sewing invisible zippers into garments.

PREPARATION

Zippers with cotton tape must be preshrunk before they are applied. Rinse the zipper in hot water and allow it to dry.

The tape on all zippers should be pressed to remove any folds. Care should be taken not to press the teeth of nylon or polyester zippers. A hot iron could melt them.

CENTERED ZIPPER

The slot, or centered, zipper is usually placed in the center back seam or center front seam of a garment. The zipper is centered in the seam and is evenly stitched on each side of the seam. Both

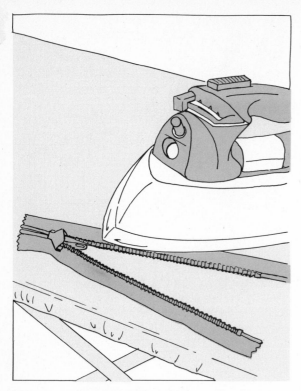

Zippers are often folded for packaging. The zipper tape should be pressed to remove the creases. This helps the zipper to lie flat for application to your garment.

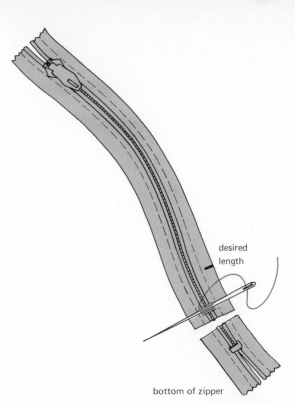

desired
length

bottom of zipper

To shorten a zipper, cut it about 1 inch [2.5 centimeters] beyond the desired length. Hand stitch across the teeth several times to form a new bottom stop.

rows of stitching are visible, and the laps formed on each side cover the teeth of the zipper.

1. Stitch the seam up to where the bottom of the zipper will be placed. Baste the rest of the seam closed. Press it open.

2. Open the zipper. Center the zipper, tab side down, on the basted seam. Beginning at the top, pin one side in place to the seam allowance. Place pins at right angles to the seam line. Be sure the zipper teeth line up evenly on the seam as you pin.

3. Machine baste along the zipper guideline, through the zipper tape and the one seam allowance.

4. Close the zipper. Place the zipper flat against the fabric. Pin through all thicknesses: the tape, seam allowance, and garment.

5. Stitch down the length of the zipper, pivot at

the bottom, stitch across, pivot again, and continue up the other side. Some sewers prefer to use directional stitching—from the bottom up on each side of the zipper. Some also prefer to stitch along the zipper guidelines, while others prefer to stitch an even distance from the basted seam on the right side of the fabric.

6. Remove the basting stitch the length of the zipper, and press.

LAPPED ZIPPER

The lapped zipper can be used in any area of the garment, but it is most frequently found in the side seam. The single lap covers the zipper very well.

1. Stitch, baste, and press the zipper seam as for a centered zipper.

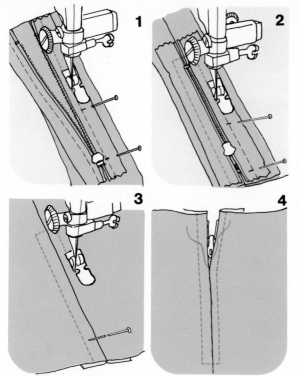

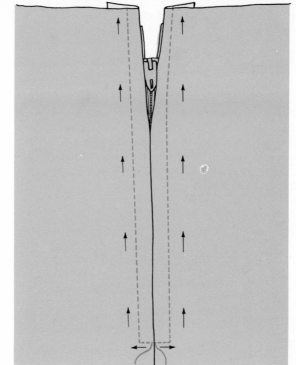

CENTERED-ZIPPER APPLICATION

1 Baste one side of the zipper to the seam allowance. The zipper tab should be facing the fabric, and the teeth should be directly on the seam.

2 Pin the closed zipper to all thicknesses of the garment. Starting at the top, sew along the stitching guide. Pivot, stitch across the bottom of the zipper, pivot again, and continue stitching up the other side.

3 You can also stitch the zipper from the right side of the garment. Mark and stitch each side an equal distance from the seam.

4 Remove the basting stitches to open the seam.

2. Open the zipper. Position it tab side down on the right-hand seam allowance. Pin the tape along the guideline. As you begin, be sure the zipper teeth line up on the seam.

3. Machine baste through the zipper tape and the seam allowance along the guideline.

4. Close the zipper and turn it so that the right side is up. This will make a fold along the seam

It can sometimes be difficult to stitch a smooth, even centered-zipper application. If this is the case, try stitching both sides of the zipper in the same direction—from the bottom up.

just sewn and the zipper teeth. Machine stitch close to the fold from the top to the bottom of the tape.

5. Place the zipper face down against the other seam allowance. Pin through all thicknesses of fabric: the tape, seam allowance, and garment. Stitch along the guideline. At the bottom of the zipper, pivot and stitch across to the seam. Pull the threads to the wrong side and tie.

6. Remove the basting stitches and press.

The fly-front zipper is a variation of the lapped application. The difference is that extra fabric is added to the seam allowance to make the lap wider. When using this type of zipper application, follow the directions in the guidesheet carefully. How you fold and stitch determines whether the lap opens on the right or left side.

classroom
experiences

Mastering sewing skills takes practice and experience. Sewing in a classroom with other students gives you and others many opportunities to learn from each other. For example, you can learn to apply a zipper or pocket, even if your project has neither, by watching another person do them and by seeing the results.

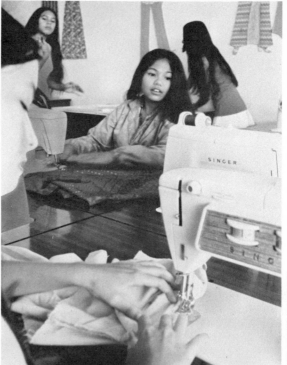

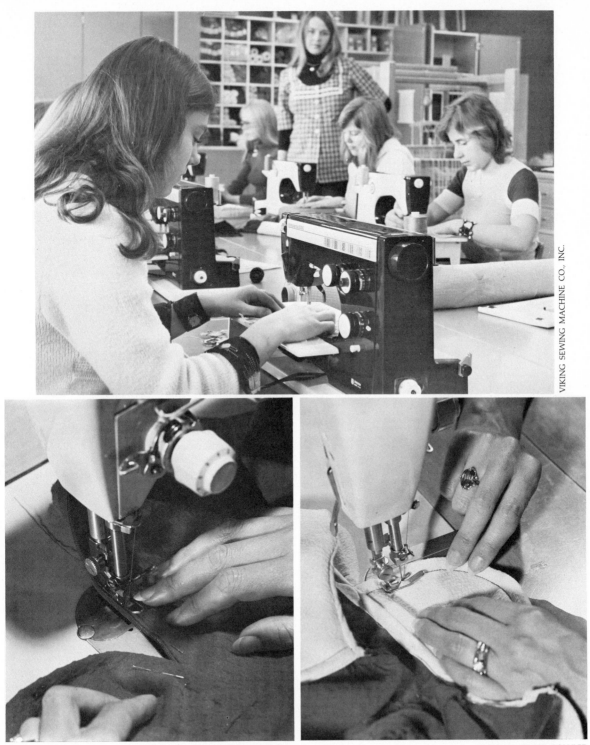

MASSEY JUNIOR COLLEGE   MASSEY JUNIOR COLLEGE

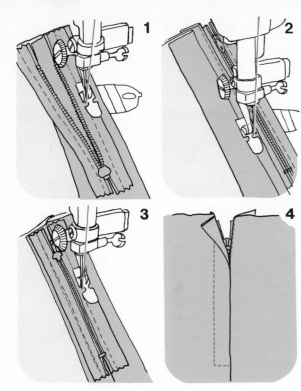

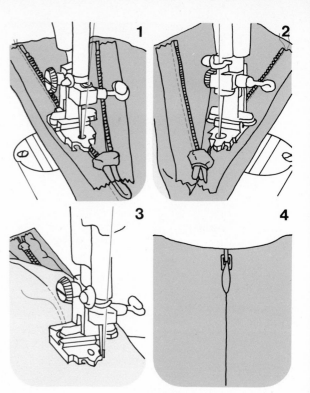

LAPPED-ZIPPER APPLICATION

1 Machine stitch the right-hand zipper tape to the right-hand seam allowance.

2 Close the zipper and turn it over so that the tab is up. Stitch along the fold created by the first row of stitching.

3 Return the zipper to the facedown position. Stitch the other side along the guide, pivot, and stitch across the bottom of the zipper.

4 Remove the basting stitches to open the seam.

INVISIBLE ZIPPER

The invisible zipper cannot be seen from the right side of the garment. The pull tab is the only way of telling it is there. This zipper is suitable for medium- and heavyweight fabrics, but not for sheer and lightweight fabrics.

1. Leave the entire zipper seam open. Machine baste each side of the garment on the seam line of the zipper opening.

INVISIBLE-ZIPPER APPLICATION

1 Machine baste the stitching lines on each side of the garment. Place the zipper on the right side of the garment with tab down and coils on the stitching line. Position the coil in the invisible-zipper foot and stitch from the top. Back stitch at the bottom for reinforcement.

2 With the zipper still open, place and stitch the other side of the zipper.

3 Close the zipper, and adjust the zipper foot so you can sew a seam. Beginning about ¼ inch [6 millimeters] above the bottom of the zipper, stitch the rest of the seam closed.

4 The zipper cannot be seen except for the tab at the top.

2. Place the opened zipper, tab side down, on the right side of the cloth. Allow about 1 inch [2.5 centimeters] from the top of the garment to the zipper teeth. This will provide enough room for a seam allowance to finish the edge above the zipper and for the zipper tab to lock in place and lie flat. Position the zipper teeth (coils) on the seam line.

3. Adjust the invisible-zipper foot so the machine needle goes into the hole at the center of the foot. Place the zipper coil in the groove of the foot with the teeth upright.

4. Machine stitch from the top of the tape to the tab at the bottom of the zipper. Back stitch to lock the stitches.

5. Place the other side of the zipper facedown on the right side of the other seam allowance. Stitch along the seam line with the zipper teeth held upright in the groove of the foot. Back stitch the end.

6. Close the zipper. Slide the foot to the left so that the needle is positioned in the right-hand notch. Put the seam allowances together and insert the needle $\frac{1}{4}$ inch [6 millimeters] above the bottom end of the zipper. Keep the needle slightly to the left of the zipper stitching and on the seam line. Stitch the seam.

7. Press the finished seam open.

EXPOSED ZIPPER

The exposed zipper is decorative since the teeth and tape are not concealed by any lap or seam. It is especially appropriate for casual knit clothes and can be used in an area where there is no seam. Boldly printed and large-teeth zippers, designed to add decoration to your garment, and conventional zippers work well with this application.

1. Place the zipper where you want it to be sewn on the garment. Mark the center line and bottom of the zipper on the right side of the garment.

2. Remove the zipper and machine baste $\frac{1}{4}$ inch [6 millimeters] around the markings to reinforce the area. Pivot to make square, even corners.

3. Cut through the center marking to within $\frac{1}{2}$ inch [12.7 millimeters] of the bottom stitching. Carefully clip diagonally to each corner.

4. Fold the edges along the stitching to the wrong side of the garment and press.

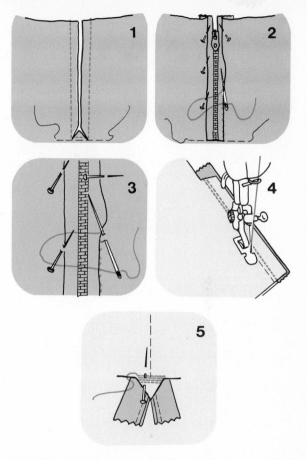

EXPOSED-ZIPPER APPLICATION

1 Mark center and bottom of zipper on garment. Machine stitch ¼ inch [6 millimeters] around markings, pivoting to make corners. Cut through center to ½ inch [12.7 millimeters] from bottom; then cut diagonally to corners.

2 Fold edges under along stitching. Center zipper in place and pin the folded edges to the tape. Slip-baste each side, beginning at the bottom.

3 To slip-baste the zipper in place, slip needle through fold, then through zipper, using even spaces and stitches.

4 Turn to the wrong side. Place the zipper, tape side down, in the machine and stitch close to the stitches done in the beginning. Stitch one side, then the other, beginning at the bottom each time.

5 Secure the bottom of the zipper by making several rows of stitches through the tape and small triangle.

When applying the zipper, be sure that it is even on each side of the opening. The amount of fabric covering the zipper teeth should also be even. If the stitches are too close to, or too far away from, the teeth, the zipper will not open and close easily. *Simplicity Pattern Co.*

5. Center the zipper in place and pin the folded edges to the tape. Slip-baste (see page 223) along the fold working from the bottom up on each side of the zipper.

6. Use a zipper foot to stitch on the wrong side of the garment.

7. Place the zipper, tape side down, on the machine and stitch right alongside the basting stitches made in step 2. Stitch one side, then the other, beginning at the bottom each time.

8. To secure the bottom of the zipper, stitch the fabric triangle to the zipper tape with several rows of stitches.

FACINGS

A facing is a piece of fabric used to finish a cut edge. Facings are found at the waists of pants, skirts, and shorts when a waistband is not used and at the armholes of sleeveless garments. Facings are also used to complete neck edges and front openings of some jackets, shirts, and dresses.

Some facings are cut from separate pattern pieces and stitched to the garment. Others are cut as part of a major garment section and folded over. Another type of facing is cut from a strip of bias fabric.

FACING A CURVED EDGE

1. Prepare the facing as directed on the guide-sheet. This usually includes sewing the facing pieces together and finishing the outer edges. Clean finishing (see page 214) is commonly used with facings made of light- and medium-weight fabrics.

2. Pin the facing to the garment edge with right sides together, matching notches and seams. Stitch.

3. *Grade*, or layer, the seam allowances by trimming them separately to different widths. For example, allow a $\frac{1}{4}$-inch [6-millimeter] seam allowance on the facing and a $\frac{1}{2}$-inch [12.7-millimeter] seam allowance on the garment.

4. Clip the seam allowance toward the stitching line at $\frac{1}{2}$-inch [12.7-millimeter] intervals. This helps the facing to lie flat when it is turned to the inside of the garment.

5. Press both seam allowances toward the facing.

6. From the facing side, stitch through the seam allowances and facing very close to the seam line. This is called *understitching*. It keeps the facing from turning to the right side of the garment.

7. Turn the facing to the inside of the garment. Press, being sure the seam line does not show. Tack the facing to the garment at the seams.

BIAS FABRIC FACING

The true bias is the stretchiest part of the fabric and can be ideal for finishing a curved edge.

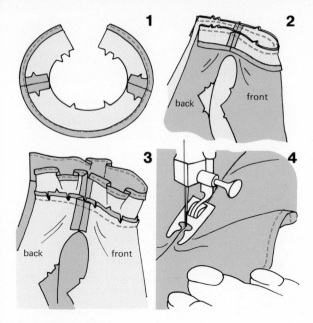

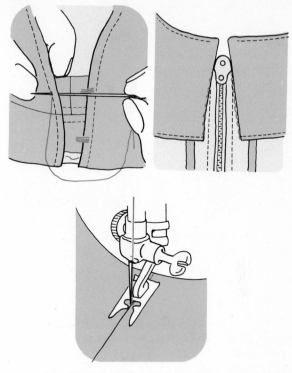

FACING AN EDGE

1 The facing is ready to be attached to the garment when all the pieces are sewn together and the outer edge is finished.

2 Pin and stitch the facing to the garment with right sides together. Match notches, seams, center markings, and any other markings.

3 Trim and grade seam allowances. Clip toward the stitching line as often as is necessary so that facing lies flat.

4 Understitch through the facing and seam allowances, very close to the seam line.

Find the true bias by folding the fabric diagonally to make the crosswise grain parallel to the lengthwise grain. A bias pattern piece may not be included in the pattern envelope. However, when a bias facing is needed, written instructions for making one are generally found on the guidesheet.

1. Begin by cutting the bias strips as directed on the guidesheet. Use fabric scraps left from cutting the garment. Sometimes, short bias strips must be sewn together to equal the length you need.

To help a facing lie flat, tack it in place at the seams, or slip-stitch the edges of an opening to the garment. You can also use the sewing machine to stitch in the seam, catching the facing underneath.

2. Turn under one end of the bias strip ½ inch [12.7 millimeters], and pin the bias strip to the garment edge with right sides together. Stitch. Allow ¼ inch [6 millimeters] of the bias fabric to lap over the beginning folded edge. Trim the excess.

3. Turn the outer edge of the bias facing under ¼ inch [6 millimeters] and press. Pin the folded edge to the inside over the stitching line. Hand or machine stitch in place.

COLLARS

If you visited a clothing store and began looking at neckline finishes, you would see a large variety of collar shapes and sizes. Some are rounded

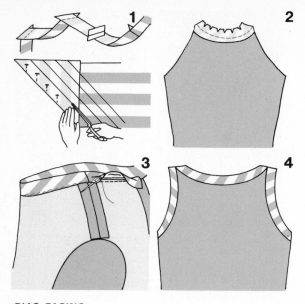

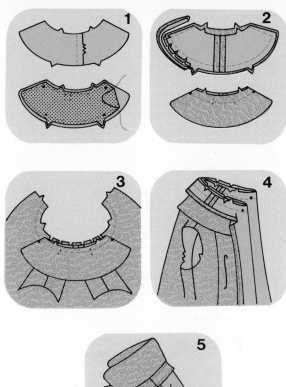

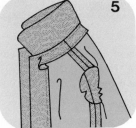

BIAS FACING

1 Cut bias strips from leftover fabric. Stitch the strips together for necessary length. Press any seam allowances open.

2 Stitch the bias tape to garment edge with right sides together. Allow for overlaps at garment's opening.

3 Trim seam allowance and clip to stitches. Encircle the raw edges with the bias tape. Fold under its outer edge and stitch the tape in place.

4 The bias tape smoothly wraps around the curved edges of the garment.

on the edges; others are pointed. Some stand up; others lie flat on the shoulders. Some are finished with a facing; others are finished with or without a band to conceal stitching and seam allowances.

Most collars are interfaced for shape and body. The interfacing is usually cut from the same pattern piece as the collar and attached to the wrong side of the upper collar. The upper collar is the part of the collar that can be seen when the garment is worn. The under collar is like a facing—it finishes the edges of the collar.

TWO-PIECE COLLAR CONSTRUCTION

1 Stitch together the sections of the under collar. Interface the upper collar.

2 With right sides together, match notches. Pin and stitch the two collar pieces together, leaving the neck edge open. Trim and clip the seam allowance and turn to right side. Press.

3 Baste across the neck edge of the collar. Pin collar to garment, matching notches and other construction markings. Clip garment to staystitching, where necessary, to relieve any strain. Baste.

4 Prepare facings and stitch to garment, as directed in pattern guidesheet.

5 The facing covers the raw edges of the collar. Tack the facing at the seams.

Many different styles of collars finish the garment and frame the face. All collars should be even on both sides and lie smoothly where they are attached to the garment. *Simplicity Pattern Co.*

MAKING A SIMPLE TWO-PIECE COLLAR

1. Cut and mark the collar sections carefully.
2. Interface the upper collar.
3. Pin the upper and under collar pieces with right sides together. Stitch along the outer edges on the seam line. Leave the neck edges open.
4. Trim the interfacing and seam allowances across the corners and around the seam edges. With heavy fabrics, grade the seam allowances to eliminate bulk.
5. Clip or notch the seam allowances, depending upon the type of edge and fabric. Turn the collar to the right side.
6. If you want the collar to lie flat, understitch the under collar along the seam line. Start and stop 1 inch [2.5 centimeters] from squared corners, or along the entire curve of a rounded collar. The row of understitching *will* show on the under collar. Topstitching can also be used to keep the collar flat and to decorate the garment.
7. Press the collar on the right side. Baste the collar neck edges together.
8. Matching notches, pin the collar to the neck edge of the right side of the garment.
9. Prepare the neck facings.
10. Place the facing over the collar with the right sides of the fabric together. Match notches and pin. Baste, if necessary. Stitch the neckline seam.
11. Grade, clip, and understitch the neck seam allowance to the facing.
12. Tack the facing to the shoulder seam allowances.

SLEEVES

The sleeve line of a garment varies according to the style. Sleeves can widen or narrow the shoulder line. They can differ in length, width, and fullness. They can have a variety of detail, such as darts, tucks, or gathers. They can be finished with a simple hem, a drawstring casing, or a fitted cuff.

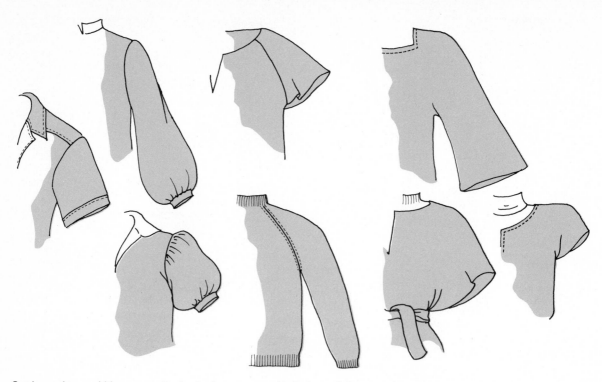

Set-in, raglan, and kimono are the basic sleeve types. Variations of these produce many different fashion looks.

Even with all these variations, there are only three basic sleeve types: the *kimono* sleeve, the *raglan* sleeve, and the *set-in* sleeve. These types are determined by how the sleeve is attached to the garment.

KIMONO AND RAGLAN

Kimono sleeves are cut as part of the front and back pattern sections of the whole garment. The sleeve and side seams are sewn with a continuous stitching line.

This one-step construction makes the kimono sleeve very easy to sew. The underarm area does need to be reinforced because it gets a great deal of stress. To strengthen the underarm area, clip the seam allowance to the stitching line every $\frac{1}{2}$ inch [12.7 millimeters] and then stitch the seam again. After clipping the seam allowance,

you can also reinforce the stress area by stitching bias tape over the seam.

Raglan sleeves are also part of the body of the garment. From the arm, the sleeves continue up over the shoulder to the neckline. They are attached in front and back by seams diagonal to the underarm. Usually a shoulder dart or seam is added for shape and fit.

Raglan sleeves are open and flat when they are attached to the front and back garment pieces. The sleeve and side seams are then stitched in one continuous operation, like the kimono sleeve. Reinforcing the underarm seam is important here, too.

SET-IN

Set-in sleeves are stitched where the arm and shoulder meet. They are found in tailored

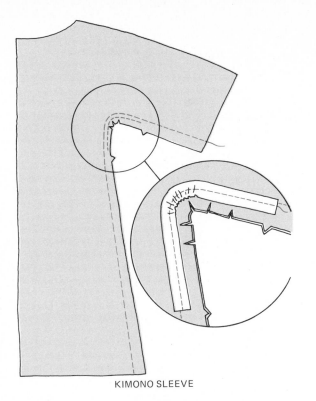

KIMONO SLEEVE

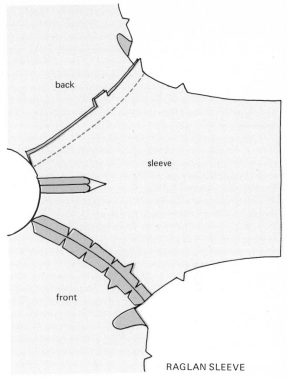

back

sleeve

front

RAGLAN SLEEVE

clothing because they give a straight, neat appearance. They are usually made separately and then attached to or "set in" to the body of the finished garment.

1. Make two rows of ease stitching in the seam allowance between the double and single notches, as directed by the guidesheet of your pattern.

2. Match the sides of the sleeve and stitch the seam. Press it open. Complete whatever seam finish is necessary for the type of fabric you are using. Turn the sleeve to the right side and slip it on to mark for length. You can sew the hem now or after the sleeve is attached to the garment.

3. Gently pull the two rows of ease stitching from both ends until the cap of the sleeve begins to take shape. The appearance must be smooth yet cupped to fit evenly into the armhole area.

4. With right sides together, match and pin together the underarm seams of the bodice and the

sleeve. Be sure the seam allowances are pinned open.

5. Match the single and double notches, and then the shoulder seam of the garment, to the marking at the top of the sleeve. Keep easing the sleeve where necessary. Place the pins close together at right angles to the stitching line with the pin heads in the seam allowance.

6. Begin stitching at one of the notches and continue around the entire opening. Stitch slowly and remove the pins as you stitch. You can reinforce the underarm area where there is a lot of stress by stitching a second time around.

7. Place the armhole seam over a tailor's ham. Using the point of the iron, press the seam allowance into the sleeve cap.

8. Clip the seam allowance in the underarm area to relieve tension.

The set-in sleeve can also be applied to the garment before side and sleeve seams are sewn.

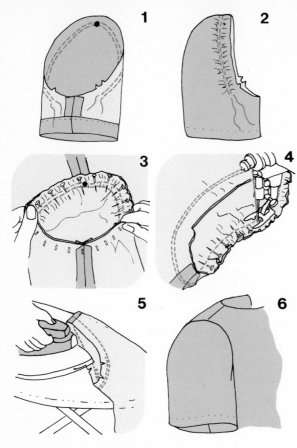

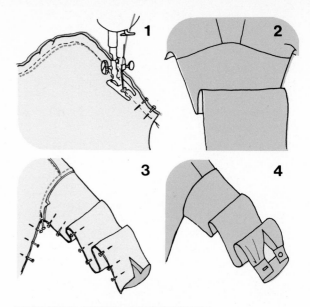

SET-IN SLEEVE CONSTRUCTION

1 Make two rows of ease stitching between notches on open sleeve. Stitch the sleeve seam and press seam allowance open. Mark and hem the bottom edge now or later.

2 Gather the sleeve cap by gently pulling the threads from both ends.

3 Pin the sleeve to the garment with right sides together. Match notches, seams, and other markings. Distribute the fullness, easing where necessary. Place pins close together to ensure an even fit.

4 Slowly stitch around the seam, removing pins as you sew. Reinforce the underarm area with a second row of stitches.

5 Press so that the seam allowances stay in the sleeve. Clip the seam allowance to relieve stress.

6 The finished sleeve should look neat and tailored.

OPEN-SEAM SLEEVE CONSTRUCTION

1 Prepare garment and sleeve as in set-in sleeve construction, but leave seams open. Ease the sleeve to fit the armhole area. Match and pin notches, construction markings, and edges. Stitch.

2 Press the seam allowance toward the shirt. You can then topstitch about ¼ inch [6 millimeters] from seam.

3 Stitch the sleeve and side seams in one operation. Clip underarm area.

4 Finished sleeve.

This method is usually used on tailored shirts. The shoulder seam can be topstitched.

1. Stitch the shoulder seams of the garment. Leave the side seams open.

2. Ease stitch the sleeve cap. Leave the seam open.

3. With right sides together, match and pin the notches, circles, and underarm edges. Evenly ease the sleeve to fit the shoulder and armhole area, and stitch.

4. To topstitch the shoulder seam, press the seam allowances toward the shirt, and then stitch them in place about ¼ inch [6 millimeters] from the seam.

5. Stitch the sleeve and side seams in one operation.

WAISTBANDS AND SLEEVE CUFFS

A waistband and a sleeve cuff are made and sewn to the garment in a similar manner. Both types of bands, waist and cuff, may be made from one piece of fabric folded in half or two pieces seamed together. Both can be interfaced to add body and to prevent stretching.

1. Cut and mark the waistband or cuff as directed on the pattern and guidesheet.

2. Pin and stitch the interfacing to the wrong side of the fabric. If the fabric is to be folded, interface only to the fold. The interfacing should be on the top piece of the finished band. If the band is made from two pieces of fabric, interface only the top piece.

3. With right sides together, pin the band to the garment edge, matching all markings carefully. The band should be long enough to overlap and to make finished edges at both ends. The garment may have to be eased or gathered to fit the band. Stitch the seam.

4. Finish the ends by folding the band in half with the right sides of the fabric together. Pin and stitch the extensions. One end of the band will turn at the garment edge. The other end may turn at the edge or beyond it for overlap according to the pattern design. The overlap provides a smooth closing and a place to put a fastener. If necessary, clip the curves and trim the seam allowances, especially at the corners, so the band will have neat, angular ends.

5. Turn the band to the right side, being sure that corners are pointed and curves lie flat. Press.

6. Turn the unfinished edge under along the seam line. Pin and hand stitch it in place. Press again.

The band may also be finished with machine stitching. If the fabric is bulky or does not fray, do not fold the unfinished edge under. Instead, pin it flat over the inside seam line. Then stitch from the right side of the garment. If you want the stitching to show, sew along the bottom edge of the waistband. To sew the waistband in place

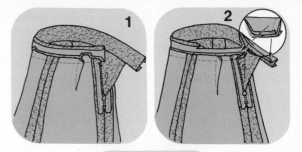

ATTACHING A WAISTBAND

1 Pin band to garment, matching notches, seams, and other markings. Stitch.

2 With right sides together, fold band in half. Stitch the edges.

3 Turn band to right side. Fold under seam allowance and slip-stitch in place. Attach the recommended fasteners.

without the stitches showing on the right side, stitch directly on the seam line.

7. Complete the band by sewing fasteners as indicated by the pattern.

POCKET KNOW-HOW

Pockets can be both useful and decorative in many different areas of garments. Some pockets are hidden in seams. An example is the pocket set into the side seams of slacks, dresses, and other garments. Other pockets, like those on trousers and jeans, add a decorative line from the waist across the hip to the side seam. Still other pockets are made by slitting the garment, then

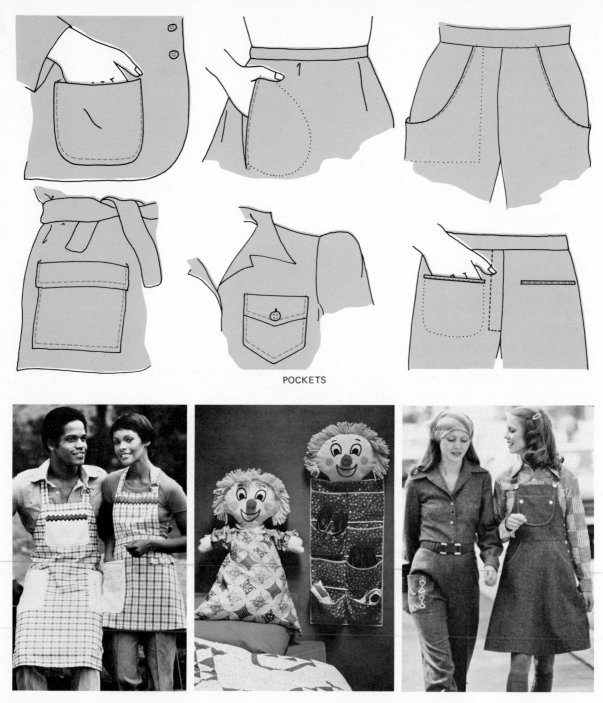

POCKETS

Pockets are used for many purposes. Those that are straight and even give a look of quality to an item. *Butterick Fashion Marketing Co.* (**left and center**); *Simplicity Pattern Co.* (**right**)

binding the cut edges, and lining. Pockets that are sewn on the outside of the garment are called patch pockets. They can be stitched by machine or hand sewn onto the garment. Patch pockets can be pointed, square, rounded, or just about any decorative shape. Thus, they are the most popular type of pocket found on clothing.

Pockets must be carefully sewn if they are to enhance the appearance of the garment. When your pattern has pockets, mark them and their position on the garment accurately. The guidesheet will give you step-by-step instructions for their application.

If your pattern does not have pockets and you would like it to, add patch pockets. Decide what size and shape you would like the pockets to be, add a seam allowance to three sides, and 1 to 2 inches [2.5 to 5.0 centimeters] to the top for the hem. Make a paper pattern. Mark the stitching lines around the three sides, and the fold line for the hem.

THE PATCH POCKET

1. Turn the upper edge $\frac{1}{4}$ inch [6 millimeters] to the inside. Stitch along the folded edge.
2. With right sides together, fold along the hem line. Sew the pocket through the hem and along the stitching line of the unfinished edge. This row of stitching finishes the hem and helps the cut edges to fold over evenly.

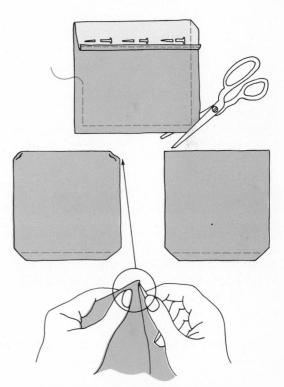

For sharp corners when you turn the pocket hem, use a pin to gently pick out the folded-in fabric.

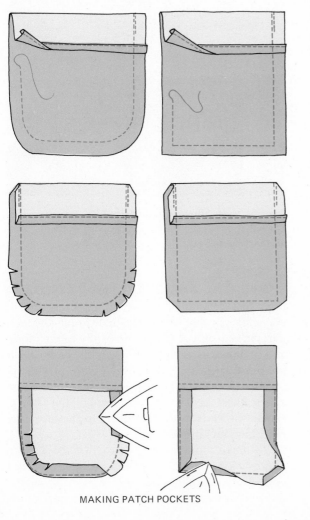

MAKING PATCH POCKETS

3. To eliminate bulk in the hem, trim the seam allowance and cut diagonally into the corners.

4. Turn the hem right side out. Fold and press the seam allowances to the inside, so that the line of stitching does not show on the outside of the pocket.

5. The seam allowance of pockets can be further treated to eliminate bulk. Corners can be *mitered*, or trimmed and folded at an angle to make a square finish, and rounded edges can be notched as in finishing a curved seam. Both of these steps will help you to make patch pockets with smooth, even edges that will lie flat when sewn to your garment.

6. Pin the pocket to the right side of the garment and stitch it in place.

CASINGS

A casing is used to hold an elastic or a fabric tie. Casings are found at the bottoms of sleeves, at the tops of skirts or pants that do not have waistbands or facings, and at the waistlines of dresses, jackets, or shirts. Casing stitching shows on the right side of the garment. When the casing is threaded with the elastic or fabric drawstring, the garment looks gathered. A casing can be made with the garment fabric or with a bias seam binding.

GARMENT-EDGE CASING
Garment-edge casing serves as a hem or edge finish. It is usually made by turning a hem on the garment edge.

1. Determine the width of the casing you need by measuring the width of the elastic or drawstring which will be threaded through it and by adding $\frac{1}{4}$ inch [6 millimeters].

2. Turn the raw edge of the garment under about $\frac{1}{8}$ inch [3 millimeters]. Measure the width of the casing and fold with the wrong sides of the fabric together. Press the two folded edges.

3. Machine stitch through all thicknesses of fabric on the two folded edges. Leave an opening to insert the elastic or drawstring.

Straight, even stitching is important to casings so the drawstring or elastic can be easily pulled through. *Simplicity Pattern Co.*

4. If elastic is used, cut it $\frac{1}{2}$ inch [12.7 millimeters] shorter than the part of the body it will encircle. To thread the elastic through the casing, pin one end of the elastic firmly to the fabric and attach a safety pin to the other end. Push the pin and elastic through the casing, stretching the elastic so the ends meet. Do not let the elastic twist as it is pulled through the casing. Fasten the ends to each other or to the fabric by machine stitching.

5. To make a drawstring, you will need a piece of fabric long enough to fit and tie snugly around your body. It should be twice as wide as the finished drawstring plus seam allowances. Sew

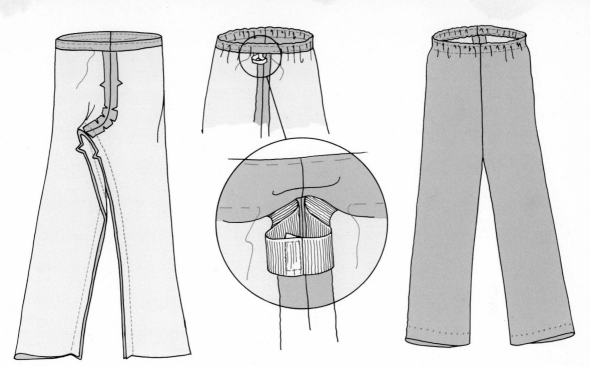

GARMENT-EDGE CASING

the right sides together, leaving an opening at the center. Trim the seam allowances. Turn the fabric by pushing an unsharpened pencil from each sewn end through the middle opening. You can also use a *bodkin*, a special sewing tool for turning casings, belts, and loops. Remove the pencil, press, and hand stitch the opening closed. Insert the drawstring and thread it through the casing.

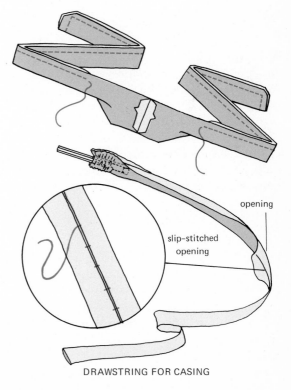

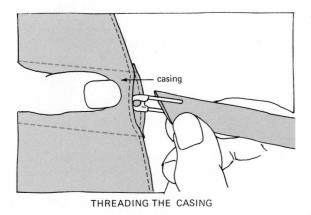

THREADING THE CASING

DRAWSTRING FOR CASING

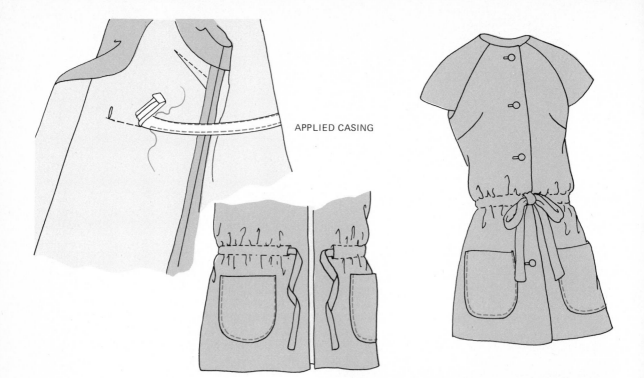

APPLIED CASING

APPLIED CASING

An applied casing is positioned away from the garment's edge. A good choice of fabric for the casing should be one that is more lightweight than the garment's fabric so the casing will gather easily without adding bulk. Bias seam binding and bias strips of fabric are recommended, since they conform to the curved areas, such as the waist and wrist, where applied casings are usually found. The casing should be slightly wider than the elastic or drawstring that will be threaded through it, so the stitches will not break.

1. Mark the position of the casing on the fabric, as shown on the pattern and guidesheet.
2. Pin the bias binding or fabric over the markings. Turn the raw edges of the material under.
3. Machine stitch along each folded edge.
4. Thread elastic or a drawstring through the casing.

Knit garments, like T-shirts, move with the body. They are comfortable and are often used for sportswear. *Wrangler Sportswear*

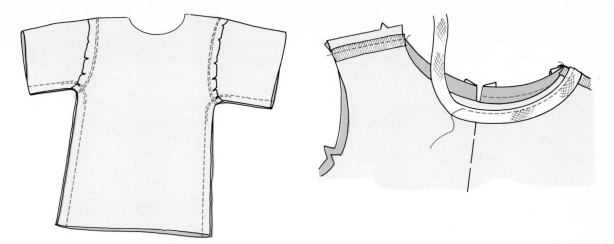

For knits, two rows of stitching strengthen the seams; bias tape on curves prevents stretching.

THINGS TO KNOW ABOUT SEWING KNITS

Zigzag and special stretch stitches are best for sewing on knit fabrics. If you have a machine that sews straight stitches only, you can still sew knit garments.

When you sew knit fabrics with a straight stitch machine, stretch the fabric slightly as the stitches are being made. When the seam is relaxed, there will be some give between the stitches. This keeps the stitches from breaking easily when the fabric is stretched.

Sewing a second seam in the seam allowance right next to the first will add strength to the seam. This is especially good for stress areas, such as sleeve and crotch seams.

Sometimes you will not want stretch in certain areas of a garment. You can reinforce shoulders, necklines, and waist seams with ribbon, seam binding, or bias tape.

Many knit garments are made with little construction detail. This is because added detail has a tendency to add bulk. Eliminating such bulk is necessary in areas where seams and darts meet other seams.

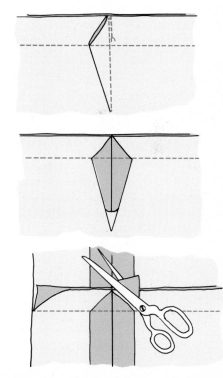

To eliminate bulk, slash darts open and clip diagonally the intersecting seam allowances.

1. Visit a fabric or notion store to do a comparison study of zippers. Select different brands and types of zippers. Make a chart showing the types, lengths, and prices of each brand.

2. Interview a local dressmaker or tailor. Find out how the person became interested in his or her job and what training and skills are needed for the job. Ask what kinds of sewing tasks are done—alterations, fittings, repairs, or making complete garments. What are the costs of these services? Report your findings to the class.

3. Demonstrate how to grade, clip, and understitch a facing. Explain when these steps are done, and why.

4. Design a bulletin board showing different types of sleeves and collars. Use drawings, photographs, or magazine clippings of current clothing styles. Label the types of sleeves and collars on each.

5. Make a sample pattern of a patch pocket. Then, using scrap fabric, make the pocket according to the directions found in this chapter. Try making pockets of different shapes. Triangles, hearts, and circles are just a few shapes you can experiment with.

6. Sew an applied casing onto a piece of fabric using bias seam binding or bias strips of fabric. Thread a drawstring or piece of elastic through the casing.

7. Make samples of some of the sewing techniques used with knit or stretch fabrics. Explain when and where you would use these techniques when making garments.

● DO YOU KNOW

casing	patch pocket
facing	raglan sleeve
grade, or layer	set-in sleeve
invisible zipper	slot, or centered, zipper
kimono sleeve	trim
lapped zipper	understitch

those important last steps

After reading this chapter, you should be able to:

- *Discuss the decorative and practical uses of fasteners.*

- *Apply buttons, snaps, and hooks and eyes to a garment.*

- *Determine the correct size machine buttonholes for your buttons and mark their placement on a garment.*

- *Mark and prepare a hem for finishing.*

- *Explain several ways to finish a hem edge.*

- *Use a variety of hand stitches for sewing hems.*

- *Discuss the importance of caring for your clothing.*

THE FASTENERS

Fasteners have a practical origin. They were invented to hold garment openings closed. While zippers are relatively new, buttons, snaps, and hooks have been used as fasteners for centuries. They are still popular, practical, and, quite often, decorative as well.

Thanks to stretchable synthetic fibers and knit fabrics, many garments do not require fasteners. However, most garments do require at least one. The types of fasteners used are determined by the garment's design and where they are placed. The recommended fasteners for your pattern are listed on the pattern envelope with other notions.

BUTTONS AND BUTTONHOLES

Buttons should be selected to complement the design and fabric of your garment. There are

BUTTERICK FASHION MARKETING CO.

SIMPLICITY PATTERN CO.

BUTTERICK FASHION MARKETING CO.

SIMPLICITY PATTERN CO.

SIMPLICITY PATTERN CO.

Taking care in completing your project will ensure a garment that is not only well made but looks and wears well, too.

Buttons can be decorative, as well as functional, when selected to contrast with the color of an outfit. *Wrangler Sportswear*

two types of buttons. Those with a little stem-like loop on the back are called *shank* buttons. Those with holes going through them are called *sew-through* buttons. Both types come in many different sizes and shapes and are made from many different materials. Wood, leather, ivory, plastic, and metal are but a few materials that are carved, molded, or shaped into buttons.

If your pattern requires buttons as fasteners, it will also require something to fasten them to—buttonholes. The location of the button-holes should be transferred to your garment along with all the other markings from the tissue pattern. Thread markings are more durable than chalk or pin markings, in this case. Check to be sure that there is equal spacing between each buttonhole, especially if you had to make a length alteration in the area. Also measure the distance from the buttonhole end to the center line or edge of the garment. The distance should be the same for each buttonhole. It is important that buttonholes be straight and evenly spaced because they almost always show.

The length of the buttonhole is determined by the size of the button you are using. Measure and add the diameter and thickness of the button. This total will make a buttonhole long enough to fit the button and to allow for ease.

sew-through

shank

BUTTONS

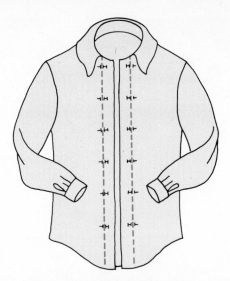

Button and buttonhole markings should be evenly spaced along the center line of the garment.

To find the correct size buttonhole for a very round or thick button, wrap a narrow strip of fabric or paper around the button. Secure the paper or fabric with a pin and slip it off the button. Fold the strip in half and measure the length from the fold to the pin.

Buttons and buttonholes for loosely woven and knit garments can pull and stretch out of shape. To prevent this, reinforce by interfacing the whole button and buttonhole area or by adding small patches of interfacing or closely woven fabric under each button and buttonhole.

There are two types of buttonholes: *worked* and *bound*. Worked buttonholes can be made by

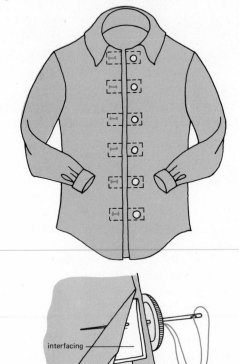

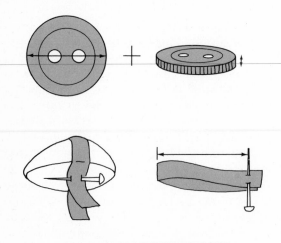

MEASURING FOR BUTTONHOLE SIZE

REINFORCING BUTTON AND BUTTONHOLE AREAS

242

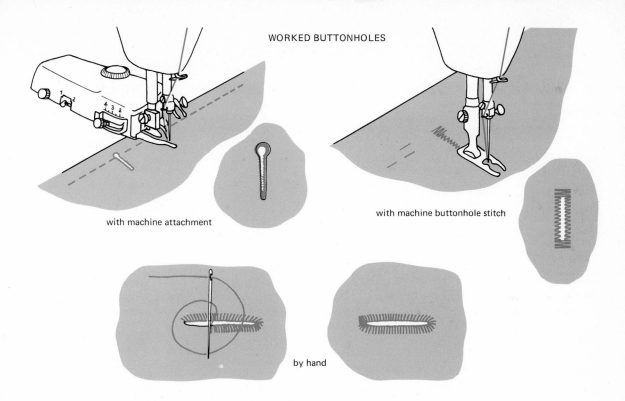

with machine attachment

with machine buttonhole stitch

by hand

hand or by machine. They are more popular than bound buttonholes on sportswear and casual clothing and are easier to do. Bound buttonholes are made with a combination of hand and machine sewing. However, they are most often referred to as handmade buttonholes. Bound buttonholes are becoming rare on garments because of the amount of time and effort needed to make them.

Most buttonholes are the worked type. There is a sewing machine attachment for making these buttonholes. With such an attachment, you can accurately make the same size buttonholes over and over again. Some newer models of zigzag machines do not even require the attachment. Instead, the zigzag stitch itself is set to the desired buttonhole size. The garment is not cut to open machine-worked buttonholes until after they are made.

To make worked buttonholes by hand, cut the buttonhole the desired length, then blanket stitch the raw edges of the opening to keep them from raveling and tearing. This method is best suited to soft or delicate fabrics.

Buttons are sewn to the garment after the buttonholes are made. To place the buttons, pin the garment closed, matching the center lines. Put a pin through the opening of the buttonhole at the end nearest the garment's edge. The button should be sewn at this mark.

The shank on a button allows the fabric around it to lie smoothly when the garment is buttoned. This is especially true on garments made of fabric that is thicker than the button. The shank should be as long as the buttonhole area is thick, plus $\frac{1}{8}$ inch [3 millimeters] for ease. To make a thread shank for a sew-through button, place a pin, toothpick, or matchstick on top of the button. Stitch over this as you sew the button in place.

To sew on a button, use double strands of regular thread or a single strand of buttonhole

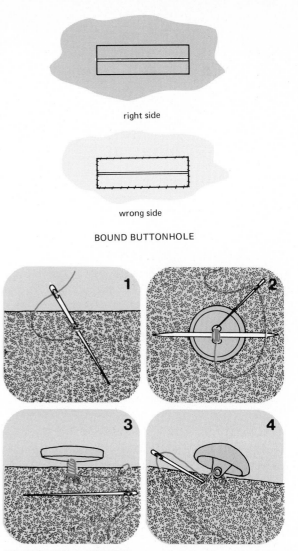

right side

wrong side

BOUND BUTTONHOLE

For horizontal buttonholes, slip a pin through the end nearest the edge of the garment. For vertical buttonholes, insert a pin through the top end.

twist or heavy-duty thread. Secure the thread to the wrong side of the garment with a couple of small stitches. Then bring the thread up to the right side and go through one of the holes in the button. Go back down to the wrong side through another hole, crossing over the pin, toothpick, matchstick, or whatever you are using to create the thread shank. Continue stitching like this until the button is secure—four to six times is usually enough. End on the inside of the garment. Remove the shank-making object and lift the button so that extra thread is then between the button and the fabric. Bring the needle back up to the right side but do not go through the button. Wind the thread around the stitches under the button to form the shank. Take the needle back to the wrong side of the fabric and secure the thread with two or three small stitches. After sewing on a button by machine, leave enough thread to wrap the stitches.

TO SEW ON A BUTTON

1 Secure the thread when you begin and end by making a couple of small stitches in the wrong side of the garment. Place the button, and bring the needle to the right side of the garment.

2 Sew over a toothpick, a matchstick, or a pin to make a thread shank on a sew-through button.

3 Remove the matchstick and wind the thread around the stitches under the button.

4 A shank-type button is sewn with small stitches going through the shank and into the fabric.

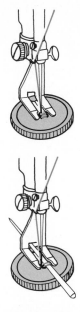

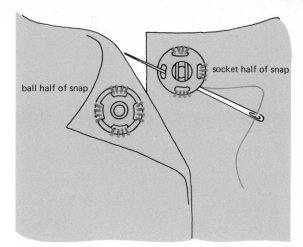

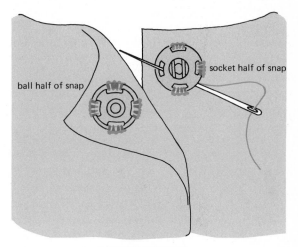

SEWING ON SNAPS

TO SEW ON BUTTONS BY MACHINE

1 Use the special button-foot attachment and follow instructions in your machine manual.

2 To make a thread shank, place a machine needle or toothpick in the groove of the button foot before stitching.

A button that already has a shank does not usually need an additional thread shank. Sew this type of button in place with small stitches going through the shank and into the fabric. As you start and finish each button, secure the thread as described for sew-through buttons.

SNAPS

Snap fasteners are best for fastening overlapping edges that have little strain. They are available in a variety of sizes to suit different weights of fabric. Heavy fabrics require large snaps, while thin, lightweight fabrics need small ones.

A snap consists of two halves. One half has a ball that fits into the socket of the other half. The socket half of the snap is always sewn on the right side of the garment section closest to the body. The ball half, however, is sewn on first to the wrong side of the overlap. Mark the position of the snap and then secure the thread to the fabric. Make small stitches, picking up one or two threads of fabric, as you go through the holes of the snap. The stitches should not be seen on the right side of the garment. A blanket stitch can also be used to hold the snap securely. When going from one hole to the next, guide the thread under the snap. After stitching the ball section in place, overlap the garment edges and stick a pin through the center of the snap to mark the location of the socket section.

The socket half of the snap is sewn in place the same way as the ball half.

Some snaps are held in place with tiny prongs or teeth rather than with stitches. These snaps are used on sportswear and children's clothing. They are stronger and larger than the sewn-on type. Because they usually show on the right side of the garment, these snaps are also made to be decorative. They should be applied according to the manufacturer's instructions.

HOOKS AND EYES

Hooks and eyes are more secure than snaps in areas, such as waistbands and neck edges, where there is some strain. Sometimes hooks and eyes are used together with snaps for added hold. Like snaps, there are many sizes of hooks and eyes. The shape of the hook is standard, but eyes are available in round and straight variations. When two edges overlap, such as on a waistband, a straight eye is used. If the two edges just meet, a round eye serves the purpose better.

The hook is sewn first to the side that overlaps or to the right-hand side of the closure if there is no overlap. It is placed about $\frac{1}{8}$ inch [3 millimeters] from the edge of the opening so that it cannot be seen. Small stitches or blanket stitches are worked around each of the loops to hold it securely in place. Keep the stitches from coming through to the right side of the garment. Slip the needle through the fabric to the curved end of the hook. Secure the end of the hook with a few stitches.

Mark the position of the eye and put it in place. Straight eyes are sewn to the top side of the underlap; round eyes to the bottom side, slightly extended beyond the edge. The eyes are sewn in the same manner as the hooks.

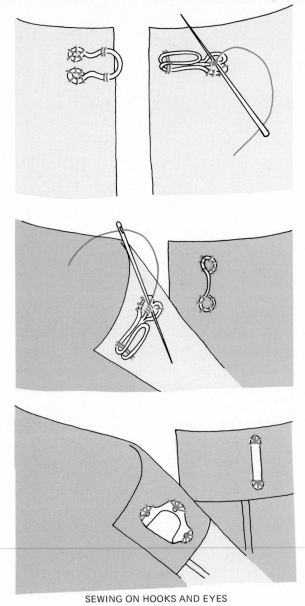

SEWING ON HOOKS AND EYES

THE HEM

Few things affect the final appearance of a garment as much as the hem does. It may seem strange, but most people do not notice the well-made hem, only the one that is poorly done. Actually, that is just the way it should be—a hem should not be obvious. Whether part of a skirt, a pair of pants, a shirt, a jacket, or a coat, a hem should be smooth, even in width, and sewn with almost invisible stitches.

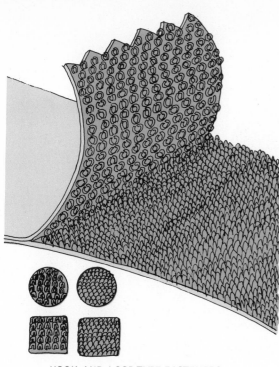

HOOK-AND-LOOP TYPE FASTENERS

MARKING

You should be ready to mark the hem when all other construction is complete and fasteners have been attached. Press the garment and let it hang overnight. This will allow the garment to fall smoothly into place and help prevent the hem from stretching after it is marked and sewn. Wear any accessories, such as a belt or jacket, and the type and height of shoe to be worn with the garment, when marking the hem. This will give you a clear picture of what the finished garment will look like.

Before you begin, turn up the hem across the front and side of the garment to get an idea of where the finished hem should be. Study yourself in a full-length mirror to check the overall proportions of the garment. Hem lengths should be stylish, but they should also be right for the person wearing them.

The hemlines of dresses, skirts, pants, or coats are usually parallel to the floor. Even with a

Fashion trends may change the length of a skirt or pair of slacks, but a neat, even hemline is always in style. *Simplicity Pattern Co.*

MARKING A HEM

chalk-type hem marker, it can be very difficult to mark an even hem on yourself. It is much easier to have someone else mark for you. You should stand still while the other person moves around you. Use a yardstick or hem marker to mark the hemline. Make chalk marks or place pins parallel to the floor and about 2 inches [5 centimeters] apart. Fold on the hemline and pin the hem allowance to the inside of the garment. Check the finished length carefully. If the hemline is even, parallel to the floor, and you like the overall look, you are ready to finish the hem.

For garments such as blouses, shirts, or jackets, and for garment sleeves, mark the hem at the depth indicated on the pattern. Use a ruler or sewing gauge and pins or chalk to mark the depth of the hem. Pin the hem in place and try on the garment. You may have to adjust the hem to get the garment to hang evenly on your body. Again, check in the mirror for the overall effect.

PREPARING THE HEM

Pin, baste, or press along the folded hem edge to keep the hemline even and in place while you

248

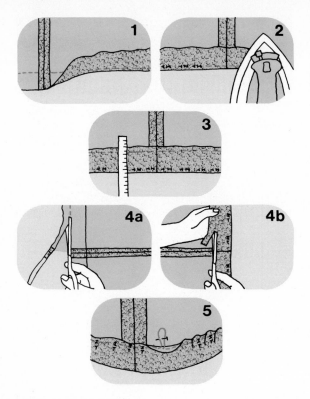

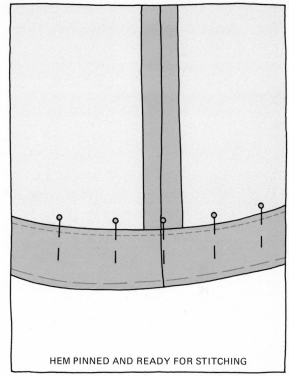

HEM PINNED AND READY FOR STITCHING

PREPARING THE HEM

1 Fold on the hemline, matching seams on the garment and hem allowance.

2 Pin, baste, or press along the fold to keep the hemline even and in place.

3 Measure and trim the hem allowance to an even depth.

4 Trim carefully
    a hem allowance flat on a table.
    b hem allowance held in one hand.

5 Ease any fullness in a curved hem.

work on it. Do not press if you want a soft, rolled look to your hem. Be sure to match the seams on the hem allowance with the seams on the garment.

The hem allowance should be an even depth all around the garment. If it is not even or if it is too deep, it should be trimmed. Measure and mark the desired depth from the hemline toward the cut edge of the garment. When trimming, hold the hem allowance flat on a table or over the inside of your hand. This will help to prevent accidentally cutting through to the garment.

How deep you make the hem depends on the type of garment and fabric and on your personal preference. The hem could be as narrow as $\frac{1}{4}$ inch [6 millimeters] for blouses, shirts, and swimwear or as deep as 6 inches [15.2 centimeters] for dresses, robes, and for making cuffs on slacks. Check your pattern to see what hem depth is recommended. Consider the weight of your fabric and the shape of the garment at the hemline. If the fabric is heavy, you will have to make the hem deep enough to hold the weight of the hem. If it is not deep enough, the hem edge could pull, ripple, or sag. If the hem area is curved, some fullness or gathering will occur in the hem allowance. This type of fullness can

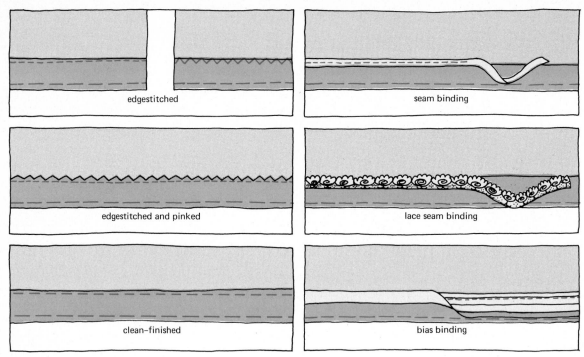

edgestitched	seam binding
edgestitched and pinked	lace seam binding
clean-finished	bias binding

HEM FINISHES

often be reduced or eliminated by making a narrow hem. Generally though, 1 $\frac{1}{2}$- to 3-inch [3.8- to 7.6-centimeter] hems can be used for most garments.

When a curved hem is *turned* (folded to the inside of the garment along the hemline), the fabric ripples where the hem allowance is fuller than the garment. This fullness can be eased to make a smooth, even hem with the same technique used for easing and gathering seams.

Sew a row of machine stitching $\frac{1}{4}$ inch [6 millimeters] from the cut edge. Pin the seams of the hem allowance to the garment seams. Continue to pin, dividing the distance between the seams as you work. Use a pin to pull the thread wherever there is extra fullness. Gather and distribute the hem allowance until it lies flat on the garment.

If your fabric will shrink, use a steam iron to press out some of the hem fullness. Place a press cloth or piece of brown paper between the gar- ment and the hem to prevent any chance of shine or press marks. Use a gentle up-and-down motion, letting the steam penetrate without putting pressure on the fabric. Allow the hem to dry completely and cool before lifting or moving it. If you do not, the hem edge might stretch and the fullness return.

Another method of taking out fullness in the hem is by making little tucks as you pin the hem to the garment. This is not always as satisfactory as easing because it can create bulk that may show through to the right side of the garment. However, it can be used with lightweight fabrics and hems that have only a small amount of fullness.

FINISHING THE RAW EDGE
If your fabric ravels, the cut edge of the hem will have to be finished. The same techniques used for finishing seams and facings are used to finish hems. Again, the method you select will depend

on the style of the garment, the fabric, and your personal preference.

If the fabric is firmly woven and does not tend to ravel, the hem can be **edgestitched** or **edgestitched and pinked.** If the fabric will ravel, the hem edge can be machine stitched and finished with an overcast or a zigzag stitch. These hem finishes can be especially useful for blouses and shirts. They make a flat hem that will not bulge or show through when tucked into a skirt or slacks.

Clean finishing is best suited for lightweight, firmly woven fabrics. Heavy fabrics and curved edges would be too bulky for this method. It is also best used with a fairly straight hem, such as a blouse or pant hem, rather than a curved hem. You clean-finish a hem the same way a seam edge is clean-finished—stitch $\frac{1}{4}$ inch [6 millimeters] from the raw edge, fold the edge under on the stitching line, and stitch a second time, close to the folded edge.

A straight **seam binding** or hem tape works well on medium or heavyweight fabrics. It is easiest to apply to straight edges, but it can be used without too much difficulty on slightly curved hems. Pin or place the seam tape on the hem at least $\frac{1}{4}$ inch [6 millimeters] from the raw edge. Be careful to cover any ease stitches. Machine stitch close to the edge of the tape.

Lace binding and **stretch lace binding** are very popular, since they are easy to apply, lack the bulkiness of either straight or bias seam tape, and make an attractive hem finish. Use either with light- or medium-weight fabrics and stretch fabrics. Place the center of the lace $\frac{1}{4}$ inch [6 millimeters] below the raw edge of the hem. Pin in place and machine stitch. A straight stitch is adequate for sewing lace tape to woven fabrics. Use a zigzag stitch to allow the lace to stretch along with knit fabrics and to maintain the cut edge of fabrics that ravel easily.

You may need the give of a **bias tape** rather than a straight seam tape to finish the edge of a curved hem or stretchy fabric. Because bias tape itself can be bulky, it should only be used

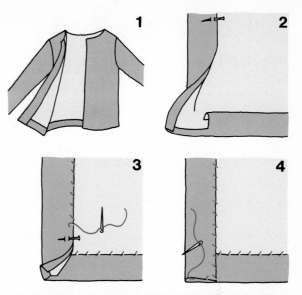

TO ELIMINATE BULK IN OVERLAPPING CORNERS

1 Determine the hemline.

2 Trim the hem allowance where the facing overlaps it.

3 Stitch the hem and facing in place.

4 Stitch the bottom of the facing closed along the hemline.

on medium- and heavyweight fabrics. To apply, open the fold along one side of the bias tape and pin the right side of the tape to the right side of the hem edge. Have the raw edges of both the tape and the hem even. Machine stitch in the fold line of the tape. The rest of the tape will return to its original fold and cover the raw hem edges.

The overlapping hem corners of such garments as skirts, shirts, jackets, and coats also require some special handling. Since there are at least four layers of fabric at each corner, bulk can be a problem. Mark, fold, and baste or press the hem in place. Trim the hem allowance where the facing overlaps it. Stitch the hem in place and slip-stitch (see page 255) the lower edges of the facing to it.

pride in having
made it yourself

BUTTERICK FASHION MARKETING CO.

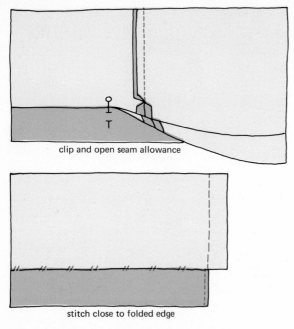

clip and open seam allowance

stitch close to folded edge

SPECIAL HANDLING OF PLEAT SEAMS

Garments with pleats added to a seam, like those in the backs of jackets, often require special finishing to eliminate bulk and to allow the hemline to lie flat. This can be done by trimming or clipping and pressing open the pleat seam. Press the seam in the fold of the pleat to one side. Clip into the seam allowance $\frac{1}{2}$ inch [12.7 millimeters] above the hemline. Press the seam open below this clip. If the fabric is heavy, you might also have to trim the seam allowances. Finish the hem and stitch in place. First press the pleat flat and then fold and press the pleat in place. If the pleat will not lie flat, stitch through the inside fold of the pleat. Be sure to stitch close to the folded edge through all thicknesses of the hem.

SECURING THE HEM

Whether made by hand or by machine, hem stitches should be almost invisible. When hand stitching, use a thimble to help you control the needle and to protect your finger. To begin, cut off a length of thread about 18 inches [45 centimeters] long. Cut the thread at an angle to make it easier to pass it through the eye of the needle. Most hand sewing requires a single thread and a fine needle. Most hand stitches are done from right to left. If you are left-handed, reverse the direction.

Use a small back stitch or knot to secure the thread in the hem edge. Keep your stitches evenly spaced and loose so they do not pucker the fabric. There are a number of hand stitches that can be used to hold a hem in place. Select one suitable to your fabric, the type of hem finish, and your own skill and preference.

The **hemming stitch** is used on clean-finished hems and hems finished with seam tape. To make a *slant* hemming stitch, secure the thread in the hem edge and take a tiny stitch by picking up one or two threads in the garment. Bring the needle up diagonally through the finished edge of the hem allowance. The thread will lie across the hem on a slant. Take another stitch in the garment about $\frac{1}{4}$ to $\frac{3}{8}$ inch [6 to 9 millimeters] to the left of the first stitch and repeat across the hem.

To make a *vertical* hemming stitch, secure the thread end and bring the thread up through the hem edge. Take a tiny stitch in the garment directly under where the thread came up through the hem edge. The thread will lie straight up and down across the hem. Slant the needle to the left and bring it through the hem edge $\frac{1}{4}$ to $\frac{3}{8}$ inch [6 to 9 millimeters] away from the first stitch. Repeat across the hem.

The **slip stitch** is used on hems that have been clean-finished or finished with bias tape. It makes a very secure and neat hem since the thread is hidden and protected in the fold of the hem edge. Secure the thread in the fold and pick up one or two threads in the garment so that a small vertical stitch is made. Place the needle into the fold of the hem directly above where the needle comes up out of the garment. Slide the needle through the tunnel formed by the fold for a distance of about $\frac{1}{2}$ inch [12.7 millimeters]. Bring the needle out of the fold and back down into the garment to make another stitch. Continue across the hem.

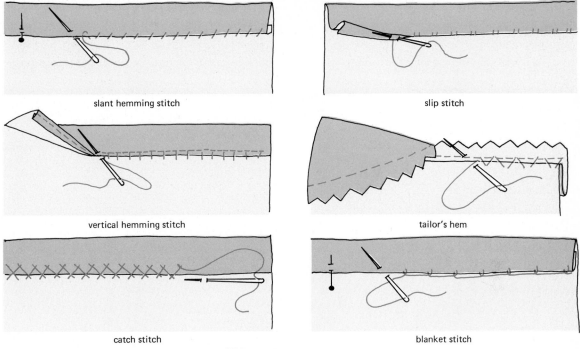

slant hemming stitch

slip stitch

vertical hemming stitch

tailor's hem

catch stitch

blanket stitch

STITCHING A HEM BY HAND

The **catch stitch** is ideal for stretch or knit fabrics because it has some give to it. Unlike the other stitches, the catch stitch is worked from left to right. Begin by securing the thread and making a small horizontal stitch in the garment near the hem edge. Again, pick up one or two threads of the fabric so that the stitch is tiny and all but invisible on the right side. Put the needle into the hem allowance about $\frac{1}{4}$ inch [6 millimeters] from the first stitch and make another small horizontal stitch. Then, moving diagonally, put the needle back into the garment and continue to stitch. Because the needle is inserted from right to left and the thread is carried from left to right, a crisscross pattern will be formed. Do not pull the stitches tight. Keep the thread relaxed so that the stitches will be able to stretch.

The **tailor's hem,** or **blind stitch,** is invisible from both sides of the garment. Because the stitching is hidden inside the hem allowance and the garment, it is less likely to wear or snag. The blind stitch is like slant hemming sewn under the hem edge instead of along the top of it. Turn the finished hem edge back $\frac{1}{4}$ inch [6 millimeters]. Take a small horizontal stitch in the garment. Then move horizontally to the left and pick up a small stitch in the hem allowance. Move back to the garment with a third horizontal stitch. Continue until the hem is completed.

A hem can be **topstitched** in place with one or more rows of regular, zigzag, or decorative machine stitching. Some machines also make a blind stitch for hemming. Hems that receive a lot of wear or stress or are washed often may be secured with machine stitching. Play clothes, sportswear, and children's clothes are examples. The hems of blouses and shirts are often not very noticeable and may also be machine stitched.

Machine topstitching can also be used to make a decorative hem and to make a smooth, sturdy hem in a bulky or heavy fabric. Topstitching can be done in place of, or in combination with, hand stitching. For topstitching use the same color thread that was used for sewing the garment, or

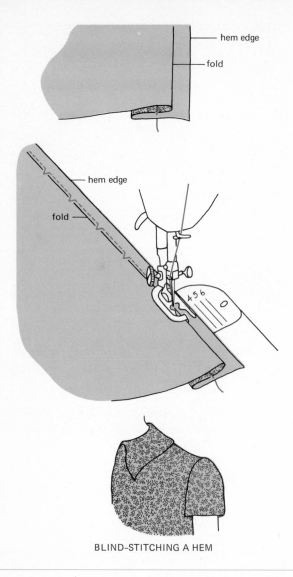

hem edge

fold

hem edge

fold

4 5 6

BLIND-STITCHING A HEM

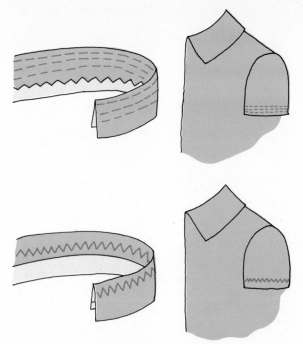

STITCHING A HEM BY MACHINE

Special fusible materials can be used to hold or bond a hem in place on a garment. Heat applied with an iron causes the bonding material to melt, thereby fusing the hem allowance to the garment. These fusibles look like a spider-web. They are sold in different widths, by the yard, and packaged in short lengths. They can be used with washable and dry-cleanable fabrics. Always check and follow the manufacturer's directions carefully. Test a sample piece of fabric first to be sure that a good bond can be obtained. Also check for any changes in the color or texture of the fabric as a result of the bonding or pressing. Be careful not to let the iron touch the actual bonding material. This material will be very difficult to remove if it melts and sticks to the iron.

Take extra care if your fabric is one of the synthetics that has a low melting point. Use a press cloth or heavy brown paper while bonding the hem, to prevent any damage to the fabric or iron.

use contrasting thread. Use buttonhole twist for extra emphasis or for stitching heavy fabrics. Adjust the stitch length to make it a little longer than for regular stitching. If you are using buttonhole twist, you may also have to adjust the tension and use a larger needle. Practice on a scrap of fabric until you get the right combination of thread, stitch length, and tension for your fabric. Use a quilting attachment, stitching guide, or a hand-basted line to help you keep the topstitching straight and even.

BONDING A HEM IN PLACE

THE FINAL CHECK

Your garment is not really complete until it is pressed and ready to wear. Make one final check of all construction and pressing details.

- Are all basting threads removed?
- Are any chalk or thread markings still visible?
- Are all the threads securely fastened and trimmed close to the fabric?
- Does your garment need a final pressing? If you have been careful to press each construction detail, it should only need a light touch-up. When pressing, try not to handle the garment any more than is necessary, and do not overpress.

CARE OF THE GARMENT

After all the time and effort you have put into the construction of your garment, you will want to keep it looking its best. Your care will keep it looking new for a long time. Care means hanging up a garment or folding it neatly when it is not being worn. Care means cleaning and pressing. It also means watching out for repairs. Buttons may eventually work loose or fall off, hems may pull out, and tears and snags might accidentally happen. If these are taken care of as soon as they are noticed, you will be able to save your garment before a rip becomes too large

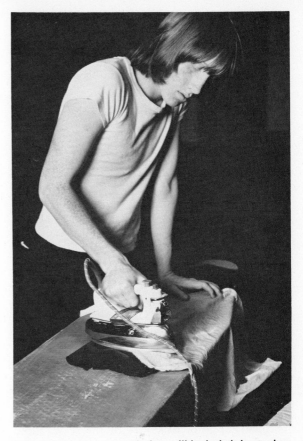

Because you care, your clothes will look their best when you wear them. *Co-ed, Scholastic Magazine, Inc.*

to fix, a button is permanently lost, or the garment is too soiled to ever get clean.

REPAIRS
There is no better way to practice clothing ecology than by repairing your favorite torn or worn garments. *Mending* is done to repair or improve. It can take on many forms, from ironing on a patch to reinforce a worn area, to adding a decorative appliqué that conceals an unfortunate stain.

Darning is most frequently used for small worn areas and for holes where you would prefer not to have a patch. It is like weaving, done with matching thread to make the repair less noticea-

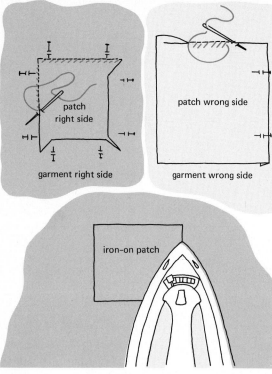

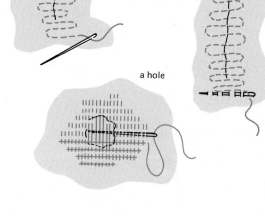

a tear

a hole

DARNING

PATCHING A GARMENT

ble. A thread can be pulled from a scrap of the garment fabric or from one of the seam allowances.

To darn, make rows of very small running stitches going back and forth in one direction until the area is filled. Then weave in and out of the stitches with others going across them. Begin and end the rows of stitches far enough beyond the hole so they are secure. Keep the stitches parallel to the yarns of the fabric. Darning can also be done on the sewing machine, but is usually more noticeable because you have less control of the stitching.

Replacing a stretched-out elastic waistband on a favorite garment can make it look and feel as good as new. Sometimes the elastic is threaded through a casing. Other times it is stitched directly to the garment's edge. When you remove the old elastic, take note how it was originally applied. If the elastic is threaded through a casing, see page 235 in Chapter 12 for "how-to"

instructions.

When applying the elastic directly to the garment, use a length of elastic ½ inch [12.7 millimeters] less than your waist measurement. Overlap the ends and stitch them together, forming a circle. Quarter the elastic and the garment edge. Pin the elastic to the garment, matching the quarter markings. To stitch the elastic in place, use a zigzag stitch. To fit the garment evenly, stretch the elastic as you stitch.

One type of repair especially common for knits is getting rid of those unsightly snags that so often happen on the outside of your garment. Cutting these pulled threads is not the solution, for that may cause an even more unsightly hole in the garment. When a snag appears, gently smooth the fabric around it to work the thread back into the fabric as much as possible. From the wrong side of the garment, insert a needle threader at the base of the snag. Slip the yarn through the fine wire and gently pull the threader

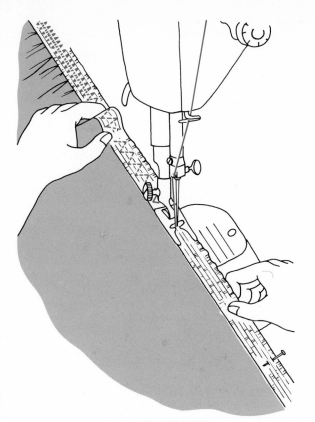

REPLACING ELASTIC

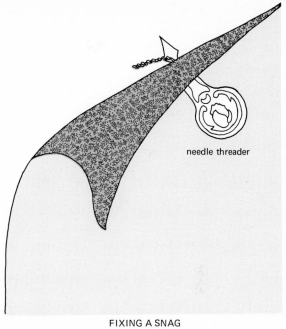

needle threader

FIXING A SNAG

back out of the garment, bringing the pulled yarn with it to the wrong side.

LAUNDERING AND DRY CLEANING

So much of our clothing is made of easy-care fabrics that we almost tend to forget the importance of laundering. A check for spots and stains after each wearing, and regular washing will keep garments new-looking and fresh. If you wash your clothes in an automatic washer, either at home or at a laundromat, be sure that you are familiar with the operation of the washer. Know what each of the cycles and water temperatures is designed for. Most washable garments can be machine washed, but be especially careful of those that might be snagged or easily torn.

These may need to be washed by hand or in a machine that has a special delicate cycle.

· Sort your laundry, first according to color. Whites and light colors should be washed separately from dark colors.
· Check the care labels for manufacturers' directions as to water temperature for each garment.
· Spots or stains should be treated before laundering. If an area is particularly heavily soiled, presoaking it in a detergent solution or treating it with a spray-on prewash product will help to loosen the dirt.
· For a cleaner wash, do not overload the machine.

Once the clothes have been washed, they can usually be placed in an automatic dryer. Here again, check the care labels for specific guides. Follow the machine manufacturer's directions for temperature and drying time. Most wrinkling can be eliminated if the clothes are removed promptly from the dryer and folded as soon as they are dry.

Blood	While stain is fresh, soak in cold water. Work in detergent paste. Launder in warm water. If the stain persists, soak again with bleach. Then relaunder.
Candle Wax and Paraffin	Place the stain between clean white blotters or several layers of facial tissues and press with warm iron. To remove remaining stain, sponge with a dry-cleaning fluid. Rinse and then launder.
Chewing Gum	Harden gum by rubbing it with ice. Scrape off excess with dull knife. If a stain remains, sponge with a dry-cleaning fluid, rinse, and then launder.
Chocolate and Cocoa	Soak in cold water. If colored stain remains, pretreat with detergent paste and launder in water as hot as is safe for the fabric.
Coffee and Tea	Pour boiling water through taut fabric. Launder in hot water.
Cosmetics	Pretreat with detergent paste. Launder in hot water.
Crayon	Loosen stain with cooking oil. Add detergent, working until outline of stain is removed. Launder.
Egg	Scrape off excess. Soak in cool water and then launder in hot water.
Fruits and Berries	For cherry, peach, pear, and plum stains, soak at once in cool water. For other fruits, pour boiling water through stain. Launder.
Grass and Foliage	Rub detergent paste into stain. If necessary, use a mild bleach. Launder in hot water.
Grease and Oil	Scrape off as much grease as possible. Rub detergent paste into stain. Launder in hot water with plenty of detergent.
Ice Cream	Soak in cool water. Then treat with detergent paste. If chocolate or fruit remains, follow directions for those stains.
Ink (ball-point)	Rub white petroleum jelly into stain. Pretreat with detergent paste and launder. If fabric permits, add bleach.

STAIN REMOVAL GUIDE FOR WASHABLE FABRICS

Mildew	Launder in hot water. If possible, dry in the sun.
Mustard	Pretreat with cool water and detergent. Launder.
Perspiration	Pretreat stain with detergent paste. If stain persists, apply ammonia to fresh stain and white vinegar to old stain. Rinse with water and then launder.
Scorch	Pretreat with hot water and detergent. If stain remains, rub with suds. Add bleach if fabric permits. Launder in hot water.
Shoe Polish	Scrape off as much as possible. Pretreat with detergent paste and then launder.
Soft Drinks	Sponge immediately with cool water. Launder.
Tomato	Sponge area with cold water. If stain remains, pretreat with detergent paste. Launder in hot water with bleach.

Some fabrics require dry cleaning to keep them looking new. The professional dry cleaner can do a better job for you if advised of spots or stains. Dry-cleanable garments can also be cleaned by you in a coin-operated cleaning machine. There is usually a savings in cost and you can wait while the garment is being cleaned.

Before cleaning, brush the garment thoroughly and pretreat any stains. There is usually an attendant on duty who can advise you on stain removal. Follow the machine directions carefully and avoid overloading the machine. When the cycle is complete, remove the garments and hang them on hangers. This will give them a chance to air out and prevent excess wrinkling.

Before modern day conveniences and synthetic fibers, ironing garments to keep them fresh looking was a must. Today, ironing is still an impor-

tant way to make your clothing look its best, but it is not always a necessary part of your care routine. In fact, if you hang up or fold your clothes when they are not being worn, they may never need to be ironed. If and when you do need to iron your clothes, keep the following in mind:

· Be sure the iron is clean. Any residue or film on the iron may come off onto your clothes.
· Check the temperature setting. Wrinkles will not come out of a cotton garment if the temperature is not hot enough, and a synthetic fabric may melt if it is too hot.
· Use steam when possible. Wrinkles disappear quicker and with less effort with steam than with a dry iron.

1. Make a bulletin board on buttons and other fasteners. Include as wide a variety as possible.

2. List different types of fasteners and their uses. Explain how to select and apply each type.

3. Prepare a display showing how to mark and turn a hem, finish a raw hem edge, and stitch a hem in place.

4. Select three or four different pieces of fabric. Discuss how each fabric might be finished and sewn to make hems on different garments. Give your reasons for each choice.

5. Visit a clothing store. Look at casual and dressy clothing and coats and other outerwear for men, women, and children. Compare the hems and fasteners used. Are the hems always neat and even? Does the stitching show on the right side of any of the garments? Are fasteners securely in place? Are buttonholes neat and strong?

6. Bring to class a garment that is in need of some kind of repair. Ask your classmates to do the same. Discuss ways to repair each of the garments.

7. Survey your family, friends, and classmates to find what types of clothing stains are most often a problem to them. Do some research to find the best ways of handling these stain problems. Make a stain-removal chart showing the results of your research.

● DO YOU KNOW

bias tape	hemming stitch
blind stitch	hooks and eyes
buttons	laundering
buttonholes	mending
catch stitch	patch
darning	seam tape
dry cleaning	shank
fasteners	slip stitch
fusables	snaps
hem allowance	tailor's hem
hemline	topstitch

GLOSSARY
and INDEX

glossary

allowance The amount of fabric between the stitching and the cut edge of a garment. Also, the extra fabric within the garment to allow for construction details such as gathers, darts, and tucks.

altering Changing the length or width of a pattern piece or a garment.

applied casing A bias strip of fabric attached to the garment for a drawstring or elastic to be threaded through.

appliqué Small piece(s) of fabric attached to a background fabric by hand or machine.

armscye The armhole, or the opening in a garment for the sleeve.

arrowhead tack A small, triangular, hand-embroidered trim to reinforce the ends of pleats, vents, pockets.

back stitch A small hand stitch that looks like a machine stitch on the right side. On the wrong side, the stitches overlap.

bands Strips of fabric applied to garments, to finish the edges or to decorate them. Bands may be cut on the bias or on the straight of the grain.

basic pattern A pattern sewn together and altered for correct garment fit, then used as a guide for making alterations on other patterns.

basting Making long, loose stitches by hand or machine. The stitches are usually temporary, made with a different color thread from that of the garment.

belt carriers Thread or fabric loops for holding a belt in place.

belting Stiff banding used inside a waistline as a stay or covered with fabric for use as a belt.

beveling Another word for layering seam allowances.

bias The diagonal of a fabric, which has more "give," or stretch, than the straight grain.

bias band, facing, seam binding Strips of bias-cut fabric used to finish or trim curved edges.

bias tape Double or single folded bias fabric used to bind, face, or trim curved edges.

blanket stitch A decorative hand-embroidered edge finish, formed by interlocking stitches.

blend A combination of two or more different fibers in one yarn, or of different yarns in one fabric.

blind stitch A stitch made by catching only one thread of the outer fabric, so it cannot be seen easily.

bodkin A long, blunt needle with a large eye or a pin on one end. It is used to turn drawstring and tubing and to thread tape, elastic, or ribbon through a casing.

body measurements The actual measurements of the body, used to select the correct pattern size.

box pleat A two-sided fold in the garment resembles a panel. The edges face opposite directions.

braid A decorative trim that comes in a variety of widths and weights. It can be attached to the garment by hand or machine.

canvas A type of fabric often used for coat or jacket interfacing.

cartridge pleats Folds in the garment with unpressed, rounded edges.

casing A hem or a strip of fabric attached to a garment, with an opening so that a drawstring or an elastic can be pulled through.

catch stitch A crossed stitch made by hand and used to hold a hem in place.

chain stitch A hand-embroidered stitch formed by interlocking loops.

chalk The substance used for transferring pattern and fitting marks to a fabric.

clean finish The treatment of an edge on non-bulky fabrics that ravel.

clip A short cut into a seam allowance of a garment to help curved areas lie flat without strain.

cording A cord covered with bias fabric often used as a decorative finish on edges.

crease A folded line pressed into a fabric or a garment.

crosswise grains The yarns of a fabric that run across the fabric from selvage to selvage. They should be at right angles to the lengthwise yarns.

crow's foot A triangular-shaped, hand-done thread design used for reinforcement at the beginning of pleats and pockets.

dart A fold of fabric stitched to a point at one or both ends. It gives shape to a garment.

diagonal basting A slanted, temporary stitch for holding layers of fabric together to control the amount of slipping.

directional cutting, stitching, and pressing Working with the grain of the fabric to retain the grain and shape of a garment section and to prevent raveling.

dress form A duplicate of the human figure often used in designing and fitting a garment. It can be made of foam rubber, cardboard, or plastic and covered with fabric.

dressmaker's carbon Colored paper used with a tracing wheel to transfer construction details from pattern to fabric.

ease To make one section of a seam which is slightly fuller or longer than its joining section fit the narrower or shorter section without gathering or puckering.

ease allowance Added room to allow for comfort and movement in a garment.

edge finish A treatment used on the cut edge of fabric to prevent raveling. Examples are binding, hemming, overcasting, pinking, stitching, trimming, or zigzagging.

edging Any type of trim with one decorative edge and one straight edge.

edge stitch Functional or decorative stitching made close to a garment's edge.

elastic thread Thread made with a stretchy core. It is used for gathering and is applied by hand or machine.

embroidery Decorative stitching done by hand or machine.

emery bag A small bag filled with coarse grains used to polish and clean pins and needles.

even basting Temporary, large stitching often used for marking. The stitches and the spaces between them are equal in size.

eyelet A small hole in a garment, finished with hand stitches or a metal ring. It is used for lacing ribbon, yarn, or leather strips and to hold the prong of a buckle.

facing A piece of fabric used to finish the edges of a garment, such as the neckline, armholes, and front or back openings.

fagoting A decorative trim placed within a seam.

fastenings Items such as buttons and buttonholes, hooks and eyes, and snaps, which are used to close garments.

feather stitch Slanted, blanket stitches that are used for a decorative effect.

fibers Natural or synthetic threads used to make yarn for fabrics.

figure type The classification of various body shapes according to height and body proportions. Each figure type consists of various size ranges for pattern selection.

filling See crosswise grains.

findings See notions.

fish dart A double-ended dart that comes to a point at each end.

fitting Adjusting a pattern or garment to fit you.

flap A piece of fabric that is attached to the garment by one side only. It is often found on pockets.

flat fell A seam used on tailored garments and jeans. After the seam is stitched, one seam allowance is trimmed and the other is stitched over it.

fly front A means of concealing buttons or a zipper in the front of slacks.

french knot A decorative hand-embroidery stitch in which the needle is wrapped with thread and brought down through the fabric at almost the same spot where it came out, forming a small, raised dot.

french seam A double-stitched seam first stitched with the wrong sides of the garment together, then with the right sides together. It looks like a plain seam on the right side and a small, neat tuck on the wrong side.

fringe A decorative edge finish formed by raveling the edge of the fabric. It can be purchased by the yard.

frog A decorative fastener associated with Oriental clothing. It is made with braid, bias binding, or cording.

gathering Even distribution of fullness formed by pulling threads of basting stitches.

glove stitch Decorative hand topstitching made by taking stitches of equal size on both sides of the work.

godet A triangular piece of fabric that is set into garments for added width at the bottom.

gore A piece of fabric that is narrow at the top and wide at the bottom, added to a garment to make it flare.

grading Eliminating bulk within a seam by trimming the seam allowances to different widths; also known as beveling or layering.

grain The direction of fabric yarns. The lengthwise grain runs parallel to the selvages; the crosswise grain runs from selvage to selvage.

grain line The line printed on a pattern to show the grainline for each garment piece.

grainline The lengthwise or crosswise yarns of a fabric forming the grain.

guide sheet The printed sheet that is included with each pattern and contains general information about the pattern and how to use it, as well as instructions for cutting and sewing your project.

gusset A small, triangular piece of fabric set into a slash or seam for added ease, shape, and comfort. It is usually placed at the underarm of a kimono sleeve.

ham See tailor's ham.

hand pricking See prick stitch.

hand-rolled hem See rolled hem.

heavy-duty thread A strong thread used for sewing on buttons or stitching on heavy fabric.

hem The fabric folded to the wrong side to finish the garment's edge.

hemline The bottom edge of a garment where the hem turns up.

inset An extra piece of fabric added to a garment. Sometimes it is necessary for fitting the garment; other times it is used for decorating.

interfacing A special fabric that helps to shape and add body and strength to collars, lapels, waistbands, and cuffs.

interlining An extra layer of fabric sewn between the garment and lining to provide warmth.

inverted pleat A fold in the garment with two edges facing each other.

invisible stitch A stitch worked from the wrong side that cannot be seen on the right side of the garment.

kick pleat A short pleat at the lower edge of a tapered garment. It makes movement less confining without changing the line or shape of the slim garment.

kimono sleeve A sleeve extended from the front and back bodices.

knife pleats A group of one-sided pleats that face the same direction.

lap A piece of fabric or side of a garment placed over another.

lapel The upper front edge that turns away from the center on a coat or jacket.

lapped seam A decorative seam with one seam allowance folded under and placed on top of the other seam allowance. Stitching is then done on the right side of the garment next to the fold.

layering Another term for grading the seam allowance.

layout The way each pattern piece is placed on the fabric for pinning and cutting.

lazy daisy stitch A hand-embroidery stitch that groups chain stitches together to form a flower.

lengthwise grain The yarns in the fabric that run the length of the fabric and parallel to the selvage. They should form right angles with the crosswise yarns.

lining A means of protecting and concealing the inside construction details of a garment.

lock stitch A machine stitch used to knot thread at the beginning and end of stitching.

loop The part of the fastener that extends beyond the finished edge of a garment to fasten onto a hook or button. It can be made of thread, fabric, or metal.

machine basting The longest stitch on the machine. It is used for marking construction details and joining seams temporarily.

machine hem A machine-stitched hem; it can be decorative or reversible.

marking Transferring construction details and symbols from the tissue pattern to the fabric.

measuring stick A ruler, yardstick, or meterstick used for determining garment length and small distances.

miter A diagonal seam stitched at a corner to eliminate bulk.

nap The surface texture of some fabrics, like corduroy, having short fibers which feel smooth when brushed in one direction and rough when brushed in the other.

needles Necessary tools for sewing. They carry the thread through the fabric.

needle board A pressing aid with fine metal or nylon teeth set vertically into a flat board. It is used for pressing corduroy and other nap or pile fabrics.

notch A small wedge cut out of curved seam allowance to help the seam lie flat. Also, they are the diamond-shaped markings through the cutting line of the pattern. They are used for matching one section of the garment to another.

notions The items in addition to the pattern and fabric that you will need to sew and finish your project.

outline stitch A hand-embroidery stitch using a short back stitch and working from left to right.

overcasting Making small, slanted hand stitches over the cut edge of fabric. This helps to keep the edge from raveling.

overlap The part or side of a garment that laps over another part. See lap.

permanent basting Basting stitches that remain in the finished garment. They are usually made with matching thread.

piecing Sewing two or more pieces of flat fabric together for additional width.

pile Loops or extra fibers on the surface of a fabric, formed during weaving. Corduroy, terry cloth, velvet, and velveteen are examples of fabrics with pile. See nap.

pin basting A means of joining garment sections together with pins before permanently stitching them.

pin fit To pin the garment together as you try it on before permanent stitching.

pin tucks Thin tucks stitched close to the edge at the fold.

pinch pleats A type of pleat made by dividing one pleat into two or three smaller ones.

pinking A means of finishing a seam by trimming the cut edge with pinking shears.

pins Dressmaker or silk pins used to temporarily attach pattern pieces to fabric and garment sections. Fine, sharp pins are used with woven fabrics and ball point pins, with knitted fabrics.

piping Bias fabric, folded, or a braid inserted into a seam as a trim.

pivot A technique for stitching sharp corners.

placket A reinforced opening in a garment. It is usually closed by snaps, hooks and eyes, or buttons and buttonholes.

plain seam The most popular seam for joining two pieces of fabric.

pleats A design element used for control of excess fabric or fullness. The fabric is folded at specified distances.

pocket stay The reinforcement of a pocket opening which is achieved by stitching a strip of fabric to the wrong side of the pocket.

preshrink Treating fabrics before cutting or

sewing so that the size of a finished project will not change by washing or dry cleaning.

prick stitch   A type of back stitch used to insert zippers. Tiny dotlike stitches are visible on the right side, while they overlap on the wrong side.

quilting   Stitching through several layers of fabric.

raglan sleeve   A type of sleeve that continues from the arm up over the shoulder to the neckline. It is attached to the garment with diagonal seams.

ravel   To pull yarns from the cut edge of the fabric. This is sometimes done to find the grain but can also be done to form a decorative fringe.

reinforce   To add extra stitching or strips of fabric to areas of stress.

remnant   A short length of fabric that was left on the bolt after the last sale.

reversible   Fabric or a garment that has been finished so both sides can be the right side.

rick rack   A zigzag trim made of fabric.

rip   To remove stitches to open a seam.

rolled hem   A hem finish done by hand and formed by rolling the raw edge between the fingers and then stitching. It is recommended for sheer fabrics, scarves, and handkerchiefs.

ruffle   A type of edge trimming made by a strip of fabric that is gathered or pleated.

running stitch   A hand-basted stitch that is equal on both sides of the fabric.

saddle stitch   A decorative, hand-sewn topstitch. Longer stitches appear on top, and shorter ones underneath. This is often done in contrasting thread.

sag   A stretch in the fabric which causes the hem to be lopsided or causes stress areas to be baggy.

satin stitch   A hand-embroidery stitch using long stitches placed close together.

scallops   A row of connected semicircles finishing an edge.

seam   The line created when two pieces of fabric are stitched together.

seam allowance   The fabric between the cut edge and the stitching line.   The usual seam allowance is $\frac{5}{8}$ inch [15 millimeters].

seam binding   Strips of fabric for finishing raw edges of a garment. They come woven, for straight edges; cut on the bias, for curved edges; and lacelike, for decorative effects and knit fabrics.

seam finish   The way in which the raw edges are treated to reduce fraying and to eliminate bulk after the seam has been stitched.

seam roll   A firmly padded pressing aid resembling a long tube; it is used for pressing seams.

selvage   The tightly woven edges along the length of the fabric.

set-in sleeve   A sleeve attached to the garment at the place where the arm and shoulder meet.

shank   The stemlike loop on a button or a stem of thread made when sewing the button onto a garment. The shank allows the fabric around it to lie smoothly when the garment is buttoned.

shape makers   Refers to sewing techniques and fabrics used to preserve the grain of the fabric and the shape of garment pieces.

shirring   Gathering done with two or more rows of visible stitching.

shrinking   Contracting fibers, causing the fabric to become smaller.

side pleats   See knife pleats.

slash   A quick, even cut into the fabric along a straight line. It is a longer cut than a clip and is usually done on a foldline to eliminate bulk.

sleeveboard   A small ironing board. It is used for pressing sleeves, shoulders, and other hard-to-reach places.

slip basting   Hand basting that cannot be seen. It is done by making longer and fewer slip stitches from the right side of the garment.

slip stitch   Tiny hand stitches made by slipping the needle through folds of fabric, causing the stitching to be invisible.

slot seam   A seam with a piece of fabric underneath it which is topstitched in place at equal distances from each side of the seam.

smocking   Gathering fabric in a decorative manner for distribution of fullness.

stay   A strip of fabric stitched to the garment for reinforcement of the area.

staystitching A line of regular-length machine stitches made along curved areas of each garment piece to keep the edges from stretching and to hold the grain in place.

steam press To press a garment using steam produced by a hot iron and moisture.

straightening Refers to making the grain of the fabric straight so that the lengthwise grainline and the crosswise grainline meet at right angles.

stretch stitch A machine stitch recommended for knit fabrics. It goes forward, backwards, and then forward again, and is more durable than the regular straight stitch. It will not break when knit fabric stretches.

tacking Making tiny hand stitches to hold two pieces of fabric together.

tailor's ham A padded cushion resembling a ham. It is used for shaping and pressing curved seams and garment pieces, such as collars.

tailor's tacks Simple hand stitches made with loose loops of thread. They are used for marking pattern symbols onto fabric.

taping Refers to reinforcing points of stress by attaching strips of fabric or tape to seams and to the wrong side of the garment.

tension The control of the needle thread and the bobbin thread of the sewing machine. The tension regulates the amount of slack necessary for making even stitches.

topstitching Decorative stitching which is visible on the outside of the garment. It is usually done close to a seam or a finished edge, outlining construction details.

trapunto A type of quilting in which only the design part is padded for emphasis.

trim To reduce the size of the seam allowances after the seam has been stitched or to make a ragged edge even.

true bias The "stretchiest" part of the fabric found by folding the fabric diagonally to make the crosswise grain parallel to the lengthwise grain.

tubing Tubelike strips of fabric used for loops and trim.

tucks Folds of fullness stitched straight.

twill tape A strip of twill fabric weave used for stays or ties.

underlap A section of a garment that is lapped over by another.

underlining Lining a garment by sewing the outside fabric and lining fabric together as one. The seam allowances remain exposed.

understitching Stitching through the facing and seam allowances that are very close to the seam. It keeps the facing from turning to the right side of the garment.

unit construction The completing of sections of a garment before joining them together.

vent A lapped, pleatlike opening on the bottom edge of a jacket or skirt.

warp See lengthwise grain.

welt seam A type of seam where the seam allowances are trimmed to different widths, creating a padded effect when the seam is topstitched.

whip To encase two edges together with tiny slanting stitches.

with nap Refers to all fabrics that require that pattern pieces be laid in the same direction on the fabric for cutting.

yardage Refers to how much fabric is necessary to make a particular project. The width of the fabric, as well as your size, is taken into consideration.

zigzag stitch A machine stitch made by the needle moving from side to side. It can also be made with the help of an attachment that moves the fabric from side to side.

index

Corduroy, 45
  pressing of, 157
Corners, stitching of sharp, 136
Corporation, 19
Cosmetic product
  representative, 83
Costume designer, 10
Cotton, 26, 33–36, 40, 43
  care of, 36
Cotton gin, 35
Cotton thread, 174
Crafts, 91–120
  appliqué, 117–118
  crocheting, 106–107
  embroidery, 92–95
  knitting, 101–105
  macramé, 112–114
  needlepoint, 95–100
  patchwork, 116–117
  quilting, 114–116
  rug making, 111–112
  weaving, 108–111
Credit, 22-23
  advantages of, 23
  disadvantages of, 23
Crewel embroidery, 93
Crewel needle, 93, 153
Crochet hooks, 106
Crochet yarns, 106
Crocheting, 105–107
Cross stitch, 96
Cubed-cross stitch, 100
Cuffs, 231
Curved edges:
  bias facings for, 224–225
  clipping of seam allowances
    on, 210
  facing, 224
Curved hem, easing of, 249–250
Curved lines, 54–56
Curved seams, 202, 210, 211
  location of, 210
  pressing of, 210
  stitching of, 136, 210
Customer benefits, 19
Customers:
  cash, 23
  credit, 23
Cut edges, matching of, 209
Cutting lines, 181

Cutting of pattern, 193, 194
Cutting tools, 145–147

Darning, 257
Darts, 182, 206–207
  alteration of, 205
  horizontal, 207
  location of, 206
  markings for, 181–182
  pressing of, 154, 157, 207
  shape of, 206
  stitching of, 207
  vertical, 207
Decoration, body, 6
Dental care, 78
Dental floss, 78
Design:
  in a garment, 57
  quilting, 115
Designer:
  costume, 10
  fabric, 57
  fashion, 58
  textile, 45
Designs in fabric, 48
Diagonal basting, 206
Diagonal lines, 54, 55
Dietitian, consulting, 75
Directional stitching, 203
"Divide and pin"
  technique, 209
Dots, as pattern markings, 182
Double crochet stitch, 107
Double-cross stitch, 97
Drawstring, making a, 234
Dressmaker pins, 152
Dressmaker shears, 147
Dry cleaning:
  clothing care guide for, 30
  of garments, 261
Drying, care guide for, 30
Dyeing, 48

Ease, 207–208
  in patterns, 159
Ease stitching, 207–208
Easing, 182
  of curved hem, 249–250

Easing (*continued*)
  markings for, 181–182
  in seams, 209
Ecology, clothing, 257
Edgestitching:
  as hem finish, 251
  seam finishes, 214
Eisenhower jacket, 10, 12
Elastic:
  measuring for casing, 234
  threading through casing, 234
Elastic thread, 174
Electric scissors, 147
Embroidery, 92–95
Embroidery hoop, 93
Embroidery needle, 153
Embroidery scissors, 146
Embroidery stitches, 94, 96–97
Emery bag, 153
Energy:
  food, 69–70
  relation of food to, 69–73
  using up, 69–70
Even basting, 206
Exercise, 73, 75, 78
Exposed zipper:
  application of, 223–224
  as decorative trim, 223
Eye color, 84–85

Fabric, 33–50
  blended, 41, 43
  on bolts, 170
  bonded, 46
  buying, 170–174
  calandering of, 47
  care labels on, 26, 155, 170
  chart of finishes for, 49
  designs in, 48
  double-knit, 46
  embossed, 47
  factory cuts, 171
  felting, 46
  finding straight grain of,
    187–189
  finishes for, 47–48
  fold of, 181
  gingham, 45
  irregular, 170–171

1 2 3 4 5 6 7 8 9 10 VHVH 85 84 83 82 81 80 79 78 77 76